Lanza's Mob

THE MAFIA AND SAN FRANCISCO

Christina Ann-Marie DiEdoardo

An Imprint of ABC-CLIO, LLC

Santa Barbara, California • Denver, Colorado

Library of Congress Cataloging-in-Publication Data

Names: DiEdoardo, Christina Ann-Marie, author.
Title: Lanza's mob : the Mafia and San Francisco / Christina Ann-Marie DiEdoardo.
Description: Santa Barbara, California : Praeger, 2016. | Includes bibliographical references and index.
Identifiers: LCCN 2016011098 | ISBN 9781440842160 (hard copy : alk. paper) | ISBN 9781440842177 (ebook)
Subjects: LCSH: Lanza, Francesco, -1937. | Mafia—California—San Francisco—History. | Organized crime—California—San Francisco—History.
Classification: LCC HV6452.C29 D35 2016 | DDC 364.10609794/61—dc23
LC record available at https://lccn.loc.gov/2016011098

ISBN: 978-1-4408-4216-0
EISBN: 978-1-4408-4217-7

20 19 18 17 16   1 2 3 4 5

This book is also available as an eBook.

Praeger
An Imprint of ABC-CLIO, LLC

ABC-CLIO, LLC
130 Cremona Drive, P.O. Box 1911
Santa Barbara, California 93116-1911
www.abc-clio.com

This book is printed on acid-free paper ∞

Manufactured in the United States of America

Dedicated to my Mother, Shirley, who taught me
my love of reading and learning.
And to my Father, James Anthony ("Tony")
who made me Italian American.

Aren't we the Commission? What would the Commission be for if it did not understand these things? The Commission knows all these things—it is human—the Commission may be right or may be wrong, but it is human.

—*James "Jimmy The Hat" Lanza, October 16, 1964, FBI Wiretap*

Contents

Preface

Growing up in New York City in the early 1970s, the Mafia seemed to me to be as much as part of the landscape as subway cars covered in several layers of graffiti, the unique smell of New York subway stations, which was equal parts allure and menace, hot dog pushcart vendors selling roasted chestnuts every winter and church carnivals with the sweet aroma of cotton candy and *zeppole*.

So when I visited the National Museum of Organized Crime and Law Enforcement shortly after it opened in 2012—which is located in the very building where Sen. Estes Kefauver grilled Las Vegas's politicos, casino owners, and "legitimate businessmen"—I was surprised to learn that the last boss of the Mafia in San Francisco, where I now live, was "James Lanza."

"Who the hell is that?" is what I said next. My quest to answer that question led to the book you are holding.

It is ironic and unfair that Lanza was mocked during his lifetime as the leader of "a tiny, ineffectual squad" as *Time* magazine quipped in the 1960s. In sharp contrast to his colleagues like Joseph "Joe Bananas" Bonanno (whom Lanza successfully helped hide at the Jack Tar Hotel in San Francisco when Bonanno was dodging both federal subpoenas and equally urgent summonses from the Mafia's Commission) and Joe Profaci, who, unlike Lanza, managed to get caught when the cops swarmed the Mafia's sitdown at Apalachin, Lanza tried to stick to the shadows whenever possible and often succeeded. Although that makes a historian's job more difficult, it also makes for a more interesting story.

As you see from the following pages, when not engaging in real estate development in San Francisco, settling disputes among the Italian American community—and, according to an illegal FBI wiretap, incessantly complaining about taxes—the Lanzas allegedly smuggled morphine across the country in olive oil barrels.

The family they led is believed to have approved or been involved in at least two high-profile hits (that of Nick De John in 1948 and of Joseph "The Animal" Barboza in 1976), which took place in San Francisco, even though most people believe that the murders were done for the benefit of and carried out by other families (the Chicago Outfit for DeJohn and the Patriarca family for Barboza).

Those of us who appreciate history can be grateful the Lanzas never successfully placed a rumored contract on Jimmy "The Weasel" Fratianno who—despite being a member of the Los Angeles Mafia family and the Chicago Outfit at various times—operated mostly without supervision in San Francisco, since then we would be deprived of Ovid Demaris's work *The Last Mafioso*, which discusses the Lanzas during Fratianno's time in San Francisco when he was running scams and corrupting Teamster officials, much to Lanza's evident annoyance at the heat and media attention the Weasel was bringing to his ordered kingdom.

The Lanzas had an effect on national politics too, although it was not by anything they intentionally did. After the FBI declared James Lanza a "top hoodlum" and the bureau illegally bugged his office for several years, it learned of the relationships between Joseph L. Alioto, then a hotshot attorney working his way toward the mayoralty of San Francisco with dreams of higher office to come, and Lanza.

Although James Lanza was a Republican—and Alioto a scion of the Democratic Party—Lanza took no *schadenfreude* in the leak of the FBI's illicit wiretap evidence to *Look* magazine in 1969, which plastered his name and Alioto's across the country. Neither did Alioto, who launched the local equivalent of Charles Dickens's *Jarndyce v. Jarndyce*, the case in his classic *Bleak House* that goes on for so long it consumes all of the resources of the parties.

Per Dickens, by the time Alioto's case reached a verdict 12 years later in 1981, *Look* was no more and Alioto's $12.5 million lawsuit had been whittled down to a $350,000 judgment, which was promptly seized by one of Alioto's professional creditors on an unrelated matter.

The Lanzas affected architecture too. The iconic Transamerica Pyramid now stands on the site of James Lanza's former headquarters, whereas the Exposition Fish Grotto, the restaurant that his father Francesco owned with Alioto's father, was one of the anchor establishments on Fisherman's Wharf for years.

Although they may not be as famous—or infamous, depending on your perspective—as Capone and Fratianno, the Lanzas occupied an important social and economic niche in San Francisco from Prohibition until the early Noughties. It is time for their tale to be told!

—Christina Ann-Marie DiEdoardo, Esq.,
January 2016

Acknowledgments

No one writes any history worth reading without the support and assistance of scores of people whose names do not appear on the spine of the book. This overall truism applies with even greater force to *Lanza's Mob*, since by the nature of its subject, creating it required the bringing together of historical resources from a plethora of state and federal sources in Italy and the United States.

First and foremost, I want to thank my acquisitions editor at ABC-CLIO, Catherine Lafuente, who was the first person I pitched this project to (at a New Year's Eve party, of all things), and Kevin Downing, ABC-CLIO's editorial director of books. Kudos are also due to Erin Ryan at ABC-CLIO, who helped with permissions, and to Silverander Communications, whose team developed the great cover on the book you hold in your hands.

Of course, I would never have met Catherine if it had not been for Coda Gardner and Jeff and Jeannie Anderson (see what happens when you invite me to New Year's Eve parties?). So I owe all three a huge debt of gratitude for their support then and since. On that note, double *gratsis* with a cappuccino are due to my dear friend and writing buddy Holden Karau for keeping me on task and on message through many work sessions on our respective books-to-be.

Archives and Special Collections libraries—whether state or federal—can be intimidating places. Thankfully, all of the staff at the National Archives in Washington, D.C., Archives II in College Park, Maryland, and at the National Archives and Records Administration in San Bruno,

California (where I was apparently the first researcher to peruse the case files of *Alioto v. Cowles Communications* since they passed to NARA's custody) were the picture of grace and professionalism. The same goes for their colleagues at the California State Archives in Sacramento and the New York State Archives and the New York State Library in Albany, New York. I am fortunate both for living within a few blocks of the Central branch of the San Francisco Public Library and being able to spend many hours researching and writing this book there.

A special *brava* goes to the staff of the *Archivo Centrale Dello Stato*, the Central Archives of Italy. Despite my inability to speak Italian beyond a few dialect phrases (none of which are suitable for polite company outside of Queens or South Philly), they quickly tracked down what I needed and got it to me in digital form. The good people at the *Istituto nazionale di statistica* (The Italian National Institute of Statistics) also deserve praise for making so many of their collections accessible in English over the Web and for graciously responding to my communications with them.

Both New York City and San Francisco have undergone major changes to their street grid during the period of time covered by this book. Without the help of Miriam Bader and David Favaloro at the Lower East Side Tenement Museum in New York City, I never would have been able to match the barely legible records of the 1905 state census (that showed Francesco Lanza's first recorded address in the United States) to the street where it was then located. Thanks to the David Ramsey Map Collection/ Cartography Associates, I was able to show you where that street—which no longer exists—was located in 1905.

For whatever reason, I am most productive as a writer when I am working somewhere other than my office. Thank you to the very understanding staff at SAM's Diner, San Francisco, who kept me in bottomless Diet Cokes, and always asked how the book was going and graciously let me occupy booths to write in. The same goes for the amazing management and staff at Wicked Grounds, the pearl of San Francisco's South of Market area, who let Holden and I write for days on end (or so it seemed) with no complaints.

Speaking of friends, I owe a special debt of gratitude as well to all the amazing people who kept me sane through their administration of encouragement, kudos, and—when necessary—kicking my ass, especially my sister Julie Kelsey and brother-in-law John Kelsey, my best friend Amy Larson and her husband Joel Becker, as well as Jennifer Kathleen Rice and Sky Beaber.

Extra special thanks are due to Madeleine Ariadne Bair for her support and love during a lot of anxious days and nights (not all of which were related to this book)—and to another Madeleine who gave me a guided tour of San Mateo and shared some amazing stories of trick-or-treating at James Lanza's house in the 1970s, as well as what it was like playing steps away from the home of a mobster.

Thanks to everyone for their support and assistance!
Avanti! (Forward!)

—Christina Ann-Marie DiEdoardo, Esq.,
January 2016

Notes on Terms

During the period under discussion, U.S. media and government agencies frequently had difficulty with Italian names, which often—particularly in the 1920s and 1930s—resulted in gross inconsistencies in terms of reporting.

For example, Chicago's most famous second-hand furniture dealer Al Capone was referred to as "Alphonse Caponi" by both the *Chicago Tribune* and the *New York Times* for years.[1] When there has been a dispute over how a subject's name is spelled, I have endeavored to either use their preference or—when none was recorded—to go with the consensus spelling by which they are best known.

As I know from personal experience given my own last name, to be Italian sadly often means accommodating oneself to endless typos when being written about, so I have done my best to clear up that confusion rather than create more. As an example, Francesco Lanza (formerly Francesco Proetto) is sometimes referred to as "Francisco Lanza" or "Frank Lanza" in contemporaneous sources. In the interest of clarity and consistency, he will be referred to here as "Francesco."

In situations where there are multiple conflicting references to a subject's address and residence, I have made every effort to confirm the correctness of the one cited through other sources such as City Directories and census records as well as other clues, like the presence of spouses or family members at the address.

Except for the word "Mafia" or "mafia," Italian or non-English words are *italicized*, for example, *zeppole* or *caporegime*.

San Franciscans refer to their city—and no other, regardless of whether
the competing metropolis is San Mateo, New York, or Las Vegas—as
"The City." Indeed, libeling their beloved City by referring to it as "Frisco"
is still considered an offense almost worthy of a punch in the mouth in
some circles of natives and longtime San Francisco residents, including
the author. Since this is a San Francisco story, that convention will be followed here except in quoted matter.

—Christina Ann-Marie DiEdoardo,
January 2016

Chronology

October 8, 1872: Francesco Lanza, *nato* Proetto, is born in Castelbuono, Sicily.

October 23, 1902: James "Jimmy the Hat" Lanza is born.

July 11, 1904: Francesco Lanza is believed to have arrived in New York according to the FBI.

February 10, 1905: James Lanza and his siblings arrive in New York (according to DHS records).

1915: The Harrison Narcotics Act is passed by Congress and is signed into law by President Wilson, marking the first foray of the federal government into antidrug work.

February 12, 1916: Joseph L. Alioto is born in San Francisco when family living at 572 Filbert Street.

September 1918: Congress passes the Wartime Prohibition Act, which ends the manufacture of most beers and wine in the United States after May 1919 and the sale of all beverages with an alcohol content greater than 2.75 percent after June 30, 1919.

January 17, 1920: The Volstead Act, the main federal statutory means to enforce Prohibition, begins to be theoretically enforced—and practically violated on a mass scale.

1920: The Lanzas are living at 1830 Coney Island Avenue, Brooklyn, NY, before moving to California later that year.

May 25, 1921: Francesco Lanza becomes a U.S. citizen in San Francisco, California.

November 24, 1928: Jerry Ferri murdered, allegedly by his then partner Alfredo Scariso, who is himself murdered about a month later.

July 30, 1929: Frank "Strong Man of the Sicilians" Boca is shot, stabbed, and left in a bloody car for the police to find.

February, 28, 1930–April 15, 1931: Castellammarese War breaks out between loyalists of Giuseppe "Joe The Boss" Masseria and partisans, including Joseph "Joe Bananas" Bonanno, of Salvatore Maranzano.

October 13, 1930: Gennaro Broccolo aka "Don Broccolo the Magnificent" killed by Ralph, aka Raffaele, Esposito, who is later acquitted on the grounds of self-defense.

April 1931: Masseria is executed at the Nuova Villa Tammaro restaurant in Coney Island while at dinner with Charlie Lucky, aka Lucky Luciano (who, conveniently, is in the restroom when the hit goes down). Beyond ending the Castellammarese War, the event inspires the hit on Virgil "The Turk" Sollozzo in Mario Puzo's *"The Godfather."*

September 10, 1931: Maranzano is whacked in his own New York office by non-Mafia gunmen posing as federal officers, believed to have been hired by Luciano.

October 18, 1931: Frank Grupico—Ferri's former sidekick and Wortova's paramour—and Luigi Malvese are arrested as part of a counterfeiting ring.

May 16, 1932: Frank Grupico is shot in a botched attempt to shake down reported bootlegger Edward Giubbiny.

May 18, 1932: Luigi Malvese murdered in front of the Del Monte Barbershop, where Ralph Esposito works.

May 24, 1932: The San Francisco Police Department (SFPD) begins mass arrests after the hit on Malvese. It nabs Al Capone's former tailor but fails to locate anyone with any useful information about Malvese's killing.

December 5, 1933: Prohibition ends in the United States.

June 14, 1937: Frank Lanza dies, apparently of aplastic anemia.[1]

June 1937: Tony Lima succeeds Frank Lanza as boss of the family.

May 9, 1939: Caterina Lanza dies.

January 30, 1942: U.S. Attorney General Francis Biddle bars all aliens, including Italian permanent residents who are not U.S. citizens, from Fisherman's Wharf.

November 5, 1942: Secretary of the Navy Frank Knox allows the Italians to return to the Wharf.

May 7, 1948: Nick DeJohn is murdered. Lanza soldiers are suspected of doing the deed as a favor for the Chicago Outfit.

May 2, 1950: U.S. Senate Special Committee on Organized Crime in Interstate Commerce (Kefauver Committee) established.

November 1950: The Kefauver Committee holds hearings in San Francisco.

1953: Mike Abati succeeds Lima as boss of the San Francisco family.

November 14, 1957: James Lanza represents the family at the Appalchin summit, where he apparently shares a room with bosses from Los Angeles and elsewhere, but escapes the police dragnet.

February 20, 1958: FBI designates James Lanza as a "Top Hoodlum."

March 20, 1958: FBI begins 30-day mail cover (i.e., mail interception) of 559 Washington Street, the headquarters of Lanza Brothers.

April 1, 1959: FBI HQ approves the San Francisco Field Office's request to install an illegal microphone at the Lanza Brothers' place of business.

November 8–9, 1960: John F. Kennedy is elected with heavy assistance from the Chicago Outfit.

January 21, 1961: Robert F. Kennedy is sworn in as attorney general.

May 30, 1961: Gov. Pat Brown signs a bill repealing California's vagrancy statute, thereby depriving the SFPD of its favorite tool to harass suspected mobsters, minorities, and anyone else the police did not like.

1961: Abati allegedly names Lanza the boss of the family.

November 22, 1963: John F. Kennedy is assassinated in Daley Plaza.

July 11, 1965: Lyndon Baines Johnson orders the suspension of all illegal wiretaps except those specifically authorized by the attorney general in "National Security" matters.[2]

July 12, 1965: According to the FBI, Lanza electronic wiretap terminated.

September 5, 1969: Alioto files libel suit seeking $7.5 million in actual damages and an additional $5 million in punitive damages against *Look* magazine's founder and publisher Gardner Cowles and his publishing company, Cowles Communications, in the U.S. District Court for the northern district of California.

   After four inconclusive trials and two appeals to the Ninth Circuit Court of Appeals (including an unsuccessful request for U.S. Supreme Court review), Alioto is ultimately awarded $350,000 in general damages, plus costs, when the case concludes in 1981.

September 1969: *Look* magazine, relying, in part, on the fruits of past illegal FBI surveillance, publishes an article claiming to link Lanza and other organized crime figures to the then San Francisco Mayor Joseph Alioto, previously a leading contender for vice presidential slot on the Democratic Party's 1968 ticket.

October 15, 1970: Congress passes the Organized Crime Control Act of 1970 (Public Law 91-452), the best known portion of which permitted RICO prosecutions for the first time.

September 16, 1971: Blaming an increase in postal rates, Gardner Cowles announces that *Look* magazine will cease publication with its October 19, 1971 issue.

February 11, 1976: Joseph "The Animal" Barboza is murdered in San Francisco by Joseph J.R. Russo of the Patriarca family.

October 1977: The body of Peter Catelli is found in a trunk of a car in San Francisco. Both Angelo and Salvatore Marino are charged with the crime. Two trials and appeals later, Salvatore's conviction is overturned.

February 14, 2006: Joseph "Jimmy the Hat" Lanza dies at 104.

June 21, 2014: Pope Francis declares Mafia membership incompatible with participation in the Catholic Church, stating in Calabria, Italy "Those who in their lives have taken this evil road, this road of evil, such as the mobsters, they are not in communion with God, they are excommunicated."

Chapter 1

Disarming the Bodyguard: San Francisco Mafia Myths and Realities

Truth deserves a bodyguard of lies.

—*Winston S. Churchill*[1]

Before diving into the saga of Francesco and James Lanza and what they did, it is important to take a moment to clear up what they *did not* do, but sadly, are often either blamed or credited for. In addition, this is a good time to discuss some common misconceptions about *La Cosa Nostra* and organized crime generally, because, as Churchill noted, unless we disable those bodyguards of lies, we will never get to the truth.

Fortunately, in this case—as in so many others—the truth is far more interesting than the myth.

MYTH NO. 1: "THERE'S NO ORGANIZED CRIME IN SAN FRANCISCO" AND "THERE'S NO MAFIA IN SAN FRANCISCO"

Organized crime has been with us ever since criminals first realized that they could accomplish more in concert than they could individually. Indeed, it has been a documented part of San Francisco's history since the City passed under U.S. control in 1848. As word of the California gold rush spread around the world, San Francisco became an attractive place for some of Down Under's worst residents to find new prey. Indeed, according to Herbert Asbury, "by the early autumn of 1849, the arrivals from Australia had become so numerous, and so thoroughly dominated the

underworld, that the district in which they congregated began to be
known as Sydney-Town, and it was so called for some ten years."[2]

Asbury notes that the residents of Sydney Town (who came to be
called the Sydney Ducks by other San Franciscans) "opened lodging-
houses, dance-halls, groggeries and taverns."[3] When underworld commerce became tiresome, on multiple occasions they attempted to burn
the City down both as a cover for looting and burglary[4] and as a signal
of their displeasure with City authorities.[5]

The San Francisco Police Department (SFPD) and the district attorney
were as ineffective in dealing with the Sydney Ducks, as they would each
later prove to be with the Lanzas and their considerably less public (and
less violent) operations. Even so, no city with aspirations to greatness can
allow a mob of arsonists and thieves to operate unimpeded without *any*
consequences, so in 1851, a group of citizens decided to organize an
insurrection and claim the power of life and death over their neighbors.[6]

What would ultimately become known as the Committee of Vigilance
of 1851[7] quickly distinguished itself by defying the governor of California and lynching three Sydney Ducks in short order,[8] without any apparent legal consequences to the members of the committee—all leading
citizens—when conventional authority was eventually restored. Seeing
their members swinging in the breeze evidently had the salutary effect on
the Ducks that the committee had intended, because for the next two
years, according to Asbury, "San Francisco was as peaceful and law-
abiding a city as could be found on the American continent."[9]

Through our modern eyes, *both* the Sydney Ducks *and* the Committee
of Vigilance qualify as organized crime entities—the only difference is
their degree of organization. From what we know, the Ducks operated
under a loose hierarchy, and although they might come together and
assist each other for certain capers (e.g., the multiple attempts to burn the
City down), the group lacked a formal chain of command. In contrast,
the Committee of Vigilance had both a written constitution and formal
lists of officers.[10]

The Mafia in San Francisco and elsewhere would fall between these
two extremes. Although dons like Francesco and James Lanza could and
would exercise tighter control over their soldiers (sometimes, much to
their great annoyance) than any leader of the Sydney Ducks could dream,
they would have considered producing a written constitution to be the
depth of foolishness. Then again, the Committee of Vigilance never had
to worry about being prosecuted under the Racketeer Influenced and Corrupt Organizations ("RICO") Act.

The other difference between the Mafia and these two groups is that the
Sydney Ducks lacked the desire or the ability to plan for its continued

existence, and the Vigilance Committee was explicitly intended to be a short-term project by its creators. The Mafia, in contrast, is designed to *survive* for the ages. That is why—as we see later on—the Lanzas passed on inducting new members in the 1950s and 1960s due to concerns about heat from the FBI and others.

Although the Ducks were largely done with San Francisco after the events of 1851, some in the City had not quite had their fill of using organized crime to punish lawbreakers and political rivals, as evidenced by the formation of a second Committee of Vigilance in 1856. The said committee proceeded to hang Charles Cora, the boyfriend of Belle Cora (then a local madam) for killing—in a duel—a man who had insulted Belle's honor,[11] as well as a local politician who had murdered a muckraking journalist.[12] As in 1851, the governor fumed impotently, but the members of the committee escaped any real punishment for their actions.[13] Given these events, anyone who claimed organized crime was absent from San Francisco in the 19th century would have been deemed naive at best or a dangerous lunatic at worst.

As for the Mafia, the first mention of it in the *San Francisco Chronicle* appears to have been on October 18, 1874, where the paper's London correspondent told readers about "a more numerous band of cut-throats called the Mafia [that] keeps the inhabitants of Palermo, in Sicily, in terror."[14] By the 1890s, the *Chronicle*'s competition the *San Francisco Call* regularly kept its readers enthralled with tales of Mafia (sometimes misspelled "Maffia") wars in New Orleans[15] and elsewhere. Indeed, the paper quoted one alleged *mafioso* cooling his heels in a New Orleans lockup as saying, "They have got the Mafia society everywhere. *They have it in San Francisco, Chicago, St. Louis, New York and here*"[16] (emphasis added). According to the *Call*, the Mafia was "simply a murderous, blackmailing, terrorizing association of criminals, similar [sic] but probably more formidable than the Chinese highbinders of San Francisco."[17]

Although the tongs the *Call* found wanting in criminal ability when compared to the Mafia might take offense at that estimation, it was likely accurate at the time. Although criminal tongs in San Francisco and elsewhere wreaked criminal and economic havoc on the Chinese American communities, they generally lacked either the inclination or the ability to expand their operations to the City as a whole, particularly after the passage of the federal Chinese Exclusion Act in 1882.

In any event, much of the *Call*'s coverage of the period focused on the aftermath of the slaying of New Orleans Chief of Police David C. Hennessy, allegedly by the *mafioso*, on October 15, 1890. After their acquittal for murder charges, the accused were promptly lynched while in police custody by a different sort of New Orleans mob, leading to anarchy in

New Orleans and a period of severe diplomatic tension between the United States and Italy.

Of course, being a San Francisco paper of its time, the *Call* declared in an editorial: "*We are not yet in possession of all the facts* leading up to and in connection with the lynching of the Italian prisoners at New Orleans. *Until we are*, it will be *impossible to form an opinion* as to the full measure of provocation which induced the action of the people"[18] (emphasis added). In other words, maybe the spectacle of city residents breaking into a jail and lynching several men who were just acquitted *is not* so bad if the residents were aggravated, perhaps by a criminal court verdict they did not like. One wonders whether the *Call* would have felt the same if San Francisco had not had the experiences it did with both Committees of Vigilance.

Shortly thereafter, San Francisco had its own alleged Mafia atrocities for its newspapers to write about. Readers of the February 5, 1892 edition of the *Call* were greeted with: "TERRIBLY SLASHED: Mrs. Rosie Campagna Wounded by Antonio Lalla."[19] According to the article, Campagna's husband had gotten into a dispute with another merchant, Domencino Parenti, which led to an argument with butcher knives and chains. Although the SFPD arrested both Mr. Campagna and Mr. Parenti, they were both quickly released with their charges dropped. At that point, Lalla—who was Parenti's brother-in-law and who previously claimed to have been a member of the Mafia who fled New Orleans after committing a murder—slashed Ms. Campagna from chin to ear in three different places.[20] Tellingly, once he was arrested, Lalla apparently rediscovered *Omertà* and refused to talk to the *Call*'s reporter, much to their evident annoyance.[21]

Some of the other stories about the early Mafia in San Francisco read more like dark slapstick comedy than hard news. My personal favorite is the piece the *Call* ran on December 7, 1898 entitled: "RIVALED THE FROG, NOT THE NIGHTENGALE: Di Franchi Thought He Could Sing."[22] Despite what its title suggests, the article is not about a *mafioso*—Di Franchi—turning informer, but about an account of what may be the most ridiculous ways for a man of respect to meet his end. Di Franchi bet another bar patron a dollar that he could outsing him (with the bartender as judge) and, after Di Franchi lost, drew a gun on the barkeep who, alas for Di Franchi, shot first and did not miss.[23]

By 1905, the *Call* was confident enough to declare without equivocation: "The Mafia exists in San Francisco. Indisputable evidence of this fact is in the hands of the police."[24] The 1906 quake and fire turned the attention of the San Francisco papers to other topics, but at this point, they had not yet lost interest in *La Cosa Nostra*. On March 15, 1909, the *Call* reprinted (in English) an editorial from *L'Italia*, one of San Francisco's Italian newspapers,* regarding the assassination of New York Police Department Det. Joseph Petrosino in Sicily. Because it was written by Italians for an Italian audience, part of the editorial is worth quoting in full: "No matter how their organization be defined—call it Black Hand or Mafia or any other name—*the gravest and most painful thing for us Italians is that no longer can we deny the existence of wide associations of criminals who can boldly operate their deeds, both in Sicily and in America*"[25] (emphasis added).

The desire on the part of some to deny the existence of the Mafia specifically, and organized crime in general, only slowly came to San Francisco, but it appealed to those with either short memories or credulous natures. In 1943, district attorney candidate (and future California attorney general and governor) Edmund G. "Pat" Brown proclaimed, "There is no organized crime in San Francisco; the crime is all organized by the police department."[26]

Brown was right in stating that bent cops have been as much a part of the San Francisco scene as sourdough bread since the days of the gold rush. Besides the vigilance committees in the 1850s (which were, in part, a reaction to a police force rendered useless by corruption), another scandal in the 1930s would disclose the almost wholesale compromising of the police force by underworld interests—and the subsequent ham-fisted attempts by the City to unsuccessfully cover it up. However, the fact that corrupt cops were apparently as common as fog in the City by the Bay does not address the unspoken meaning in Brown's quip.

As noted above, crime that consists of a conspiracy of more than two people is by definition "organized" whether it is committed by police officers or civilians, so read literally, Brown's statement makes no sense.

The only way for it to *make* superficial sense is if the phrase "organized crime" is understood—as Brown apparently intended—as a synonym for *La Cosa Nostra*. In other words, Brown was engaging in what Ian Henry López calls "Dog Whistle Politics"—that is, using coded language to refer to a particular racial or ethnic group (in this case Italians and Italian Americans who happened to be members of *La Cosa Nostra*)—without explicitly saying so.[27] Given that he was running for office in a city with a large Italian population at the time he made his statement, Brown's attempt at discretion was tactically understandable, although offensive.

---

* *L'Italia* would go on to become one of the two most important Italian newspapers in the United States, as we see in Chapter 7.

In addition to being obnoxious, Brown's statement was manifestly inaccurate. Throughout the Prohibition Era, as this book shows, with the exception of the McDonough brothers (as seen in Chapter 4), the top bootleggers (at least those the newspapers apparently knew about) were almost exclusively Italian or Italian American.

After the booze wars petered out in the late 1920s, the *San Francisco Chronicle* generally (and conveniently) lost interest in the City's organized crime enterprises until the slaying of Nick DeJohn in the late 1940s—and got disinterested again for decades thereafter after Brown (who was, by this time, the district attorney) aborted the prosecution of the men charged with DeJohn's murder *after* the case had already gone to the jury.

It is true that there were many organized criminal activities, such as Elmer "Bones" Remmer's gambling operations in San Francisco (at the Menlo Club and elsewhere) and around the Bay during this period, that were not—strictly speaking—Mafia owned, operated, or affiliated, to say nothing of the prostitution enterprises run by Sally Stanford and others. Indeed, Remmer as a non-Italian and Stanford as a woman were disqualified for membership in the Mafia even if they had *wanted* to join. As the above record indicates, organized crime has been part of the DNA of San Francisco since the City first passed under U.S. control in the mid-18th century. Claims to the contrary are simply not supported by the facts.

Although this book focuses on what is generally considered to be the American Mafia's "modern" period, which began after the organization of the commission by Salvatore Lucania (aka Lucky Luciano) after the aftermath of the Castellammarese War in 1931, the overall history of the Mafia in the United States predates the commission by decades.

MYTH NO. 2: THE LANZAS CREATED FISHERMAN'S WHARF

The original Fisherman's Wharf was built in 1853—almost two decades before Francesco Lanza was born in Sicily—by a man named Henry Meiggs[28] and was first located at the intersection of what was then Jefferson and Powell streets.[29] After the waterfront area was expanded by adding landfill and moving the shoreline further out into the Bay, the wharf was relocated several times. A 1911 map by August Chevalier places it just north of the intersection of Beach and Jones streets. Today, the wharf is sited at Taylor Street and Embarcadero.

As for how the wharf came to be in the first place, Meiggs was a wood merchant from upstate New York who managed to sell his cargo at an astronomical profit[30] in a city plagued with gold rush fever. He built the wharf as an appendix to his real estate interests in North Beach—ironically, he saw it as a place to unload lumber rather than as the base it later became for fishing and crabbing operations, much less as the restaurant destination it later became under the Lanzas and others. Also, given that Meiggs was also an assistant city alderman, at the time he built the wharf, he evidently felt pretty confident that he would be able to tilt the regulatory table his way with regard to building permits.

In 1850, San Francisco had what amounted to a bicameral municipal legislature, with one house being the "Board of Aldermen" and the other being the "Board of Assistant Aldermen." Each of the city's wards got to send one representative to each board, and when the boards met together, they became the "Common Council" or the body analogous to today's board of supervisors. Alas, after the state legislature passed the Consolidation Act in 1856, the boards of aldermen were combined into one board of supervisors.

Beyond being legislated out of a job by meddlers in Sacramento, Meiggs had other problems. Things did not quite work out as he had planned with his real estate development, so, facing a cash squeeze, Meiggs helped himself to some $800,000 in City warrants, signed by the mayor and the comptroller in advance (and who apparently knew nothing of his scam).[31] Meiggs ultimately fled to South America a step ahead of the law.[32]

As Asbury notes in *The Barbary Coast*, Meiggs made another fortune and attempted to repay part of what he owed (or had stolen). Although the California Legislature was willing to pass a bill granting Meiggs amnesty, the governor was less forgiving, and Meiggs was barred from returning to the United States—at least as a free man.[33]

Although Italian and Italian American fishermen were major players in what the wharf ultimately became and Francesco Lanza was an early partner in the Exposition Fish Grotto with Giuseppe Alioto, father of future San Francisco Mayor Joseph Alioto, the Lanzas cannot be credited—or blamed—depending on one's opinion of the current wharf and pier 39 area, for creating it in the first place.

MYTH NO. 3: IF ONE MEMBER OF THE FAMILY IS IN THE MAFIA, ALL OF THEM AUTOMATICALLY ARE/MYTH NO. 4: MAFIOSOS ONLY ENGAGE IN ILLEGAL BUSINESSES

In the first recorded sociological study of a Mafia crime family, *A Family Business*, Francis A.J. Ianni and Elizabeth Reuss-Ianni refuted both of these myths. With regard to the first myth, as Ianni and Reuss-Ianni point out, although a family connection is helpful to secure membership in a crime family, the usual approach is for *some* male members of a biological family to join, not all of them. As of this writing, there has been no documented instance of a woman being inducted into the Mafia in the

United States, although the history of the Mafia in Sicily is more ambiguous on this point.

This appears to be in accord with what we know of the Lanzas. The FBI never believed that James's brother and business partner was involved in anything that was not a legitimate activity (despite sharing an office with Jimmy that had been illegally bugged by the bureau). Similarly, the children of James Lanza had no reported or suspected involvement with organized crime.

As for the second myth, Ianni and Reuss-Ianni state that the crime family they observed (whom they gave the pseudonym of the "Lupollos") frequently used their resources and assets for both legal and illegal businesses, depending on the circumstances and the opportunity.

I would suggest that it is best to think of *mafioso* not as criminals who occasionally engage in business but as businessmen who acknowledge no limit on their freedom of action, save force or the credible threat of it (either from the government, a competing family, or from personnel higher than them on the Mafia food chain). From this point of view, there is little difference between, say, insurance brokerage (James Lanza's primary business during the 1950s and 1960s) and the narcotics smuggling the government thought he was involved in, other than in terms of differing levels of risk and reward.

MYTH NO. 5: JAMES LANZA WAS A FAILURE AS A MOBSTER

This is probably the most pernicious claim of all the myths. When seen from the perspective of men engaged in a dangerous business, where both the government and their competitors were literally their lethal adversaries, it is difficult to imagine a higher level of success than surviving to enjoy a comfortable retirement as a free man. James Lanza lived to be 104 and got to enjoy decades of his favorite pastime—watching the horses run at the Bay Meadows racetrack—while colleagues, adversaries, and others like Joe Bonanno, Jimmy "The Weasel" Fratianno, John F. Kennedy, and Joseph Alioto had long gone on to their rewards.

Thus, in some ways, the fact that Lanza is not a household name like Al Capone or John Gotti is an indicator that he did his job far better than they did, rather than the reverse. Unlike Capone and Gotti, he did all he could to *lower* his public profile, maintain his operational and personal security, and stay out of the news. Although Lanza did not always succeed in flying completely below the radar, he *was* good enough to frustrate state and federal law enforcement for decades, despite his primary adversary during this period being J. Edgar Hoover—who, as we see, was more than happy to tear up constitutional guarantees against illegal searches as long as he was not likely to get caught.

For this reason, this book is different from most studies of the Mafia, which—whether they focus on mobsters in a particular city or a particular crime family or limit their scope to a single person (e.g., Al Capone or John Gotti)—tend to rely heavily on court records to discuss their protagonist(s)' rise and fall *because* those individuals were actually arrested and brought to trial. The genius of the Lanzas, in contrast, was *avoiding* that kind of legal scrutiny, which is one of many reasons their tale has not been told in detail until now.

Thanks to illegal FBI electronic surveillance beginning in the late 1950s, we have a lot more direct evidence about what James Lanza was up to when he led the family than we do about his father, Francesco or Tony Lima and Mike Abati, the men who preceded James as bosses of the San Francisco family. For that reason, think of this book as your guide on a trail where the Lanzas have a head start, but we are in hot pursuit. Their footprints may be faint at the beginning, but they will increase in frequency and intensity as we go along.

It is now time to begin the journey at its start point in Sicily, which we do in Chapter 2.

Chapter 2

Sicilian Realities and American Dreams

To most people, Castelbuono, Sicily, is known for two things: the fortress in the center of the town built by Count Francesco I of Ventimiglia[1] in 1316 and the cultivation of manna (i.e., crystalized sap)[2] from certain varieties of ash trees, which is supposedly referenced in Exodus 16:14–16[3] and is used as a natural remedy for a host of aliments as well as a diabetic friendly sweetener.[4]

However, Castelbuono is important for another reason. It is where Francesco Proetto, who would go on to become Francesco Lanza, and then on to lead the San Francisco family of the American Mafia, first blinked his eyes open on October 8, 1872.

In Francesco's[5] day[6] and our own,[7] around 10,000 people called it home. In a bit of ironic foreshadowing, like much of modern San Francisco, today's Castelbuono is densely built and street parking is extremely scarce.

But the Count of Ventimiglia, who was Francesco's eponym, did not build a castle there for the hell of it. Although Castelbuono's official municipal Web site waxes elegiac about the town's "rich memories" from the period it was under "Greek, Roman, Byzantine and Arabic" rule,[8] this is a subtle reminder of Castelbuono and Sicily's place in what has been a rough neighborhood for centuries.

Sicily is named for the Sicels, the Italic people who occupied the island from approximately the Iron Age until they were wiped out in the Peloponnesian War during one of the myriad of invasions that the land was seemingly condemned to suffer by history.[9] Indeed, from approximately

439 C.E. (when the Vandals ripped Sicily from the side of the barely breathing Roman Empire) until 1860 and the landing of Giuseppe Garibaldi's Redshirts, *all* choices that mattered for Sicilians were made by foreign overlords. Whether those particular overlords happened to be Vandal, Arab, French, or Spanish or Bourbon was relatively immaterial to the average Sicilian, since the said overlords saw Sicily and its people as sources of wealth to be extracted, rather than as human and physical capital to be developed.

Not surprisingly, this led to multiple uprisings, most of which were bloodily suppressed. Even those who "succeeded"—like the Sicilian Vespers of 1282 or the Second Italian War for Independence in 1860—merely traded one foreign king or distant overlord for another, most of whom were strikingly disinterested in building a civil society for the average Sicilian, let alone arbitration of disputes and control of brigands. Because politics, like nature, abhors a vacuum, the stage was set for the entry of an organization that *would* provide, in Castelbuono and elsewhere, the services the government would not.

ENTER THE HONORED SOCIETY

Although the development of the Mafia may have been inevitable given the conditions in Sicily just before and after the Second Italian War of Independence, the exact path of its development remains a mystery. However, two main theories exist. As *should* be the case in an Italian story, the first theory is ridiculously sentimental, but unlikely, whereas the second is far less interesting, yet far more probable.

First, there is the "sentimental" version. According to Selwyn Raab in *Five Families: The Rise, Decline, and Resurgence of America's Most Powerful Mafia Empires*,[10] "[A] Sicilian woman died resisting rape by a French soldier and, in revenge, her fiancé slaughtered the attacker." According to the legend, "The fanciful episode supposedly sparked the creation of a rebellious, acronymic slogan from the first letter of each word: '*Morte alla Francia Italia anela*' ('Death to France is Italy's Cry')," that is, "Mafia." However, the more probable explanation, according to Raab, is that the word Mafia is derived from "a combined Sicilian-Arabic slang expression that means acting as a protector against the arrogance of the powerful."[11]

Similarly, as Salvatore Lupo points out in his seminal *History of the Mafia,* some who should know better have claimed, "If a shapely young woman walks by, a Sicilian will say she is a *ragazza mafiosa* (mafiosa girl), and if a young man is quite alert and intelligent, he will say that the boy is quite *mafioso*."[12] Lupo notes that this line of thinking is often used to justify the idea that the Mafia does not exist, either in the United States or in Sicily, as a criminal organization, but is instead some sort of cultural eccentricity peculiar to Sicily.

Although the overwhelming majority of scholars who have examined the subject (including Lupo and myself) agree that the only reasonable inference to be drawn from the evidence is that the Mafia *does* exist as an organized criminal enterprise, there is likewise a general agreement that part of the reason the Mafia has flourished for so long in Sicilian and U.S. soil is through its appropriation and use of cultural models for its own benefit. As Lupo points out: "The *Mafia d'ordine* (order-keeping Mafia) always presupposes a disorder that needs to be organized and kept firmly under control, whether during post-Risorgimento Sicily or during the more recent process of criminal escalation."[13] Similarly, although the word *omertà* is usually misunderstood as the duty of a *mafioso* to remain silent, several commentators have asserted that its true meaning is far deeper and more nuanced.

Cesare Mori, Mussolini's "Iron Prefect," who is thought to have done more damage to the Mafia in Sicily than to any other antagonist until the late 20th century, defined it this way: "In its original meaning *omertà* also implies exemption from the common law: as such it embodies the pride of all rebels against justice and tyranny, in every age an country, besides a particular view of questions involving personal honour." Furthermore, said Mori, "It is easy to understand, then, that *omertà*, in its original sense, has always exerted a special influence over the masses, *for the masses love the man who can take the law into his own hands to revenge an injury better than him that can forgive*"[14] (emphasis added).

Lupo generally concurs with Mori that *omertà* means much more than simply not reporting crimes to the authorities or cooperating with their investigations. "In the nineteenth-century organizations of freemasonry, even outside of Sicily, the informer was deemed *infame*, or infamous. From the Masonic concept of humanity derives the Camorristic concept of humility—that is to say, subordination to the wishes of the organization. Hence, according to one interpretation, by converting the 'l' sound to an 'r' sound, which is typical of the Sicilian dialect, the word *omertà* is derived."[15]

Given this background, it is not surprising that Raab would note, "To a nineteenth-century Sicilian with a cultural heritage of centuries of danger and oppression, true manhood was said to consist of an independent arrogance in which a man kept silent in the event of a crime. The Sicilian reserved the right of personal *vendetta*, vengeance, for offenses committed against himself and his relatives."[16]

A SHOTGUN WEDDING LEAVES SICILY AT THE ALTAR

Thus, when Garibaldi landed in Sicily with a thousand men at Marsala in 1860[17] to strike the first blow for the unification of Italy against the Bourbons of the Kingdom of the Two Sicilies—who were the latest batch of foreigners and their local henchmen to claim the island—it surprised no one when several thousand Sicilians flocked to his banner. As Raab points out, some of these men—when not fighting the Bourbons—"alternated between working the fields and holing up in caves as bandits . . . they were glorified by Garibaldi as his 'Squadri della Mafia,' Mafia squadron."[18]

Although the Mafia and other Sicilians helped purchase Italy's freedom with their sweat and blood, the new government in Rome failed to honor that debt. Indeed, after Garibaldi was effectively sidelined during the first years of the new Italian state, there is little historical evidence that his successors, who were predominantly from the north of Italy, even *wanted* to help improve the lives of Sicilians. Instead, those elites developed the doctrine of *trasformismo*,[19] whereby control of the new central government was virtually ceded to northern Italian-based elites, whereas their Sicilian counterparts were given a free hand to govern—or in practice, misgovern—the island for their own purposes. To the new regime in Rome, Sicily might as well have been a bandit-infested island on the other side of the world.

In fairness to the Piedmont elites who dominated the new centralized government in Rome, Sicily was not the only problem they had to contend with. Active resistance to the Italian *Risorgimento* (reunification) movement—notably by the Catholic Church, which "[declared] war on liberalism" in 1864[20] and arguably created the doctrine of papal infallibility to increase its ability to stop observant Catholics from participating in Italy's new political system[21]—impeded the ability of the new central Italian government, which did not even control Rome until the departure of French troops after the latter's defeat in the Franco-Prussian War[22] and which then had to govern a mostly illiterate population[23] to improve the lives of Sicilians even if it had wanted to.

Sadly, in the early years of the Kingdom of Italy, the central government quickly chose the tools used by every other despot who had controlled Sicily before them. As Lupo notes, "The fact that Sicily never experienced a large-scaled outbreak of pro-Bourbon brigandage did nothing to prevent the government from extending the Pica Law of 1863 to Sicily, establishing martial law on the island as well."[24] Under the said statute "in provinces which were declared 'in a state of brigandage,' groups of three or more found in the countryside with the apparent intention of committing crimes would be judged by a military court, while those who resisted arrest could be shot."[25]

By grasping an iron fist around Sicily's throat, the central government on the mainland only succeeded in making a bad situation worse. As Lupo points out:

The measures General Giuseppe Govone and the prefect-general Giacomo Medici took to round up the numerous men avoiding the draft called for general sweeps of whole provinces in western Sicily; towns and villages were surrounded and occupied by armed soldiers, and the relatives of those avoiding the draft were persecuted, in line with the concept of collective community guilt in the eyes of the military authorities. But by theorizing and implementing these systems, the generals succeeded only in achieving the opposite of what they had hoped, swelling the already vast ranks of draft-dodgers and deserters ... with a huge number of individuals who had become fugitives from justice precisely in the wake and a direct result of the army's actions (it would be no exaggeration to call them terrorist actions).[26]

As a result of these and other pressures, in September 1866—a mere six years before Francesco was born—Palermo rose in revolt against the central government, with several Mafia *cosca* in the vanguard of the rebels.[27] According to Lupo, "At the climax of the revolt, on 19 September, there were 12,000 armed rebels in the city, 1,200 of whom had come in from the countryside and 'two thousand citrus gardeners, peasants, *carretieri* (teamsters), and the most ferocious of them all, who live in the *sobborghi,* or outlying districts, and in the *casolari,* or farmhouses, surrounding Palermo.' "[28]

Other *mafioso* fought for the forces of property and the central government, which ultimately crushed the revolt.[29] But no matter who *formally* controlled Palermo and its environs, including Castelbuono, real power over the economic assets of the area remained in the hands of the Mafia.

WHEN SICILY GIVES LEMONS, THE MAFIA TAKES LEMONADE

Although the historical and political factors set forth in the preceding sections set the stage for the foundation of the Mafia, to some observers it was the *type* of economic inputs that existed in Sicily in the 19th century, which were the most critical ingredient in the spread of the Mafia's tentacles into the pockets of Sicilians and into the heart of their government. In a 2012 article, "Origins of the Sicilian Mafia: The Market for Lemons," Arcangelo Dimico, Alessia Isopi, and Ola Olsson argued that the presence of lemon groves generally served as an effective proxy to determining whether or not the Mafia was present during the 19th and early 20th centuries. As an initial matter, the island's climate of small landholdings and sharecropping bred trouble.

In 1887 the share of citizens that owned the land was still the lowest in Italy with an average of less than 2.05 owners per 100 citizens, compared to for instance 15 owners per 100 in Piedmont. . . . In addition, almost 56 percent of the population employed in agriculture owned less than one hectare of land and most of them were hired by the landlord on a daily basis at less than one lira per day rate.[30]

After the scurvy-deterring effects of lemons became known in the late 18th century, Sicily was transformed into—at least to some observers— "a vast lemon juice factory."[31] By the time Francesco was born, "Sicilian production of citrus fruits represented almost 73 percent of the total production in Italy."[32] By the early 20th century, those who owned the lemon groves in Sicily grossed an estimated net profit of approximately $150 an acre in 1908 dollars[33] (or $3,947.37 per acre in 2015 dollars),[34] serving the needs of the United States, the United Kingdom, and Austria– Hungary for citrus products.[35]

Although this was undoubtedly sweet on some levels, the cultivation of lemons created certain challenges in a place like Sicily. As Dimico and his colleagues note, "Compared to other agricultural goods like grapes or wheat, lemons are very easy to collect quickly by a prospective thief, and the price per stolen bucket is further very high. These factors contributed to lemon plantations being in particular need of protection."[36] This is the sort of enterprise that plays directly to the Mafia's primary economic strength—that is, that of being a "rent seeker," or an entity that seeks to obtain the profits of others without giving anything of value in exchange.[37] If, as Lupo has noted, the Mafia can create the conditions that *require* protection while simultaneously *providing* that protection, particularly in industries like lemon cultivation that can be disrupted by actions at a few key choke points (e.g., theft or destruction of crops, interference with irrigation, and so on), then it effectively becomes a silent partner in that economic activity without having to invest a lire. Moreover, because it is an *export* industry, trade in lemons offered the Mafia the ability to spread its reach across the Atlantic. As Lupo notes, "The first documented Mafia presence in the United States is in the port city of New Orleans, and that presence is clearly closely related to the substantial trade in lemons and oranges that ran through that southern port."[38]

A later study—*Poor Institutions, Rich Mines: Resource Curse and the Origins of the Sicilian Mafia*[39]—determined that the presence of sulfur mines, which are clustered in southern and western Sicily, had a similar spurring effect on Mafia activities. According to the authors: "[W]e do not claim that sulfur was the sole cause of the emergence of Sicilian Mafia. What we claim is that the effect of Sulphur on the emergence of Mafia is the only one (i) clearly identifiable and (ii) empirically robust."[40]

As a reflection of the weak rule of law on the island, "a set of laws regulating within-mines penal responsibilities was approved only in 1893."[41] Thus, "Due to the lack of organized law enforcement, each miner had to protect his extraction from other miners, as raw material extracted by miners was usually only paid only once a week *and the material extracted each day was two or three times worth the daily wage of a worker*"[42] (emphasis added).

The rewards—both on a micro level in terms of worker's wages and on a macro level in terms of net profits—were huge. By 1893, Sicily extracted 83 percent of all sulfur mined across the entire world,[43] which was used to make materials as varied as from manufacturing acids and alkalis to gunpowder.[44] Although the Sicilian export market peaked around 1900, with the development and exploitation of other sources of sulfur around the world coming online,[45] resulting in the sulfur industry going into decline (other than a boomlet between the 1920s and through approximately the 1940s, which was likely driven by the preparations for World War II), Sicily would deal with the aftermath of Mafia control over the industry for generations to come.

Lupo poses the question: "As the Sulphur industry began to decline, might the structure of the mining crews have served as a scaffolding for the construction of the Mafia crew as a self-motivating franchise?"[46] The answer of history, based on the *Poor Institutions* article and similar works, would appear to be "yes."

As for Castelbuono, beyond its geographical proximity to the Mafia's hub at Palermo, given that manna was one of its primary crops, it seems reasonable to infer that the same "curses" lemons and sulfur brought to the rest of the island would apply with equal force to manna cultivation. An ash tree, after all, is just as vulnerable to interference with its irrigation system as a lemon tree—and manna can also be stolen if those who are supposed to watch it for the landlord have been co-opted or neutralized by the local Mafia.

A LANCE BY ANY OTHER NAME WOULD NOT BE AS SHARP?

On September 23, 1894, Francesco married Caterina Albanese, when he was 22.[47] His son, Mariano Vincenzo Proetto—whom we would know as James Lanza—was born on October 23, 1902. After he emigrated to the United States, Francesco's brother[48] obtained a decree changing Francesco's name and that of his wife and children from "Proetto" to "Lanza"[49] on June 10, 1926. The move would cause his son James no end of headaches in the years to come, and the reasons *why* Francesco did it remain elusive. It does not appear that he did it because Proetto was "shameful" or "ridiculous" or would have revealed that he or any of the members of his family were born out of wedlock, at least according to investigators for the United States Immigration and Naturalization Service (INS).[50]

When the INS finally got around to asking James Lanza about this in the early 1970s, he claimed he was ignorant of the entire procedure and asserted that he had only been known as "Lanza" from his earliest days.[51] Where this caused him trouble down the road is that he was listed on the S.S. Sicila's manifest as "Mariono Vince Proetto."[52] Although James was two years old at the time, his sister Grazia and brothers Natale and Gandolfo who accompanied him *all* had Proetto as their last name as well.

Although the matter cannot be settled definitively based on presently available information—especially since James Lanza's file with the Department of Homeland Security remains heavily redacted for public viewing nearly a decade after his death—there are two potential explanations. First, Lanza is a well-known name with an exceptionally deep lineage in Sicily. As Italian historian Luigi Barzini has pointed out: "The Lanzas are one of the first families in Sicily. They arrived one thousand years ago, fought at the side of Frederick II of Hohenstaufen, King of Sicily and Emperor, in the thirteenth century."[53] Not surprisingly for the holders of a surname that literally means "Lance," during the Middle Ages, the Lanzas were members of the *Ordine della Stella*, or the "Order of the Star," a military order founded in 1595 in Messina for sons of the leading noble families in the area.[54]

More recent famous holders of the Lanza name have included Ferdinando Lanza, who commanded (and surrendered) Neapolitan forces near Palermo to Garibaldi during the unification of Italy,[55] and Prince Raimondo Lanza di Trabia (the "di Trabia" refers to his fiefdom of Trabia), who managed to survive both World War II and his friendship with Count Gian Galeazzo Ciano, the former foreign minister of Fascist Italy and Mussolini's son-in-law,[56] to become the playboy sidekick of Aristotle Onassis for a time.[57]

Given this background, the Lanza name *would* have more cachet, at least among Sicilians and southern Italians in New York City and elsewhere, than "Proetto." It may be for this reason that Francesco used "Lanza" from the earliest period we can document during his time in New York City, as the 1905 New York State Census indicates.[58] However, given the timing of the order changing his name—which he obtained almost two decades after leaving Italy—we can also wonder whether the second potential reason is related to the first. At the time Francesco obtained the decree in 1926, the New York docks and the Fulton Fish Market were under the control of Joseph "Socks" Lanza and the Genovese crime family. Given that in 1915, Francesco gave his occupation as "liquor store" owner to the U.S. Census,[59] it may have been helpful for him to give the impression that he was related to Lanza as a way of deterring demands for extortion and the petition could have been a way to satisfy those who might seek to verify that claim in Sicily.

According to James Prisin-Zano, a relative of James Lanza, a Black Hand ring once demanded $5,000 from Francesco,[60] and Francesco "got in touch with the Mafia boss and received word the 'black hand' demand did not come from the Mafia."[61] Prisin-Zano's statement is consistent with what we now know about *La Mana Negra* or "The Black Hand." For years, it was commonly confused with being either an antecedent organization of the Mafia or a competing organization to the Mafia. In point of fact, it was neither.

The so-called Black Hand crimes—typically, but not exclusively, extortion rackets—were in vogue during the early part of the 20th century in New York and other cities on the Eastern seaboard.[62] Because it was advantageous for the persons doing the extorting to assert that they were part of a vast conspiracy in order to strike fear in the hearts of their victims, many understandably did exactly that. However, we now know today that most groups engaged in "Black Hand" crimes were small— usually, under 10 persons—and some were not even Italian, let alone Sicilian.[63]

Indeed, as a 1906 article pointed out, "the Black Hand was not Italian in origin at all, but Spanish . . . The name Black Hand had 'probably passed into the consciousness of the Latin mind as bound up with organized anarchistic or terroristic warfare on society,' [the author] observed 'and on that account the name is used whenever an Italian with criminal tendencies, if not record, starts out to even up some old score or to get a slice of some other man's cake.' "[64]

The Black Hand is best understood as a descriptive term for criminal behavior, rather than as a separate organization. For example, we would not refer to a group of criminals who engaged in car theft as "The Car Theft Organization"—they could be Mafia, unaffiliated, or members of some other criminal group. Similarly, many Blackhanders were unaffiliated, some had Mafia ties or connections to the Camorra or the Ndrangheta and some just claimed they did.

Because the Black Hand crimes rose in frequency during an era when Italian Americans were fighting against severe discrimination—and because many in the Italian American community feared the imposition of tighter immigration laws if the presence of the Mafia on U.S. shores was admitted as a fact—much time and energy were wasted claiming that the Black Hand either did not exist at all or that the Black Hand was a competing group to the Mafia.[65] This evolved into some in the Italian American community being willing to accept "Black Hand" as a euphemism for the Mafia (which, supposedly, did not exist in the United States), and even led to the short-lived formation of the so-called White Hand groups to work with the police to combat the Black Hand, particularly in Chicago.[66]

Francesco's decision to seek the aid of the Mafia boss is not remarkable given the time period and—with the notable exception of the late Lt. Joseph Petrosino, who founded the NYPD's "Italian Squad" and was assassinated in Palermo in 1909 for his trouble—the general lack of interest in Black Hand crimes among U.S. law enforcement at the time.[67] What does seem unusual is that he was reportedly able to contact the boss *and* get an answer—and that he apparently *never* paid the requested tribute and lived to tell about it.

But all that lay ahead. In the summer of 1904,[68] after the central government had suppressed the *Fasci Siciliani*[69] socialist movement, Francesco—like so many other young Sicilian men—decided to trade Castelbuono's manna groves for the mean streets of New York, as seen in Chapter 3.

Chapter 3

To the Mean Streets
of New York

Francesco Lanza picked a particularly opportune time to relocate to New York City from Sicily with his family in July 1904.[1] The first trains of what would become New York's legendary subway system would begin operation in October of that year,[2] and both the nation and New York were getting back on their feet as the recession of 1902 drew to a close,[3] so the economy was picking up.

That recovery was fortuitous, given that more than *3 million people* who needed to eat already called Manhattan, Brooklyn, and Queens home as of 1900[4] before Francesco and his brood arrived. By comparison, the *entire* population of Sicily was estimated at 3.6 million in 1904,[5] and San Francisco—which was picking itself up from the Barbary Plague of 1900 to 1904[6]—had about 360,000 residents[7] at the time.

Most importantly for our purposes, the first few years of the 20th century marked the last gasp of the gangs, which had held sway over much of New York from about 1825 onward.[8] Their passing—and the dramatic influx of immigrants from Italy like Francesco and his family into the city—created a space for new criminal elite to arise. As Frank J. Cavaioli points out, from 1901 to 1910, a total of 8,795,386 people emigrated to the United States from all over the world,[9] and 23 percent of them—or 2,045,374—were Italian.[10] Since most of those immigrants would ultimately settle in and around New York City, often in Italian enclaves due to nativist prejudice,[11] both New York and the nation were in for a revolution that affected both the upper- and the underworld.

FROM "DEAD RABBITS" TO LA COSA NOSTRA . . . EVENTUALLY

Almost 100 years after it was first published, Herbert Asbury's *The Gangs of New York* remains the seminal source for historians of the New York underworld of this period. Although Asbury got a few things wrong—among other things, he missed the likely involvement of the Mafia in the assassination of chicken dealer Barnet Baff in a 1914 trade war[12]—and some of his language to describe African Americans is extremely problematic, most of his factual reportage is sound.

According to Asbury, the Forty Thieves were the first group of criminals organized enough to deserve the title of "gang": in the Five Points neighborhood of lower Manhattan.[13] They were followed in quick succession by a slew of imitators, including the Dead Rabbits, so named, wrote Asbury, because in gang slang a rabbit "was a rowdy, and a dead rabbit was a very rowdy, athletic fellow."[14] As with the Mafia later on, the gangs of this era prospered because they provided services the population wanted *and* because the gangs were useful to local politicians, specifically in this era, to Tammany Hall—the political faction that mostly controlled the Democratic Party in New York through saloons and political clubhouses[15] and through them, the machinery of city government.

The bargain struck between Tammany politicos and the gangs was simple—the gangs encouraged (at the point of a fist, knife, or blackjack if necessary) voters to cast ballots for the machine[16] when asked (and/or voted multiple times themselves for Tammany candidates, depending on the circumstances) and, in return, Tammany encouraged police to ignore gang activities.[17] Some gang members did quite well from this symbiotic relationship—in 1863, 26-year-old William Walsh went from the Dead Rabbits to the presidency of the City's Board of Aldermen, an ancestor of today's city council.[18]

However, this cozy system started to fall apart shortly before Francesco landed at Ellis Island. In August 1903, a gunfight between partisans of Monk Eastman and members of Paul Kelly's (who was an Italian originally named Paolo Antonini Vacarelli)[19] Five Points gang broke out after a group of Five Pointers tried to knock over one of Eastman's card games at Allen and Rivington streets, just outside of what is now modern Little Italy.[20] When the police tried to intervene, *they* became targets as well.[21] Almost a half-hour of armed anarchy elapsed in lower Manhattan before order of a sort was restored.[22] This sort of thing was about as welcome to Tammany as a clean election, so, according to Asbury, "[T]hey called upon Eastman and Paul Kelly and impressed upon them the obvious fact that *such wholesale combat jeopardized their usefulness*"[23] (emphasis added).

Under pressure from Tammany, Kelly and Eastman made peace—but thanks to a series of convenient (for Tammany anyway) events, both soon faded from the New York scene. In early 1904, Eastman made the mistake of trying to rob a mark who happened to have an armed bodyguard— and when he regained consciousness, Tammany ensured that he would be relocated to prison for the next decade.[24] Shortly thereafter, Kelly decided to relocate uptown and later still to enter labor racketeering, which caused less umbrage to Tammany and fewer headlines.[25]

Even as the visibility and power of the Five Pointers faded, they played an important role as an arena for future organized crime chieftains like Johnny Torrio (who would go on to found the Outfit in Chicago) and Al Capone, as well as Charles Lucania, later better known as "Charlie Lucky," aka Lucky Luciano,[26] to cut their teeth and plan for the future.[27]

But the Mafia was not the only game in town, as Barnet Baff learned to his cost. As David Critchley points out in *The Origin of Organized Crime in America: The New York City Mafia, 1891 to 1931*, attempts to control the market for live poultry probably qualified as the most ancient "racket" the city had.[28] Even so "despite its apparently favorable conditions for racketeers, Mafia involvement in the poultry market was puny. The predominant ethnic makeup of the industry in question was the key to understanding this apparent anomaly."[29] In other words, Creighton found "where an industry remained solidly 'Jewish' in its workforce composition, the Mafia was generally absent."[30] Instead, the Mafia turned its attention to industries that were rich in unskilled or semi-unskilled Italian workers, like the docks in Brooklyn or the construction and garbage cartage across the entire city.[31]

Still, the Mafia *was* available to help their criminal colleagues address economically disruptive annoyances like Baff, who managed to aggravate both union members (he ran his own trucks) and the poultry dealers (by his pricing power stemming from his control over the kosher slaughterhouses where the birds were killed), as well as for his resistance to a nascent poultry trust designed to illegally control prices.[32] When verbal entreaties by others failed, the Mafia provided the men who could make arguments that were impossible for Baff to answer—that is, the ones that come from the barrel of a gun.

Although the Mafia never managed to displace existing racketeers in certain industries like poultry during this era, there were enough opportunities for graft to keep them busy. Some of this was an outgrowth of the *Padrone* system, which, from the late 19th century to the first quarter of the 20th century, was the main way Italian laborers found work.[33] Rather than personally interview prospective workers, the contractor entered into a contract with a *padrone*, whose job it was to locate and sign up the workers. On the surface, in return, the *padrone* got to run the commissary on the construction project and keep between 90 and 100 percent of the profits.[34] In reality, that was just the beginning. *Padrones* got a cut of the workers' wages every week, and sometimes also got paid for their work as foremen by the employer.[35] Lacking access to union organizers and, in some cases, the ability to speak English, the Italian laborers were easy prey for exploitation by their own countrymen, some of whom served as the laborer's banker, landlord, and legal adviser—with fees being charged at every step of the way.[36]

The *padrones'* wings were clipped by the Emergency Quota Act of 1921, which capped the yearly level of immigration from Italy to 3 percent of the number of Italian-born persons already present in the United States, as documented by the 1910 census[37] (which, since there were 1,343,125[38] Italian-born persons enumerated in the census, limited new Italian immigration to 40,294 per year for the next three years). The screws tightened further with the passage of the Immigration Act of 1924, which cut the yearly national origin quota for Italy to 2 percent of the 182,580[39] Italian-born persons documented in the 1890 census[40]—or 3,652 people. As the flow of new Italian immigrants slowed to a trickle, the *padrone* system gradually lost its economic relevance.

Even so, it remains historically important because in many ways, the neo-feudal aspects of the *padrone*–client relationship would be repeated, as the Mafia realized how much money could be made in certain industries by controlling labor unions or employer associations—and in some instances, by having *both* those who provided the capital and those who provided the labor under its thumb.

TO THE LOWER EAST SIDE, *COMPARE!*

Four decades later, the FBI speculated that Francesco had been "wealthy" during his time in New York.[41] Although he was relatively well-off by the time he left the city, when he got there, his "wealth" was conspicuous by its absence. Instead, like so many immigrants of the era, Francesco and his family ended up in the Lower East Side, on 73 Goerck Street,[42] according to the barely legible surviving records of the 1905 New York State census. Francesco listed his occupation on the 1905 census form as "grocer"[43] and his last name as "Lanza."

Sadly, Goerck Street no longer exists, thanks to the redevelopment of lower Manhattan in the 1930s,[44] but thanks to contemporaneous election records from when Francesco lived there, we can estimate its location. The building lay within the 11th Election District, within the 12th Assembly District, which at the time was "bounded by and within Rivington Street, Goerck Street, Delancey Street and Cannon Street"[45] within the heart of the Lower East Side.

In addition to its location, we can infer a few more facts about the Goerck Street building. The 1905 census indicated that Francesco and Catherine resided in the same unit with a Russian family headed by candy store dealer Jacob Lippman, which indicates they—like most immigrants of the era—resided in one of the tenements that simultaneously dominated, defined, and defiled the neighborhood.[46]

Calling the Lower East Side a rough place—even by then-contemporary New York standards—during this period is to make a gross understatement. Thanks to the predictable effects of cramming 600,000 people into an area just more than two square miles across[47] without sufficient space or sanitation, tuberculosis and other diseases spread rampantly.[48]

Microbes were not the only predators in the neighborhood. Until 1910 or so, Goerck Street was controlled by the Short Tails, a gang equally comfortable with committing murder and mayhem on the streets of the Lower East Side or aboard any vessels docked nearby.[49] For variety, they also apparently liked to stick up local bars and run off with the beer, rather than the cash.[50]

Although Goerck Street was notable at one time for more elevated pursuits—one account has early Mormon missionaries Parley P. Pratt and Elijah Fordham used Fordham's house on Goerck as their base in the mid 1800s[51]—by the time Francesco and his family got there, the neighborhood was best known for tenement squalor. Indeed, even hardened Lower East Siders tried to stay away from Goerck Street. Bella Spewack, who grew up in the area and would ultimately co-write *Kiss Me Kate*, recalled, "I went several times to Goerck Street before we moved, compelled by fear and dread."[52]

According to Spewack, "From [Goerck Street] would come every offensive in the bottle fights that would visit Lewis, Cannon, Columbia, and Sheriff streets like some short, noisy pestilence."[53]

73 Goerck Street, where Francesco would eventually live, was no exception to this general pattern. In 1862, the *New York Times* reported that: "PATRICK MCGINNIS, whose residence was at No. 73 Goerck-Street"[54] had been murdered by "repeated blows upon the unfortunate man's head with a cane."[55]

The address continued to be a favorite for some of New York's most colorful residents. In 1869, it was one of the 21 addresses around the city for "John Moran,"[56] who was allegedly engaged in a massive naturalization and voting fraud scheme. In 1891, a teenager named Charles Price who lived there would be arrested for robbing a 12-year-old,[57] to be followed by the New York police busting a husband and wife team who allegedly dealt in stolen goods—in this case, butter, of all things[58]—in 1894.

Somehow, Francesco and his family survived the microbes, the squalor, the cane-murderers, and butter-fencers—and furthermore, managed to evade further visits from nosy census takers for the next 15 years. There is no entry of him in either of the separate censuses conducted in 1910 by the State of New York and the federal government.

However, neither he nor his brother-in-law Mariano Prisinzano[59] was idle. The 1915 edition of R.L. Polk & Co.'s Copartnership and Corporation Directory for Manhattan and the Bronx shows Lanza as a partner with Prisinzano in Lanza & Prisinzano, which dealt in wines and was located at 218 Chrystie.[60] Lanza was also the president of Homecrest Building Co., at 35 Nassau No. 907,[61] which was a property developer as well as a straight construction company. In June 1915 alone, they completed 3 three-story brick tenements at East 10th Street and Avenue O for a total cost of $30,000[62] (or $706,351.49 in 2015 dollars),[63] as well as another separate project at that same address[64] for $15,000 (or $353,175.74 if it were built today). Lanza also headed the Lodi Heights Realty Co., at 218 Chrystie and 192 Bowery No. 203.[65] Although that venture did not come to the attention of the newspapers as much as his construction work, it foreshadowed the family's investments to come in San Francisco real estate.

In its pursuit of his son decades later, the FBI found even more of Francesco's business ventures—and some of his more interesting friends. A November 18, 1958, FBI report noted that "JOHN DI BELLA . . . and others knew FRANCESCO LANZA in New York City and FRANCESCO LANZA reportedly accumulated a great deal of wealth in New York City"[66] (emphasis original).

By the late 1950s, DiBella was a leading cheese manufacturer in Fond du Lac, Wisconsin, who had close ties to both Joe "Joe Bananas" Bonanno (who would go on to sit on the Mafia's commission) and Frank DeSimone, who would head Los Angeles's Mafia family, as we see in Chapters 8 and 10. Both Bonanno and DeSimone would go on to cause Francesco's son James exceptional aggravation in the years to come. But during Francesco's time in New York, according to the FBI, "The

Prisinzano-Lanza Wholesale Company . . . dealt in import and export of food stuffs."[67]

Not surprisingly, business bred litigation. The August 15, 1918, edition of the *Brooklyn Eagle* noted that Francesco and Homecrest had satisfied two judgments against them—to the amount of $338.31 (or $5,327.93 in 2015 dollars) and $116.10 (or $1,828.42 in 2015 dollars) owed to a roofing and seating company, respectively.[68]

Meanwhile, Mariano apparently had his own ventures. A 1917 report of the New York State Committee of Excise[69] shows him with a liquor license for a hotel or saloon on 1234 Avenue U in Brooklyn, which was just a few blocks away from the next Lanza family home we know of, at 1830 Coney Island Avenue.[70] The home was a big step up from the Lanzas' days on Goerck Street. Instead of contending the plague-ridden air and half-baked criminals of the Lower East Side, Francesco and his family (and Mariano and his family, who shared the home with them[71]) were now three miles away from inhaling the ocean breezes caressing Luna Park, then the city's main amusement park near Brighton Beach. Although Luna Park would sadly go up in flames on April 12, 1944,[72] by that time Francesco and his family were long gone. Ironically, given what the federal government would later suspect as to the way the Lanzas made some of their money, the lot where he lived is now home to the Dynamic Youth Community, which offers drug rehabilitation services and counseling.

In 1920, Brooklyn was the second largest borough of New York City. Indeed, with its 2,018,356 residents, it made up 35 percent of New York's total population of 5,620,048 people.[73] Approximately 90 percent of all sugar that entered the United States in 1920 passed through Brooklyn's piers and refineries, as did 70 percent of all the coffee imported into the country,[74] making it one of the busiest ports in the nation. And not all of that sugar was going into the making of *zeppoli*, the pastry that is southern Italy's culinary gift to the world.

THE DEATH OF JOHN BARLEYCORN

Brooklyn's status as a sugar hub in 1920 was not accidental. Two years earlier, Congress passed the "Wartime Prohibition Act" (ironically, 10 days *after* Germany agreed to an armistice with the United States[75] and World War I had been brought to a conclusion). The Act made it illegal to manufacture beer or wine anywhere in the United States after May 1919.[76] Wholesalers and retailers had until June 30, 1919, to dispose of existing stocks of all beverages with an alcoholic content of 2.76 percent or above.[77] After that date, alcoholic beverages subject to the Act could only be disposed of through export.[78]

Not surprisingly, this spawned litigation. The Kentucky Distilleries & Warehouse Company secured an injunction against the federal tax collector for the area, prohibiting him from "interfering"[79] (i.e., by him enforcing the terms of the Act) with their continued withdrawal of whiskey from bonded warehouses. However, a similar suit brought by Dryfoos, Blum & Co. in federal court in Manhattan did not end as well for the liquor distributors, as the Act was upheld. To resolve the conflict between the courts, the U.S. Supreme Court granted *certiorari* and agreed to review the case.

Writing for a unanimous court, Justice Brandeis found that the Act did not improperly commandeer private property for public use, and that the time given to liquor dealers to dispose of their domestic stocks was not unreasonable.[80] More controversially—especially as viewed through the eyes of later years—he also found that the Act's restrictions on the sale of alcohol did not amount to an uncompensated "taking" under the Fifth Amendment,[81] because the Act was authorized under Congress's War Powers to improve the country's fighting efficiency. To address the obvious flaw in this argument—that is, that hostilities with the Central powers had ended long before the Act went into effect—Brandeis piously wheezed that "No principle of our constitutional law is more firmly established than that this Court *may not*, in passing upon the validity of a statute, *inquire into the motives of Congress*"[82] (emphasis added).

Of course, had Brandeis and his colleagues bothered to "inquire into the motives of Congress," they might have asked themselves whether the failure of the Senate to ratify the Versailles Treaty on November 19, 1919—coincidentally, the day before the Court heard oral argument in the case—might have had more to do with the continuance of the technical state of war than anything the Germans did.

The ruling in *Kentucky Distilleries* is what modern lawyers refer to as an "outcome-determinative" decision. In other words, the Court knew what it wanted to accomplish—in this case, uphold the Wartime Prohibition Act—and just needed a rationale to get there. In some ways, the pressures on Brandeis and the Court to hold the Act constitutional are completely understandable. By the time the Court got the *Kentucky Distilleries* case, 36 of the 48 states then in existence had already ratified the 18th Amendment codifying Prohibition, thereby adding it to the Constitution.[83]

Since the constitutionality of the Volstead Act (the enforcement mechanism for Prohibition) was not being challenged in *Kentucky Distilleries*, invaliding the Wartime Prohibition Act would only have lifted the ban on booze for 30 days or less, until the Volstead Act went into effect in January 1920 and imposed even tighter restrictions on the sale of alcohol. Although this would have been a boon to sellers of alcohol like Francesco and to those who purchased it, from the point of view of the Court, it would have been unreasonably disruptive to everyone else.

As a result of the Court's decision in *Kentucky Distilleries*, as the *New York Times* pointed out, "all hopes of a 'wet' interim before constitutional prohibition goes into effect in January vanished."[84] A month later, the Volstead Act took full effect in January 1920, and it became illegal—in theory, anyway—to sell beverages with more than 0.05 percent alcohol by volume. The bonanza for organized crime that Prohibition would become had begun. However, the Lanzas would not be sticking around in New York to reap the benefits.

RIGUARDATI, (TAKE CARE) NEW YORK!

Although Francesco picked an optimal time to come to New York, his decision to leave it in 1920 seems—with the benefit of historical hindsight—less so. Francesco's experience in the liquor trade and Mariano's time running a saloon before the Volstead Act was passed would seemingly have given them a head start in the bootlegging trade if they had chosen to take it and stick around, especially given Brooklyn's status as a major port and center for the sugar trade, a key ingredient in the rivers of hooch that were soon to flow throughout the borough and the nation.

However, none of this was obvious at the time, although it probably *should* have been. As early as January 1919, the *Brooklyn Eagle* was carrying reports of bootleggers appearing before the courts (initially, for selling booze to servicemembers).[85] Another report a month later that reads like a Treasury Department press release—which it may have well been—claimed the government "will have all necessary machinery to squelch the development of the kitchen distilling industry."[86] Indeed, the Treasury Department apparently *believed* "the average American who now takes a drink of liquor will prefer to do without 'moonshine' booze. One taste of liquor manufactured in a home-made still will be enough to convince him that he wants no more of it."[87]

In May 1920, less than four months after Prohibition had taken effect, *Brooklyn Life* editorialized, "The country is as wet as ever and will never be any dryer. Only the temperate and the impecunious have become abstainers by reason of the law, and for this the constitution has been mutilated."[88]

In any event, the Lanzas picked this moment to uproot their stakes and move almost 3,000 miles to San Francisco. When James Lanza talked about this period in a 1969 deposition, he claimed that the family's main business was "wholesale groceries,"[89] completely omitting Francesco's construction and real estate interests. However, what he told his interrogator next shows the method to Francesco's apparent madness in leaving New York just as the Prohibition-fueled boom was about to begin. "We bought a ranch, and we used to ship grapes," he said. "We used to ship a lot of grapes back to New York in those days, also. We used to buy grapes and ship them back to New York, Chicago, all over."[90]

As Edward Behr noted in *Prohibition: Thirteen Years That Changed America*, grape production in the United States "increased tenfold between 1920 and 1933"[91] because wineries and vineyards were allowed to make and sell cakes or bricks of dried grapes or dried raisins.[92] According to Behr, the idea was to allow Americans to make a limited amount of nonalcoholic cider and fruit juice.[93] Of course, the effects of chemistry were far stronger and ran much further than the writ of the Volstead Act.[94] As Behr noted, "The bricks were sold with a label that read 'Caution: will ferment and turn into wine.'"[95] For those with the vision and the resources—like Francesco—being in the grape business was an easy way to make money off of Prohibition without running even the comparatively minor risks associated with bootlegging.

Under the provisions of the Volstead Act, someone who was caught manufacturing or selling alcohol for the first time faced a potential fine of up to $1,000 or up to six months in jail.[96] Although that would be more than $11,000 in 2015 dollars[97] and was presumably intended to be a serious deterrent by Congress, it failed to account for the inflationary effect Prohibition had on alcohol prices. According to Irving Fisher, an economist who *supported* Prohibition, between 1916 and 1928 the average price of a quart of lager beer increased from 10 cents to 80 cents, port wine increased from 60 cents a quart to $3.90, gin increased from 95 cents to $5.90, and brandy increased from $1.80 to $7.00.[98] At these rates, a bootlegger would have to be afflicted with a near-lethal form of lethargy to *not* be able to cover their potential fines and legal fees.

Although the penalties for a second and subsequent offense were stiffer—a fine of $200 to $2,000 and one month to five years in jail or prison[99]—they still failed to keep pace with the potential rewards available to bootleggers. However, this also meant that bootleggers had enough money to buy grapes from Francesco and his fellow grape merchants, which they presumably appreciated. In any case, Francesco and his family were headed west—and traded a city with a population of 5.6 million in 1920 for one with less than one-tenth of that. However, the Lanzas had already crossed an ocean and survived the tenements of Goerck Street in search of profit—so San Francisco presumably held no terror for them.

Chapter 4

Go West, Young Man, 'Cause It's Prohibition

RISING LIKE AN ITALIAN PHOENIX

Fourteen years after the quake and fire that had razed most of the City to the ground, by 1920, San Francisco was on its way back in a big way. With 506,676[1] residents, it was the second largest city in California, just a touch behind the city of Los Angeles's 576,673 residents,[2] the first year Los Angeles laid claim to being the biggest city in the Golden State.[3]

It was also a relatively good time and place to be Italian. In 1920, there were 23,924 foreign-born Italians in San Francisco, who made up 17.1 percent of what the census then termed the City's population of "Foreign Born Whites"[4] as compared with a mere 7,930 foreign-born Italians in Los Angeles or 7.1 percent of that city's total population.[5] Indeed, once the differences in population levels are accounted for, in 1920, Italians made up roughly the same proportion of "foreign-born whites" in New York City (19.6 percent)[6] as they did in San Francisco.

BUSINESS, LEGITIMATE AND OTHERWISE

The City by the Bay had other attractions. Since 1912, James "Sunny Jim" Rolph had occupied the mayoralty—and he considered Prohibition to be no more than an annoying inconvenience. As Jerry Flamm notes in *Hometown San Francisco: Sunny Jim, Phat Willie and Dave*, illegal alcohol was about as plentiful in the City at the time as sourdough bread. "It was made in town or outside the city in clandestine stills, or was brought in by small boats," he wrote. "On the waterfront near Fisherman's Wharf, outlaw booze occasionally was run into the city, usually about three or four in the morning."[7]

Despite being of the opposite political persuasion, Rolph reportedly was not willing to let a minor inconvenience such that the Volstead Act get in the way of hospitality to important visitors, such as delegates to the 1920 Democratic Convention. Citing an unpublished memoir of a former reporter for the *San Francisco Chronicle*, Flamm noted that Rolph "recognized that many of the anti-dry delegates were in a mood for a bit of branch water and bourbon."[8] Accordingly, Rolph apparently put the "medicinal" alcohol stores* of the City's general hospital at the disposal of the delegates, much to their glee and consequent annoyance of Prohibition agents.[9]

For those San Franciscans of less exalted stature who wanted to quench their thirst and who did not have direct access to the mayor, there were other options. "Italian women living in houses and upstairs flats in North Beach set up small 'blind pig' operations; friends and acquaintances became customers," wrote Flamm.[10] For those new to the neighborhood, "The tiny Gold Spike . . . at 527 Columbus Avenue was the Columbus candy store and fountain in the 1920s,"[11] he wrote. "In the back room, Natalina Merchetti and her husband Attilio served wine and an occasional shot of whiskey in coffee cups, together with delicious *asso buco* (braised veal shanks), tagliarini with pesto sauce and ravioli to immigrant Italian workmen employed at the nearby wholesale produce market on Front Street."[12]

Sadly, although the Gold Spike survived Prohibition, World War II and the Summer of Love to stay in the Merchetti family for three generations, it was finally laid low by a dispute over who would pay for required plumbing upgrades in 2006.[13] As the *San Francisco Chronicle*'s article on its closing notes, "Attilio and Natalina Mechetti, immigrants from Italy's Tuscany region, opened the place in 1920 as the Columbus Candy Store and Soda Fountain, *although soda was not the only drink served*"[14] (emphasis added). Nor was illegal alcohol the only vice available. As one law enforcement official told Flamm:

"Everyone made a buck. The gamblers had to pay off. The whorehouses had to keep clean girls. If you welshed on a bet, they'd close your

---

*One of the key loopholes under the Volstead Act was that otherwise-proscribed alcohol could be purchased legally pursuant to a doctor's prescription. To no one's surprise, prescribing of bourbon, whiskey, and the like for "medicinal purposes" became very popular, in much the same way that loosely regulated medical marijuana dispensaries are today in states like California.

gambling joint. If you had a bad girl in a whorehouse that tried to roll somebody, she got fired. It was a great town."[15]

Beyond the City's relatively relaxed approach to Prohibition and large Italian community, San Francisco had another attraction for the Lanzas: it was a center of trade, both agricultural and otherwise. According to *San Francisco Business*, the weekly magazine published by the Chamber of Commerce, in 1920, San Francisco and its trading partners accounted for 71 percent of the $500 million worth of agricultural products the entire state of California produced that year.[16] The City also boasted 2,500 factories, 2,296 retail shops, 500 restaurants, 1,270 "licensed" hotels, and about 60,000 hotel rooms.[17] Twenty-nine steamship companies involved in import/export made San Francisco one of their ports of call, as well as 19 other shipping companies focused on trade up and down the West Coast.[18] If one wanted to buy, sell, or smuggle something, thanks to its business and transport links, San Francisco was one of the best places to do it.

In any case, when the Lanzas first arrived, they followed their past habit of seeking anonymity whenever possible. There is no mention of Francesco or James (or the Prisinzanos for that matter) at all in the San Francisco City directories of 1921 or 1922, for example.

TRUTH AND (NO) CONSEQUENCES

However, we know they were *in* the City based on a momentous step Francesco took. On February 4, 1921, he filed a petition to become a U.S. citizen[19] with the Superior Court of San Francisco. At that time, most petitions for naturalization in California were still being heard in state courts (despite immigration being a federal responsibility), regardless of efforts by the federal government to encourage state jurists to stop hearing those petitions. According to the report of FBI Special Agent Curtis P. Irwin, who reviewed Francesco's petition almost 35 years later, in 1921, Lanza stated that he lived at 945 Jackson Street, in San Francisco.[20] For whatever reason, Lanza claimed to be born in Palermo, rather than Castelbuono, and—more intriguingly—said he had lived in California continuously before 1919,[21] but had filed his initial declaration of intent to become a U.S. citizen in New York on May 27, 1914.[22]

Two men witnessed the petition—Rinaido† Milani, who also lived at 945 Jackson Street, and Thomas Abate, who said he resided at 1050 Greenwich.[23] According to the 1921 city directory, Abate lived at 1530

---

†The FBI's report spells his name as "Rinaido," whereas the city directory lists it as "Rinaldo."

Vallejo and was associated with the California and Italian Products Company, whereas Milani had no listed occupation in that year's city directory.[24]

Today, we know that most of what Francesco Lanza told the California Court was a complete fabrication. In addition to James Lanza's testimony decades later under oath that the family relocated to San Francisco in 1920, the 1920 U.S. Census has Francesco Lanza living in Brooklyn that year[25] with his family, *including* James, who was then 16. Since Milani and Abate swore under penalty of perjury that they had each personally known Lanza since May 26, 1919, when he supposedly moved to California,[26] and that he had been present in the state since that time, one could reasonably wonder why Lanza would subject himself and his two boon companions to potential prosecution when it was not necessary.

Although the early 1920s were a difficult time for immigrants in the United States, most of the efforts of nativists in Congress and elsewhere were focused on excluding potential immigrants from China, Japan, and the rest of Asia (with the exception of the Philippines) on racial grounds, as well as reducing the overall levels of immigration, particularly from Italy and the rest of Southern Europe. Lanza had been in the United States since 1904, so although he may have found the attempts to exclude his countrymen obnoxious, it did not affect his own right to apply for citizenship. What *did* put a crimp in his plans was the family's move to California. Since the enactment of the Naturalization Act of 1790,[27] an immigrant had to be present in a particular state for at least a year before he or she could petition a court in that state to become a U.S. citizen.

Even so, there does not seem to be any reason why he could not have waited a year and applied without any drama in 1921 *without* having to both lie in his own declaration or to suborn perjury from Milani and Abate. Although California *did* pass an Alien Land Law in 1920 (which was aimed at preventing Japanese and other Asian farmers from owning or renting land), its provisions would likely have not applied to Lanza, since he *was not* statutorily ineligible for U.S. citizenship. It may have been that he saw the way the nativist winds were blowing and was determined to secure his citizenship—and through it, citizenship for his children—including James—before the door slammed shut on that opportunity.

Whatever the motivation, today similar falsehoods on a petition for naturalization—as well as Lanza's failure to disclose his birth name, Proetta—would have been potentially far more problematic. Under the Immigration and Nationality Act, intentionally giving false testimony to obtain an immigration benefit (whether the lie turns out to be material or not) means the immigrant *cannot* be found to be of "good moral character" and thus cannot be naturalized.[28] It can also subject the immigrant up to 25 years in prison under 18 U.S.C. §1546(a).

However, there is a key loophole—in order for the falsehoods to be considered "testimony" for immigration purposes, they need to be uttered *orally*. Lies in a written application—such as those Francesco Lanza made to the Superior Court—probably would not have qualified as "falsehoods," unless he orally repeated them before the judge.[29] By the time federal immigration authorities got finally interested in the Lanza family, Francesco was long dead and thereby unavailable for an interview.

Since Special Agent Irwin made no reference to a transcript of Lanza's naturalization hearing in his 1958 report, we can only conclude that either the Superior Court judge did not conduct Francesco's naturalization before a court reporter or, if they did, the transcript had been destroyed or lost between 1921 and 1958. Without that transcript, it would have been next to impossible to prosecute Francesco even if he *had* survived until the late 1950s—and likely made it far more difficult for the federal government to cause immigration problems for James later on. In any case, on May 12, 1921, the Superior Court granted Francesco's naturalization petition and issued his certificate of naturalization on May 25, 1921.[30] The Lanzas were now as American as apple pie—or for that matter, Al Capone.

IN VINO VERITAS?

With his citizenship resolved, Francesco became less reticent about his public profile. In 1923, he made his first appearance in the directory as a dealer in "grape products" at 559 Washington Street, the building where his sons would go on to run their respective business empires.[31] He also claimed to reside in San Mateo.[32]

A broker or dealer in fruit was an important cog in California's economy. By the start of the 20th century, of all the agricultural products California produced, fruit was king, thanks to the operational rail links with the rest of the country[33] and growers getting the upper hand over the pests that had plagued the state's orchards and vineyards for decades.[34] By 1920, "California fruit growers were producing a crop worth more than $250 million . . . the value of the 1880 crop stood at less than 1 percent of that figure."[35]

For grape merchants and brokers like Francesco, things were about to get a lot sweeter courtesy of the Volstead Act. As the California Department of Agriculture noted in its 1921 report, "[T]he outstanding feature of the 1921 grape crop is the astonishing increase in shipments of carlots

of wine grapes in 1921 over that of 1920."[36] Despite a lower overall crop
due to the effects of an untimely frost, that year, California's grape growers sent 20,000 carloads—or approximately 290,000 *tons*—of wine
grapes to customers throughout the United States in 1921, up from
12,015 carloads and 176,000 tons in 1920.[37] The grapes may have been
purple, but they were pure gold to those who owned vineyards.

As the California Department of Agriculture noted—apparently, without a trace of irony—"These are *very illuminating figures* when considered from the viewpoint of how home brew making of wine is being
substituted to the industrial manufacture of the same product"[38] (emphasis added). Of course, given that Prohibition had gone into effect at that
point, the department's report is almost the equivalent of a government
agency today waxing poetic about the commercial prospects of precur-
sor chemicals for methamphetamine like phenyl-2-propanone (P2P) for
"home meth cooking," with the important distinction being that the government did not try to control precursors like grapes the way it controls
P2P today.

WHEN IRISH BONDSMEN ARE SMILING . . .

Before Prohibition, no one had more control over San Francisco vice—
and through it, the police and the mayor and the board of supervisors—
than Pete and Tom McDonough. Like most good San Francisco hustles,
it started in a bar. In the late 1890s, Pete and Tom were running their
family's bar, The Corner, which was a favorite of local attorneys, when
Pete made an interesting discovery, as retold by historian Merritt Barnes.[39]
"Many attorneys bought drinks here," Pete said. "As an accommodation
we loaned some of them bail money for their clients without charge.
Then we discovered the attorneys were charging their clients for the bail
we put up. So we started working on bail bonds in between tending
bar."[40] After forming the McDonough Brothers Bail Bond Broker's Firm
in 1896 with Tom, "Pete McDonough monopolized the bail bond business in San Francisco and quickly earned a substantial fortune, which he
invested wisely."[41]

Not all of those investments were financial. As Flamm notes, "Sheriff
Tom Finn and the McDonough Brothers . . . were in the wings of the
city's political stage all during the Rolph mayoralty, directing much of the
action the public saw and most of what they didn't see."[42] According to
Flamm, Sheriff Finn handled general patronage and the McDonoughs
controlled the police, which was handy since the McDonoughs also were
the arbiters of the vice trade in the City.[43]

Almost a century later, the breadth and audacity of the McDonoughs' operation remain impressive. Although their firm is believed to have been the first modern bail bonds company in the United States,[44] both brothers apparently realized that they could not rest on founders' laurels forever. If they were going to deter competitors, they had to be able to control their environment to such a degree that only the brave or the foolhardy would attempt to challenge them for a foothold. Ironically, they did it in much the same way that Google or Facebook makes money—by finding a way to monetize what they *knew* about their customers and their customer's adversaries (like the police and the judges) better and more efficiently than anyone else at the time. As Barnes notes, "The McDonough office became a clearing house which answered all of the needs of an accused person, including bond and lawyer. But the thing that made a call to McDonough Brothers obligatory for anyone accused of criminal activity was information."[45]

San Francisco Police Department (SFPD) officers leaked the firm information on who was in jail—and as a backup, the lockups were connected by radio with the McDonoughs' headquarters, where a fleet of cab drivers who "earned the right to serve the McDonoughs by being able to locate the city's superior court judges twenty-four hours a day"[46] stood by to pick up orders from those judges to release the McDonoughs' clients. Of course, good entrepreneurs that they were, the McDonoughs noticed that although their sweet setup helped their clients after they were arrested, it did not do much to prevent them from being detained by the cops in the first place.

You can probably guess what happened next.

"Gradually, McDonough Brothers became an agency which could provide underworld operators protection *from* arrest as well as protection *after* arrest,"[47] wrote Barnes (emphasis added). "Gambling clubs operated by a 'McDonough lieutenant' apparently paid police from 'immunity from molestation.' Prostitutes contributed 10 percent of their income to the McDonoughs and 'as long as they paid they had immunity from arrest.' "[48]

Like charity, protection apparently began at home. Prohibition agents arrested Pete and Tom in April 1923 after the feds were served two drinks at the McDonoughs' bar (and sold five gallons of hooch by Pete's nephew).[49] As Barnes notes, at the time prosecutor Kenneth M. Green bragged, "At last McDonough is up against a prosecution he can't corrupt."[50]

The prosecution was one thing, but the hearts and minds of San Francisco's elite were something else. Given that Pete had enough clout with the City's elite to be a major investor in the Bank of Italy, the institution formed by A.P. Giannini (and now known as the Bank of America)[51] and enough social cachet to "marr[y] into the family of Mayor Angelo Rossi's executive secretary,"[52] it is not too surprising that he was back in action shortly after serving eight months as an involuntary guest of the feds for the bootlegging bust.[53] Indeed, four years later, Pete managed to knock off his Republican rival Sheriff Tom Finn by judicious use of that unique San Francisco institution—that of the betting commissioner.

Although gambling was technically illegal across the rest of the Golden State (and *actually* illegal for those too broke or too dumb to pay protection money in the City by the Bay), punters who wanted to bet on a particular outcome, such as an election, had no need to skulk in back alleys. Instead, they would visit a betting commissioner—who operated openly— and say, "I want to bet X dollars on Sunny Jim Rolph to win the mayoral race at Y odds." The betting commissioner would then try to find someone else to take the other side of the bet—and if they were successful, would take a commission on part or all of the transaction.[54]

In contrast, a traditional bookmaker offers gambling "action" to the public at odds the bookmaker quotes (usually relying on a "line" developed by somebody else) and the bookmaker can either make the market for the action on their own (especially when the demand for each end of the bet is equal) or (when it is not) "lay off" or sell part of their action to somebody else.[55] This way, the bookmaker has a greater likelihood of remaining solvent if a horrendously improbable event happens, like the Oakland Raiders having an undefeated season and going on to win the Super Bowl or an unbought grassroots candidate somehow getting elected mayor of San Francisco.

Although the betting commissioners were violating state and federal law just as much as the bookies were, the SFPD and the district attorney turned a blind eye to their activities for decades, to the eventual consternation of the Kefauver Committee (as we see in Chapter 9) for a variety of reasons. Among other things, they provided de facto polling data to the newspapers, since the betting odds of a particular candidate winning or losing could be examined to track rises and falls in a candidate's popularity. Although this had some accuracy problems (the odds did not track "likely" voters, but the best guesses of gamblers on what they *thought* was going to happen), one could argue that someone who was willing to place money on the line for his or her choice was more committed to that candidate than somebody who shot his or her mouth off to a survey taker.

It also provided an elegant way to encourage—or, if one wanted to be vulgar, *buy* votes—as McDonough showed Finn. In the 1927 race, "Finn charged that McDonough had bet $7,500 at odds of 1 to 3 against him, made-up 3,000 tickets at $2.50-pays-$10 and ordered his men to go 'around town giving these tickets away.' "[56] If Finn's opponent won, the holder of the ticket would clear $10—or $136.96 in 2015 dollars[57]— giving them a strong incentive to rethink their support of the sheriff. Not surprisingly, Finn was soon unelected in an upset race.[58]

As we see in Chapter 9, Edmund G. "Pat" Brown employed the betting commissioners in a similar scheme and with equal success during his 1943 run for district attorney in San Francisco. Not surprisingly, cracking down on gambling was never one of his highest priorities while in office.

McDonough also had interests in gambling and prostitution enter-prises,[59] and loaned money to the district attorney and at least one police commissioner.[60] As one might imagine, all of these investments paid divi-dends, at least in the near term. So long as McDonough was in the prime of his power, the odds of anyone else building a successful City-wide com-bination were between slim and zero. Not surprisingly, the Lanzas focused on their legitimate businesses.

FRUIT OF THE PROHIBITION-POISONED TREE

As Prohibition raged on, Francesco Lanza continued to deal in grape products in 1924[61] and in 1925.[62] Around that time, Francesco bought an interest in a vineyard in Escondido, California,[63] from an unidentified man. Whether the unidentified man sold out voluntarily or after some persuasion, his interest was soon taken over by Nick Licata, future under-boss of the Los Angeles Mafia family.[64]

In 1926, Francesco's son Anthony joined him at 559 Washington and offered "real estate, insurance and loans."[65] In 1927, Francesco dis-appeared from the city directory, although Anthony remained in the same 559 Washington location, now focusing exclusively on real estate.[66] When interviewed by the FBI decades later, James Lanza said that both Francesco and his mother had spent most of their time on the vineyard near Escondido (which is northeast of San Diego at the other end of the state from San Francisco) during this period,[67] although he would return periodically to check on things in San Francisco. James also referred to Licata as an "old friend" of the family.[68] In 1928, Francesco was back in the city directory—this time as a "fruit broker," while Anthony contin-ued to work in real estate.[69] By 1929, Francesco appears to have retired to his home at 1020 Francisco in North Beach, while Anthony pressed on with his real estate endeavors.[70]

Whether because of the rigors imposed by the Great Depression or because he was bored, Francesco was back in business at 559 Washing-ton in 1930 as a "fruit packer,"[71] which is what he was doing in 1931 as well.[72] In 1932, he became a "fruit shipper"—while still at the 559 Washington street base.[73] In 1933, he became a "fruit buyer,"[74] which continued into 1934.[75]

HOW TO BE (AND HOW NOT TO BE) A BOSS

In many ways, McDonough offered the Lanzas and everyone else in the City a tutorial on how to prosper as an organized crime boss in San Francisco. First, provide a service or product that is as necessary as it is unglamorous—in the McDonoughs' case, it was the bail bonds business, for the Lanzas, it was grape and olive oil sales and brokerage. Second, make friends with the powers that be. McDonough was wired into the local and statewide political and economic structure about as tightly as it is possible to be for someone who got most of his or her money from illegal enterprises. Third—and most importantly—stay out of the newspapers. No matter how much they are paid, it is hard for the police to remain somnolent when bodies are piling up in the street due to gangland hits.

As we see in Chapter 5, some competitors had different ideas.

Chapter 5

Ferri Meets His Maker

At first, to the police, it began—as it so often did—with a woman. More precisely, with a fight over a woman that ended with an exchange of lead between the gentlemen involved. "Beer Baron Held Slain for Revenge," screamed the November 25, 1928 edition of the *San Francisco Chronicle* when the paper informed its readers that Jerry Ferri, aka Genero Fieve, had come out on the losing end of "six bullets from an automatic pistol."[1] Based on the bloody crime scene, Ferri, who was apparently ambushed at his home at 490 Lombard Street, did not go quietly.

Since they recovered what they believed to have been the murder weapon on the steps of a building at 15th Edith Street—and seven of its eight cartridges had been fired—the police believed the attacker or attackers had fired one bullet into Ferri's door, and when he came to investigate, six more were fired into Ferri.[2]

Before ending up on the floor in a bloody heap, Ferri was on top of the world. Sure, he had to stay one step ahead of the San Francisco Police Department (SFPD), but in the 1920s, that was far from difficult for a variety of reasons. First, in 1926, the board of supervisors passed a resolution "opposing the use of city police to enforce 'on any basis' the prohibition of alcohol."[3] Second, the board of supervisors' resolution was somewhat redundant, because, as we see, the SFPD was profoundly disinterested in doing anything that would threaten the flow of payoffs from bootleggers. The police were similarly disinclined to take action that might threaten similar tributes from those engaged in gambling, prostitution, and other pursuits that were as popular in the streets of San Francisco as they were damned in the pews of the City's churches and in the halls of the state legislature in Sacramento.

Besides the benefits to be gained from *not* enforcing the law, enforcing it could be downright dangerous. The January 1929 issue of "Douglas 2-0," the department's in-house magazine, related how SFPD Corporal J.J. Muldoon got his leg shot off by a trap gun during a raid on a Bayview still.[4]

Third, although from January 1912 to January 1931, the City was under the control of Mayor James "Sunny Jim" Rolph, Jr.—who is best known for supervising the creation of the Hetch Hetchy reservoir, on which San Francisco still relies on today,[5] and shutting down the remnants of the former Barbary Coast[6]—the mayor was a friend to Ferri's class of job creators. "To say that 'Sunny Jim' enforced the Prohibition laws as little as possible, would be putting it mildly," wrote Daniel Steven Crafts. "Rolph's stand on Prohibition helped get him re-elected continuously throughout the 1920s."[7] Indeed, Crafts said, although Rolph's personal finances were a disaster area, "the [C]ity prospered along with the rest of the country. Whorehouses and gambling dens, though also flourishing, were kept under strict police supervision, and the streets remained safe."[8]

Thus, it is probably not surprising that in the months before his assassination, Ferri had beaten a rap for kidnapping two North Beach women, then fined for carrying concealed weapons, then arrested with his colleague Frank Grupico for vagrancy, possession of burglar's tools, and carrying a sawed-off shotgun and revolver. Despite this, he had no problems posting bail, in all likelihood, arranged through the McDonough Brothers. Besides, he was living with Carrie Ellsworth, who under her stage name Naana Wortova was starring in the hot play *Easy for Zee Zee* at the Green Street Theatre. Described by its author, Samuel Dickson (who would go on to host a popular radio program about local history, which eventually formed the basis for the book *San Francisco Is Your Home*) as "a disreputable affair built on the lines of the naughty French farces of years ago,"[9] *Easy* would run for almost two years. As Dickson puts it, "The disreputable stories of that disreputable play are many. There are records of weekly raids by the police, most of them organized by the management for publicity. There were murders and suicides and scandals, and the names of the cast's principals made newspaper headlines periodically."[10]

November 1928 was one of those periods. The *Chronicle* noted that Wortova had been residing with Ferri while she was still legally married to someone else and had a seven-year-old daughter, who apparently was not living with them either. The "had been" seemed like a clue to the SFPD, since she left the Lombard Street apartment to move home with her mother at 74 Terrace Avenue in Richmond, California, before Ferri took the big sleep.

The SFPD initially suspected Gigi "Babyface" Biagini of being involved in the hit, because Ferri had once kidnapped Biagini and *his* moll (who had previously dated Ferri) and threw them both out of a car on Skyline Boulevard.[11] They also wanted to talk to Wortova.[12] When they did so the next day, Wortova—like the good actress she was—played her role to perfection when asked about Ferri. "I loved him," Wortova said to the police, "But I didn't like [Ferri's] friends. They carried guns. We quarreled over that."[13] Furthermore, according to Wortova, "'Baby-Face' was too nice to me and it made Jerry jealous. He hit 'Baby-Face' over the head with a gun."[14]

The SFPD exonerated Wortova and arrested Baby-Face, but precious little came of it because of his ironclad alibi. A few weeks later on December 1, 1928, the SFPD named Alfredo Scariso as one of Ferri's colleagues and his suspected killer.[15]

For whatever reason, Lt. Charles Dullea, then the chief of the SFPD homicide squad, felt it necessary to assure the City that Scariso and Ferri's conflict "was a purely business quarrel, so far as we can discover; a difference over a woman had nothing to do with it."[16] Sadly, Wortova's reaction to this comment was not recorded.

Even better for the SFPD, Ferri's murder "solved" itself a few weeks later when Scariso—who, according to the *Chronicle*, was a "New York gangster"[17] who had come out to help Ferri with his bootlegging activities several months earlier—along with Scariso's alleged sidekick Vito Pilleggi of Morgan Hill turned up dead themselves *in someone else's jurisdiction*, near a clay road just east of Sacramento.[18] Although this may have seemed like an early Christmas present to the police at the time, it would prove to mark the beginning, rather than the end, of the Booze Wars.

NO WAY TO RUN A LEGITIMATE BUSINESS

In San Francisco during this period, a high-profile gang murder was good for at least a few days of breathless coverage in the *Chronicle* and the *Oakland Tribune*, which covered San Francisco far more intensely then than it does now. Hits that were seen as especially egregious—such as that of Luigi Malvese, who was gunned down outside a North Beach barber shop—rated breathless coverage *and* front-page editorials demanding the police to do something. In other words, "Please find us a suspect, ideally a dead one whose last name also ends in a vowel, so we can declare the crime solved and the morality play wrapped up in a nice bow that will fit the news hole we have for it."

At the time, local reporters seemed to lack either the skill or the inclination to ask the questions we would like to have answered almost a century later: Were Italians trying to compete with the McDonough Brothers by creating their own bootlegging and criminal franchise in North Beach and elsewhere? If so, what was driving the public killings? Was it because none of San Francisco's proto-*mafioso* had the sense or the wisdom to see that leaving bodies all over North Beach was the best way to shake the SFPD out of its happy state of somnolent disinterest in enforcing laws against booze, prostitution, and gambling?

If so, the lesson on why public violence was a bad idea took a long time to sink in. On December 14, 1928, Marlo Fillippi was shot in the basement of the café he operated on 28 Sacramento Street,[19] apparently as punishment for his suspected involvement in hijacking of liquor shipments.[20] Although the hit was performed in a sloppy manner—Fillippi lived long enough to allegedly tell police "Joe shot me. Joe was a friend of Tony Lauretti"[21]—it may not have mattered, since by this time Lauretti, another suspected bootlegger and gangster, had already been shot and killed by his wife.[22]

Then again, Mike Caldaralla—Lauretti's partner at the café—apparently was not a candidate for any criminal brain trusts either. In 1926, a 500-gallon alcohol still under the international hotel at 846 Kearny Street—which was "*within a block of the Hall of Justice and less than two blocks from prohibition headquarters*"—(emphasis added) exploded and, not surprisingly, attracted the attention of Prohibition agents.[23] Sure enough, the feds found "250 wine barrels, 87 of them filled with wine, two stills . . . and three five-ton trucks and trailers"[24] with "M.A. Caldaralla" stamped on most of the empty grape boxes and on one of the trucks.[25] On a more positive note, Caldaralla was also godfather (in the liturgical sense) to Lauretti's children and cared for them while Lauretti's widow was briefly jailed for his murder.[26] Caldaralla was also questioned by the SFPD about Ferri's murder, but never charged.[27]

Although the SFPD ultimately arrested Joe Brasci for Fillippi's killing, the case fell apart because of lack of evidence.[28] Still, both reporters and homicide investigators were kept busy when Frank Boca "The Strong Man of the Sicilians" was found in a bloody vehicle at 38th Noriega Street on July 30, 1929[29] after being both stabbed and shot.[30] Evidently, nobody wanted to chance a repeat of Fillippi's deathbed-excited utterances and scandalous abandonment of *omertà* when the police found

Boca, as they were apparently intended to. Or it may have had to do with the fact that Boca's mortal sin was believed to have been the involvement in Scariso's murder, rather than mere petty hijacking like Fillippi.[31] Other floated explanations included a rumored love triangle between Boca and Lina Giorgi, who was the wife of Nello Giorgi, who ran a butcher shop that Boca had invested in (which subsequently collapsed in 1928),[32] as well as the usual clichés about Boca "fall[ing] victim to one of the notorious feuds of the Latin Quarter" or "[t]hat an old family feud, involving the mysterious slaying of Boca's foster father, had been privately avenged."[33] Whatever the cause, Boca's murder—like most of those in the Booze Wars—would remain unsolved.

BRING ON THE CASTELLAMMARESE WAR!

While San Francisco mobsters whacked each other without any apparent pretense of a strategy or an attempt to build a winning coalition that could take and hold power, their counterparts in New York City were playing for bigger stakes. Although they had similar proportions of Italians in their respective populations during this period, the differentials were in the size of that population (New York City had 6.9 million people in 1930 as compared with 634,394 people in San Francisco)[34] as well as *when* they emigrated. Most of New York's Italians came, as we saw in Chapter 3, during the late 19th and early 20th centuries, long after the city's power structure had been established. Since there was little or no room for them in the existing spoils system, there was a strong incentive to *create* a parallel system, where some of their kindred could prosper, assuming conditions allowed them to triumph over the other ethnic mobs that were also in operation. As Chapter 3 noted, during this period the Mafia never really solved the problem of how to absorb or conquer rackets (like the poultry dealers) run by Jewish gangsters, at least as long as they were unable to suborn some of those gangsters to their side. However, that did not mean that there was no money to be made and business to be taken—by one means or another—from rival groups that were not as historically unified, even if it took a while.

In contrast, San Francisco has always placed a higher value on money made quickly and ideally *today*—or even better, "yesterday." This has been true from the days of the Sydney Ducks (burning down the town to make looting easier can hardly be considered a long-term strategy or even a sustainable one) to the second dot-com boom from 2010 to the time of this writing (when a majority of the City's residents and its politicos have repeatedly failed to address pressing infrastructure needs such as housing,

preferring instead to encourage additional growth that provides short-
term gains, but makes those problems worse in the long term).

New York played by different rules and for higher stakes, as the battle
between Giuseppe "Joe" Masseria—better known as "Joe the Boss"—
and Salvatore Maranzano was to show. In the middle of the 1920s, Masseria was the boss of the biggest Italian crime family in New York.[35] As
Mafia historian Selwyn Raab notes, Masseria "led a gang that killed
more than thirty opponents in battles over bootlegging territories and
illegal gambling operations. His favorite expression for ordering the
execution of a rival was instructing an underling to 'Take that stone from
my shoe.' "[36]

Most of Masseria's income came from bootlegging and extortion,[37]
much to the aggravation of underlings like Salvatore Lucania, who would
go on to become Lucky Luciano and who wanted to grab a piece of the
prostitution and labor rackets then dominated by other ethnic mobs, ideally by forming strategic partnerships with them.[38] However, Masseria,
like James "Big Jim" Colosimo in Chicago,[39] preferred to stick with the
tried and true, rather than evolve with the times. Unfortunately, in the
Mafia, those who fail to evolve also frequently fail to survive. Colosimo
was brought down by a hit thought to have been sanctioned by traitors
within his own organization, and Masseria was displaced by an outside
rival who had help from a traitor, but the main difference between the
two was the number of bodies left in the street before the conflict was
resolved.

In Chicago, Colosimo's fall only left him on the floor, yet cleared the
way for the ascendancy of Johnny Torrio and ultimately, Al Capone. In
New York, things were more complicated, thanks to two men—Luciano
and Salvatore Maranzano.

Maranzano was a seasoned Sicilian *mafioso* who quickly set up his
own bootlegging operation after arriving in New York in the mid-1920s.[40]
Unfortunately, he refused to acknowledge Masseria's claimed status
as boss of the New York families, even after the latter placed some of
Maranzano's friends into a lead sleep.[41] Alas for the Lanzas, Masseria's
gunsels never managed to kill Maranzano's soldier Joe "Joe Bananas"
Bonanno, who would go from guarding Maranzano's bootleg booze[42] to
forming his own crime family and—although ostensibly friendly—cause
the Lanzas much aggravation in the coming years.

In the present, there was only so much *agita* a proud *Castellammaresi*
like Maranzano was willing to take from Masseria or anyone else and
what would become the Castellammarese War that broke out in late February 1930.

By the following April, it had become clear to Luciano that the struggle between his boss Masseria and the upstart Maranzano was doomed to stalemate, unless one of them was removed from the chessboard. According to Joseph Bonanno, it was settled with few words.

Maranzano and Luciano engaged in one of those classic Sicilian dialogues in which every word carried manifold implications but nothing is stated directly.

—Do you know why you are here? Maranzano asked.
—Yes.
—Then I don't have to tell you what has to be done.
—No.
—How much time do you need to do what you need to do?
—A week or two.
—Good, Maranzano said. I'm looking forward to a peaceful Easter.[43]

According to Raab, there was a bit more to it than that—Luciano believed he had secured Maranzano's agreement to recognize him as the head of the Masseria organization—once Joe the boss met his pre-ordained end—and to treat him as an equal in their future (peaceful) dealings.[44]

The tale encapsulates the difference between what was happening in New York and what was happening in San Francisco. *Before* he proceeded to betray his boss, Luciano reached an agreement with his adversaries about their postwar relations. In contrast, San Francisco's mobsters could not seem to move beyond an endless cycle of vendetta for the sake of vendetta, rather than the proper use of a vendetta in their world, which is "doing business with other means" in the same way that war is "the pursuit of policy with other means."[45] In any case, the stage was set for Masseria's last supper at the Nuovo Villa Tammaro at 2715 West 15th Street in Coney Island.[46] Ironically, the restaurant was just more than three miles away from the Lanza's former residence at 1830 Coney Island Boulevard.

If you have ever seen *The Godfather*—specifically, the scene where Michael Corleone comes out of the bathroom and kills Virgil "The Turk" Sollozzo and the corrupt New York City Police Department (NYPD) captain at the restaurant—you have a good sense of what happened next, as the scene in the film is loosely based on the Masseria hit. According to Raab and others, Luciano excused himself from Masseria and his bodyguards went to the bathroom before the dessert course.[47] Shortly thereafter, Masseria ate a meal of lead and Luciano claimed to have neither seen nor heard anything.[48]

Convenient outcome, that. In any case, leadership of the Masseria family passed to Luciano, and Maranzano was free to spread his wings—briefly.

Although Maranzano's tenure as boss did not last very long, he did contribute a number of innovations that survive to this day, albeit in modified form, in the Mafia in the United States. Maranzano structured his family (and those subject to his authority) along the same lines as a Roman legion, with a "Father" or "Boss" at the top, a *sottocapo* or underboss under him, and *capodecina*s (captains) reporting to the underboss, with each captain leading a group of no more than 10 men.[49]

Aside from the replacement of the term *capodecina* with the more popular *caporegime* (literally, "captain of a regime" or a crew) and the removal of the 10-man limit on crew sizes, this is how most Mafia families continue to be structured. A large family might have multiple crews (and thus multiple captains) reporting to an underboss, who in turn would deal directly with the family's boss and the boss's *consigliere* (advisor), whereas a smaller family might only have an underboss and a single *caporegime*. In either case, the structure helps insulate the boss and his senior leadership from culpability for the crimes committed in their name, as the soldiers and associates doing the actual work can only—at worst—testify against *themselves* and their captain, rather than against an underboss or boss they had never met. As long as the system is obeyed and the captains do not rat, the boss is effectively untouchable—or was until the passage of the Racketeer Influenced and Corrupt Organizations ("RICO") Act in 1970.

With good reason given recent events, neither Luciano nor Maranzano trusted each other. Sadly for Maranzano and his Caesar fantasies, Luciano moved first by sending non-Italian gunmen disguised as federal agents to play Brutus and Cassius to Maranzano's Julius.[50] In both the ancient and modern versions of the story, the outcome was the same: Caesar and Maranzano lay dead on the floor. The difference is what happened next. Rather than continuing the cycle of vendetta, Luciano made peace with Bonanno[51] and five other key mobsters who bought into his vision who would form New York's famous "Five Families" of the Mafia.[52]

At a meeting later that year in Chicago, "[M]embers reached a decision, apparently at the urging of Luciano, to eliminate the position of 'boss of bosses' and establish a commission of six members."[53] The first members of the commission, besides Luciano, who served as "first among equals,"[54] were Vincent Mangano, Joe Profaci, Joe Bonanno, Al Capone (until he was shipped off to the Bureau of Prisons after his conviction for tax evasion shortly thereafter), and Cleveland mobster Frank Milano.[55]

The Chicago meeting marked the beginning of the modern age of the Mafia in the United States. For the first time, bosses of the various families realized that there was more money to be made by ceding some of their sovereign freedom of action to a commission of their peers. Although compliance with commission rules was not airtight—in the years to come, the commission would frequently be called upon to give an ex post facto sanction to violations of the rules that had already taken place—it played a major role in channeling the energies of violent and dangerous men toward their non-Mafia victims, rather than toward each other.

A NOT SO MAGNIFICENT END

While the blood flowed back east and Luciano was making history, San Francisco's mobsters had problems of their own.

By all accounts, 1930 was not Gennaro Broccolo's—aka "Don Broccolo the Magnificent"—best year. In May, he had to post a $5,000 bond[56] (or $71,352.10 in 2015 dollars)[57] to get out of immigration custody, whereas the federal government sought to deport him to Italy on a murder charge that was 12 years old.[58] Still, given that the Department of Labor had demanded Broccolo post a $30,000 bond, he could take some pleasure in a partial victory,[59] but that may have had more to do with who his lawyer was—John L. McNabb, the former U.S. Attorney for the Northern District of California—than with the merits of his case. Among other things, Broccolo had been convicted of murder in this country in 1925.[60]

Even so, by the end of May, McNabb had gotten U.S. District Court Judge Frank Norcross to take the question of stopping Broccolo's deportation under advisement—judicial speak for "let me think about it,"[61] but this was apparently enough to keep Broccolo in the country while destiny wrote his last act.

On October 13, 1930, Broccolo traveled to the home of Ralph, aka Raffaele, Esposito at 2780 23rd Street. It proved to be his last visit to anyone. For once, the police even had a living suspect—Esposito—although that was not because of an uncharacteristic display of competence or energy on the part of the SFPD.

According to the *Oakland Tribune*'s account of Esposito's monologue:

"I shot him twice so I could be sure he was dead", the killer screamed to police who rushed into the room a moment after the shots were fired. "He was a mafia, a blackhand. He said he would blow up my house and kill my family unless I gave him money. Hundreds now will speak who never talked while Broccolo was alive."[62]

Esposito claimed that Broccolo had demanded an additional $50 on top of the $1,500 or so (or more than $21,000 in 2015 dollars)[63] he had previously extorted from him,[64] but the circumstances of Broccolo's demise seemed a bit at odds with that story. For one thing, why would Broccolo— the reported boss of the local family—personally shake down relatively small fish like Esposito? For another, Esposito reportedly shot Broccolo in the back and then delivered the *coup de grâce* by firing a shot into Broccolo's temple.[65] The only way that could have happened would be if Broccolo—an experienced killer—trusted Esposito enough to turn his back to him. Finally, the sudden arrival of the SFPD while the gun was still warm—just in time for Esposito to give his excited claim of self-defense—seemed a tad convenient, given that it was a feat the SFPD had never managed before (or repeated since) after any other mob hit.

Besides Esposito—who was charged with murder—the SFPD arrested three men and one woman suspected of being involved with Broccolo's extortion operation.[66] More intriguingly, they also put out a call for Wortova—who was acquiring a reputation as the City's favorite moll, despite the tendency of her paramours to meet violent ends—to be brought in for questioning in the hope that they could connect the hit on Ferri with the death of Broccolo.[67]

The *Oakland Tribune* speculated that Broccolo had "formed alliances with Chicago gangsters and . . . was about to set himself up as a Pacific Coast Al Capone,"[68] but this seems like North Beach gossip, especially since the *real* Al Capone said that "the more lucrative forms of crime were so highly organized and well protected that outsiders couldn't break into San Francisco."[69]

Still, the police were starting to put together a theory of why these murders were taking place. SFPD Sgt. Allen McGinn told the *Oakland Tribune* that Scariso—the supposed triggerman in Ferri's killing—had been "traced to a place run by Frank Boca, the 'Strong Man of the Sicilians.'"[70] According to McGinn, Boca bumped off Scariso after the latter killed Vito Pilleggi.[71] "Maybe Broccolo [killed Boca], I don't know," said McGinn. "But Broccolo from that time on until his death Monday night was the kingpin of the gang."[72]

Just as Broccolo's death ended an era of a sort in North Beach, as 1930 drew to a close, another era was ending at City Hall. On December 22, 1930, the board of supervisors elected Angelo J. Rossi to replace Rolph, who had just been elected governor.[73] Rossi had served two terms on the board of supervisors[74] and as acting mayor on several occasions when Rolph was out of town,[75] but his election made history for a different reason—he was the first Italian American to serve as a mayor of a large city in the United States. He was also, even by the standards of his time, a rabid anticommunist whose actions would lead to bloodshed on the City's waterfront, as we see in Chapter 6.

In any case, in early April 1931, Esposito was released after the court accepted his self-defense claim.[76] However, he still had a part to play in this story, as we will see.

COUNTERFEITING, HIJACKING, SMUGGLING, VAGRANCY? YEAH, I DO THAT!

Six months later, Frank Grupico was back in the news after he and Luigi Malvese, another Broccolo associate, were arrested and charged with passing bogus $10 bills in North Beach.[77] Counterfeiting was an old-school Mafia crime, but still lucrative so long as one did not get caught. Then again, for Malvese, getting caught was the necessary price of doing business. According to the *Chronicle*, in a 19-month period, Malvese was collared six times, beginning on April 19, 1930, when he was busted for transportation and possession of alcohol.[78] Evidently, it was his first Prohibition offense, as he was only fined $500,[79] but Malvese applied himself. On May 8, 1931, the SFPD arrested him on a warrant from Contra Costa county, charging him with truck hijacking, and a day later, arrested him *again* on a robbery charge in the City.[80] Malvese beat both cases.[81]

This apparently earned him a place on the SFPD's list of usual suspects, because they busted him on vagrancy charges on August 14, 1931, October 17, 1931, and again on November 14, 1931.[82] It is hard not to feel sorry for Malvese on the last one, since he was arrested while *leaving* San Francisco on the way to Los Angeles, but maybe we should not, since all of the busts were dropped or kicked into the long grass.[83]

Of course, all of these pale in comparison to Malvese's alleged *tour de force* of August 1931—a screwball plan to help smuggle three automatic pistols into Folsom Prison to help convicted bank robbers Lloyd Sampsell and Ethan A. McNabb escape.[84] Sampsell and McNabb had previously terrorized banks from Los Angeles to Vancouver B.C.—and when caught in 1929, had more than $10,000[85] in booty with them (or more than $139,366.08 in 2015 dollars),[86] as well as enough weapons—ranging from tear-gas shotguns to "high powered rifles [and] guns equipped with Maxim silencers . . . in addition to a brace of automatic pistols."[87]

Evidently, although they lost their weaponry and loot, Sampsell and McNabb retained powerful friends—or the treasure on the outside to hire some. Malvese was arrested with James Palese, a safecracker part of Detroit's Purple Gang,[88] which was then led by Pete Licavoli.[89] Although the Purple Gang was a rival to rather than a component of the Mafia, it was the dominant criminal organization in Motown during this period.

It is not clear whether Malvese was busted because he really was involved or because he was tight with Palese's "local associates,"[90] but after his attorney Walter H. Duane filed a petition for a writ of habeas corpus, the police were forced to admit they lacked sufficient evidence to hold him as part of the gun plot,[91] so they slapped him with another vagrancy charge.[92] Although Malvese had to spend a bit longer in jail, in the end, the weapons case against him fell apart when Emil J. Colson—the snitch who told the police of the plan to smuggle the weapons into Folsom hidden in barrels of nails—recanted his grand jury testimony at Palese's trial.[93] Colson was later tried for and pled guilty to perjury.[94]

Not every member of the gang was as lucky. Grupico suffered a lead injection on May 16, 1932, after his botched attempt to shake down alleged bootlegger Edward M. Giubbiny.[95] Even Malvese's luck was about to run out.

DEATH AT A BARBERSHOP

Given that Malvese made a number of bad life choices throughout his criminal career and escaped unscathed, the mundaneness of his fatal error was almost operatic. On May 18, 1932, he went for a haircut in North Beach and entered history by being cut down in broad daylight at rush hour in front of hundreds of witnesses, most of whom saw nothing. As the next day's *Chronicle* told the story, "With all the melodramatic props of a Capone gang execution, Louigi [sic] Malvese, 26, San Francisco mobster, was put on the spot in the heart of teeming North Beach shortly before 6 o'clock last night."[96]

According to the *Chronicle,* Malvese was sitting in a car outside the Del Monte Barbershop on 720 Columbus Avenue when "[s]uddenly there was a commotion at the door of the barber shop. Three men appeared, two attempting to restrain the third."[97] After the man left the scrum, he blasted Malvese out of the car. "The killer stepped coolly over the prostrate man and fired four times more. With the last shot he gave the coup de grace—a bullet through Malvese's head from behind the ear."[98]

The coroner's initial report was more prosaic, but filled with more details.

This date at about 5:55 p.m. the deceased is supposed to have double-parked his Buick coach automobile outside 720 Columbus Avenue . . . the door of the machine shows two bullet holes, the lower one at the opening of the door passed through the door. The top one did not go through. Another bullet broke the window shield [sic] of the door [and] the deceased was carried to the pavement.[99]

The autopsy showed even worse shooting. Despite being at point-blank range, the killer only managed to hit Malvese three times. One bullet entered Malvese's hip, one passed through his back under his right shoulder, and another hit him in his front chest[100]—presumably this was the actual *coup de grâce*, rather than the shot to the head the *Chronicle* claimed to its readers.

Who was working at the barbershop when all this went down? Ralph Esposito, apparently the admitted slayer of Broccolo.* Perhaps it was a coincidence, and if the *Chronicle*'s account is accurate, it may have been that Esposito was one of the two men who tried to restrain Malvese's killer. Or it may have been intended to *look* that way, especially if Esposito had tipped off Malvese's enemies as to where he would be that day.

THE GREAT ROUNDUP OF 1932 OR "WHY MURDERING PEOPLE DURING RUSH HOUR IN NORTH BEACH IS A TERRIBLE IDEA"

Malvese's killing broke new ground for another reason. Ferri had been killed and found behind closed doors, as was Broccolo. Although Boca had been found in a car in public, the deed had been done somewhere else. In contrast, when Malvese's assailant cut him down, he did so in full view of half of North Beach, or so it seemed from the breathless coverage at the time. As the *Chronicle* put it, "Not only were the streets and sidewalks crowded, but behind Malvese's parked car clanged a streetcar jammed to capacity with homeward bound workers from downtown."[101]

The next paragraph in the story, however, took the cake.

On the front platform of the car was Ralph Richards, 350 Judah Street, *who witnessed the whole affair and gave police the best account of it. He was able to describe the killer minutely* and also the two men who attempted to restrain him.[102] (Emphasis added)

One can only wonder what Richards did to annoy the *Chronicle* to such a degree that they would name him to every literate mobster within circulation range as the key witness to Malvese's killing. He fled the City

---

*At the time, Esposito claimed he was not the same Esposito who had sent Broccolo to the big sleep, but a review of the city directories for this period does not show another "Ralph Esposito"or "Raffaele Esposito" living in San Francisco during this period.

shortly thereafter and—not surprisingly—never testified at the coroner's jury[†] called to review Malvese's killing.[103]

In the meantime, the only tears shed for the dead man belonged to Ramona Crawford, Malvese's *inamorata*, or sweetheart. "He was always so square, so kind, first always to help a friend, ready with his money for his pals. He never hurt anyone. Why should they kill him?"[104]

Malvese deserves credit for two things, at least. First, in sharp contrast to his predecessors, he did not date Wortova when he came into his own status as a boss, and second, he picked a partner—Crawford—who played the role of moll in the papers better than Wortova ever could. When the *Chronicle* asked her whether she knew anything about who might have killed her lover, Crawford exploded. "Oh, the rat, the rat! Whoever he is I hope he gets his," she said. "I did not know Luigi's friends or business associates. Luigi never talked business when he was with me. But if I knew I would not tell."[105]

Cue the applause and pass the popcorn. Meanwhile, the *Chronicle* went into a collective fit, demanding—in a front-page editorial—that the police "*persecute*, as well as prosecute" suspected mobsters within the City[106] (emphasis added).

As disturbing as it is, almost a century later, to see the City's newspaper of record call for the abandonment of what protection suspects had in this era, in some ways it was an echo of the City's historical tolerance of the two vigilance committees here and lynch mobs in New Orleans. However, it was the final paragraph of the editorial that *really* dared to suggest the unthinkable—that the police go so far as to enforce the Prohibition laws against known bootleggers who engaged in "murder and highway robbery."[107]

Whether because of pressure from the *Chronicle*, Rossi, or because of the mass of citizens who preferred not to watch mob hits on the way home from work, the SFPD did not need to be told twice. On May 19, 1932, it began to arrest all "gunmen, racketeers, gangsters, rum runners, hijackers, bootleggers, dope peddlers [and] vagrants,"[108] whether it had evidence against them or not. More substantially, it began cracking down on the gambling joints in the Tenderloin, filling "six patrol wagons" full of patrons from the clubs at 136 Taylor and 105 Turk streets.[109]

[†]Under California law, a coroner is obligated to conduct an inquest whenever someone dies violently, and it is generally up to them whether or not they want to do this alone or with the help of a jury. Evidently, given Malvese's prominence and the circumstances of his passing, the Coroner felt submitting the case to a jury was prudent.

Although that was aggravating enough to organized crime, the next part of the cops' plan likely drove grown men to rage. Because most of the patrons were locked up as vagrants, they *could not* be bailed out before they appeared before a magistrate and posted a $1,000 bond[110] (or $17,368.25 in 2015 dollars).[111] In contrast, as the *Chronicle* pointed out, the normal bail on a gambling bust was $25 for the organizers and $5 or $10 for the patrons,[112] so the crackdown was not turning out to be the boon for the McDonough Brothers' bail bond business they might have hoped for, especially given the impact the raids were probably having on their less legitimate operations.

To the public, the SFPD claimed it was trying to make San Francisco "'too hot' for crooks."[113] In private, both the police and the Mafia knew the crackdown had two purposes. First, to bring home the message that there would be serious consequences for future acts of colossal stupidity like murdering a boss like Malvese in public during rush hour. Second, that this would continue until the police could parade the killer or killers—or reasonable facsimiles of each—before the court and the press.

Swarming an area with police assets and engaging in aggressive enforcement of statutes until someone coughs up a name of a suspect is probably one of the oldest law enforcement tactics on record and persists because it is usually effective. Although it can attract sociopaths interested in violence for its own sake, at its core, organized crime is about making money. If bribes are temporarily ineffective at regulating police behavior and one's customers and employees keep getting arrested, even on bogus charges, it is damned hard to run a profitable gaming hall, brothel, or other illegal operation, particularly when the courts are also willing to throw seeming technicalities like the Bill of Rights out the window, as they frequently were in San Francisco during this period.

Witness this comment from one San Francisco jurist. "I am heartily in accord with the efforts of the police to rid the City of gangsters," said Municipal Judge Frank T. Deasy. "In so far as I am concerned, I shall exercise every power at my command to prevent the sorry spectacle made by other cities where gangdom has been permitted to operate unrestrained."[114] If anyone mused that judges had an obligation to remain neutral and bear fidelity to the constitution rather than to the prosecution or the defense, it went unrecorded in the *Chronicle*.

Deasy would not have had any of it anyway. In his view, "[W]hen criminality becomes subsidized there is no protection to the public, and it is high time that the courts aid the police in this menace."[115]

RUN CAMPANELLO, RUN!

Given this amount of economic and kinetic pressure, it is not surprising that the SFPD soon had a suspect for the triggerman who blew Malvese's brains out in front of half of North Beach. According to the *Chronicle*, the alleged killer was Gennaro Campanello, a 26-year-old "Sicilian Mafia member."[116] Campanello's only previous interactions with the SFPD were vagrancy busts in May 1926 and again in March 1928, but it appears that neither arrest led to a conviction.[117] It probably would have been far more convenient if the killing could have been penned on a dead mobster (as with the Ferri and Scariso murders), since then the SFPD could declare the case solved and *everyone* could get back to their various businesses, both legal and otherwise. However, witnesses do not always cooperate. The fact that the witness with the best view of what went down—Richards—had fled, thanks to his outing by the *Chronicle* did not help matters.

In contrast, Esposito—at whose barbershop Malvese was killed—kept *omertà*. Although he denied knowing anything about illegal activities at or near his place of employment, "Police . . . in checking up on automobiles engaged in illicit traffic of all kinds, have found a number of them registered to this address. The owners of these cars are always 'known' to Esposito when he is questioned about them."[118]

With Esposito being of no help and Richards out of jurisdiction, the difficulty now was *finding* Campanello. So the manhunt went on, although the fruits of it became less and less relevant to the Malvese case. On May 24, 1932, the SFPD finally took a "name"—Louis Dinato, the former tailor to Al Capone[119]—into custody. Given that Dinato had no useful information regarding the Malvese killing or Campanello's location—and that Capone had been wearing prison stripes since his conviction in 1931 for tax evasion—the tailor's capture sadly inflicted neither an operational nor a sartorial cost on organized crime.

By the time the coroner's jury met on May 26, 1932, the police had arrested almost 1,000 people, none of whom was Campanello or had any useful intel on where he was hiding.[120] Ultimately, the jury found that "persons known to the police" were responsible for Malvese's death.[121] Although their vagueness is frustrating to us now, the jury did not seem to have a lot to work with. Their key witnesses were Esposito and Nino Ieromozzo, who claimed to know nothing about the murder that had happened outside their front door, and Crawford, who said the same. In her case, it may have even been true.

Four days later, the *San Francisco Call-Bulletin* claimed to have located Campanello on a ranch in Humboldt County based on a tip from "a San

Francisco man who talked with Campanello in a small, northern California town."[122] The SFPD was apparently less confident, as no arrests resulted. Still, they were putting more energy into finding him than usual. In July 1932, Campanello hit the big time in a way—he made the cover of *Police and Peace Officers Journal of the State of California.*

In February 1933, the police believed they had just missed Campanello when they raided a safe house outside of San Jose.[123] It seems that this was as close as they were to get, as Campanello was never located.[124]

Some—like *San Francisco Examiner* columnist Paul Drexler—have asserted that Francesco Lanza was the real triggerman responsible for Malvese's death.[125] Although this would make for a cleaner historical story and tie up the progression from Ferri to Broccolo to Malvese to Lanza with a pretty bow, I am not personally satisfied, based on my review of those portions of Jimmy Lanza's FBI file that have been released so far by the Bureau as well as the other items cited here. that sufficient evidence exists to name Francesco as the shooter.

At the end of the day, it may not matter. As Sebastian Fichera points out in *Italy on the Pacific: San Francisco's Italian Americans,* "After Luigi Malvese's demise, Francesco Lanza, partners in a Fisherman's Wharf restaurant with Giuseppe Aliotto, the future mayor's father, became the City's most prominent Italian mobster."[126] Whether by plugging Malvese or by simply being the last man standing, when Malvese breathed his last, Francesco was on top.

Lanza did not need to be told that he had to avoid piling up bodies in the street, as the last four years of the Booze Wars had exposed the fallacy of that strategy. Instead, Lanza would move in the shadows and do all he could to stay out of the news. It was a lesson his successors, particularly his son James, would learn well. Unfortunately, it was not always the optimal strategy for the family as conditions changed, as we see in Chapter 6.

Chapter 6

The End of Prohibition and the Big Strike

MAFIA? THAT'S SO LAST YEAR!

While the San Francisco Police Department (SFPD) continued their fruitless pursuit of Gennaro Campanello for Luigi Malvese's killing into early 1933, Francesco Lanza focused on business. If the last few years had taught him and his son anything, it was that the tolerance of San Franciscans for *public* gang violence had long been exhausted.

As we saw in Chapter 4, Lanza's fruit brokerage business was keeping him busy at the family's 559 Washington Street headquarters, but the windfall Prohibition brought to the grape trade would soon be over. Once repeal took place that December, there would be less need for raisin cakes from Lanza or anyone else. However, the repeal of Prohibition opened up new business opportunities for the family. In 1935, Francesco's listed address in the Crocker-Langley San Francisco City Directory was his residence on 1020 Francisco, but for the first time, we see a "Lanza, J"—presumably James Lanza—as manager of the Lanza Wine Co., also at 1020 Francisco.[1]

Still, the Depression was in full swing in San Francisco, just as it was elsewhere in the country. Thanks to immigration into California from other states that were even worse off, by 1933, there were 142 farmworkers for every 100 farm jobs, according to California historian Kevin Starr.[2] The increased supply of farm workers combined with slack demand caused wages to crater, which in turn added impetus to efforts by the Cannery and Industrial Workers Industrial Union of California

(CAWIU) to organize agricultural workers to secure better wages and conditions. Although the CAWIU organized a successful general cotton strike in 1933[3] as well as a cherry picker strike in Santa Clara[4] and labor actions to benefit pear and peach pickers,[5] the union's affiliation with the Communist Party made it easy for growers to justify suppressing strikes by means that were considered foul even in that period. By 1935, it was no more—a victim of both police harassment that saw many of its leaders convicted of syndicalism and orders from Moscow to the Communist Party of the United States, ending the party's efforts to organize workers on their own.[6]

As a fruit broker—who, after all, *wanted* to keep the wholesale price of grapes low to maximize his own profit—it is unlikely that the CAWIU's demise caused Francesco Lanza any loss of sleep. However, when the general strike came to San Francisco, he missed an opportunity that could have cemented his control over the waterfront and the City as a whole for decades. Given that between 1926 and 1936, the port of San Francisco had processed 70 percent of *all* of the dried fruit leaving the United States,[7] and by the mid-1930s was the fourth-busiest port in the nation,[8] Francesco should have been paying better attention.

A TALE OF TWO CITIES

In the early 1930s, most longshoremen on the San Francisco waterfront had no job security whatsoever. "[M]en were selected for work by a 'shape up,' where prospective workers gathered at the shore end of a pier. Here a functionary called a 'walking boss' picked who he wanted. There were about 1,500 jobs a day on the waterfront, and 4,000 men looking for work. It was a situation open to favoritism and bribery."[9] Although technically a union *did* exist to protect the longshoremen, as it was controlled by the companies that were buying their labor, it is not surprising that its advocacy was less than energetic.[10]

A similar situation existed in Brooklyn, where Albert and his brother Anthony "Tough Tony" Anastasia seized control over the docks from Irish racketeers on behalf of *La Cosa Nostra*.[11] Thanks to the Mafia's control over the Brooklyn docks, stealing 10 tons of steel at a time—or an electrical generator—was child's play.[12]

Given that Albert Anastasia would go on to become the "Lord High Executioner" and "Mad Hatter" of Murder Incorporated, it is also not surprising that Tony encountered little opposition to his efforts to use his International Longshoremen's Association (ILA) local to run the docks as his personal fiefdom.[13] All of the devices used to exploit dockworkers in San Francisco (like the shape-up, the expectation that one had to pay bribes in order to work[14] and no guaranteed employment for most of them) were in full effect in Brooklyn, except on a larger scale.

Although undoubtedly remunerative, these were relatively minor scams in the Mafia's grand scheme of things. The *real* money lay in labor racketeering. If a Mafia family could gain control over a union, it could resume the economic role it played in Sicily—that of an intermediary between labor and capital that sucked money from both, as we saw in Chapter 2. A union local who cooperated with or was controlled by the Mafia offered the family that owned it a number of immediate benefits, from the ability to create "no-show" jobs for family soldiers to the opportunity to siphon off union funds as tribute. Even better, if the local represented workers who labored in an industry where time was of the essence, the Mafia family gained the ability to extort employers by threatening walkouts or labor disruptions at key points in the production cycle—for example, by refusing to unload food before it spoiled.

A great example of this was the Fulton Fish Market in New York City, which for decades was a fief of the Genovese family through the energy of their *caporegime* Joseph "Socks" Lanza.* As James Jacobs points out in *Gotham Unbound: How New York City Was Liberated from the Grip of Organized Crime*, beginning in the 1920s, "[Joseph] Lanza instructed his underlings to steal seafood from wholesalers, and then persuaded the victims to purchase theft insurance from him."[15] By the 1930s, the Manhattan District Attorney believed the wholesalers were coughing up around $25,000 a year in tribute through this method[16]—or the equivalent of about $391,356.91 in 2015 dollars.[17] Evidently, Joseph "Socks" Lanza provided value for money by ensuring that missing boxes of fish were quickly returned to their rightful owners.[18] "Wholesalers declared that they were not victims of extortion, but beneficiaries of theft insurance."[19] Thanks to "Socks" Lanza's connections with Tammany Hall "only [his] approval . . . was needed to obtain [the necessary] permits"[20] to operate at the market.

Although Thomas E. Dewey managed to put Charles "Lucky" Luciano behind bars for multiple decades for running a compulsory prostitution ring[21] in 1936, the Mafia's hold over the Fulton Fish Market and the Brooklyn docks continued into the late 20th century, long after Dewey met his Waterloo at the hands of Harry Truman.

---

*Although the FBI would spend a considerable amount of time trying to determine whether "Socks" was related to Francesco and James Lanza, it never resolved the question, at least according to those portions of James Lanza's FBI file which have been released pursuant to the Freedom of Information Act.

Indeed, it was the Mafia's control over the New York waterfront that would ultimately lead to Luciano being freed after the United States joined the Allies and entered World War II—and the Office of Naval Intelligence transforming both "Socks" Lanza and Luciano from public enemies to Nazi hunters.[22] Thanks to both men's participation in the war effort, underworld financier Meyer Lansky could boast to the authorities "They'll be no German submarines in the Port of New York. Every man down there who works in the harbor—all of the sailors, all of the fishermen, every longshoreman, every individual who has anything to do with the coming and going of ships to the United States—is now helping the fight against the Nazis."[23]

The Mafia grabbed the waterfront in New York because they realized it was valuable real estate and held onto it for decades afterward. In San Francisco, in contrast, although events were to offer Francesco a golden opportunity to do the same in his patch of ground, he failed to grasp it.

THE BIG STRIKE AND FRANCESCO'S BIG MISTAKE

As Mike Quin pointed out in *The Big Strike*, the seminal account of the labor action that would paralyze San Francisco's waterfront and with it the City, "The history of maritime labor in San Francisco is a tale of heroism and injustice. This needs little demonstration, for the bulk of all literature on the subject, either fiction or non-fiction, is in agreement on the point."[24]

After the collapse of a strike in 1919, "the longshoremen were herded into a company-controlled union, the Longshoreman's Association of San Francisco and the Bay Area, which later became known as the 'Blue Book Union,' and remained in existence on the waterfront from 1919 to 1934."[25] According to Quin, in late 1932, an underground newspaper called the *Waterfront Worker* lit the match for the general strike to come.[26] Indeed, the *Worker*'s first issue set the tone with its very first story "Christmas for the Shipowners," where it declared: "1933 will be the beginning of a new year and a new agreement . . . it has been decreed that wages will be 75¢ an hour—a 10¢ wage-cut."[27] Assuming—as the Bureau of Labor Statistics did—that a longshoreman worked a 48-hour work week,[28] this supposedly meant an income of $144 a month at a time when lunch in a family-style restaurant in North Beach could be had for 50 cents.[29]

Quin said the reality on the docks was far different due to the near-complete lack of job security. "To obtain work, men got up before dawn, hovered about the waterfront or trudged from dock to dock . . . [o]nce at work, he might labor 24 to 36 hours at a stretch and there are cases on record of men who worked as long as 72 hours at a shift."[30] However, "the job might last one day, two days, or only a few hours. Then he'd have to look for another."[31] Realizing that their odds of changing this ranged between slim and nonexistent so long as their "union" was controlled by their employers, "a strong sentiment was developed for the establishment of a local of the International Longshoremen's Association, an affiliate of the American Federation of Labor."[32] In the fall of 1933, when the Matson Navigation Company refused to hire four veteran longshoremen based on their ILA affiliation, the quartet brought charges under the National Recovery Act and won their jobs back.[33]

According to Quin, it also spelled the doom of the Blue Book Union, and soon the earlier organization "became little more than an office with a telephone number," as its former members switched to the ILA.[34] Sadly—if not surprisingly—the shipping lines preferred to negotiate with their controlled union rather than recognize the ILA as the representative of the longshoremen,[35] but even they could see the writing on the wall. By the end of 1933, Quin noted, "the employers unexpectedly raised wages from 75 to 85 cents an hour, with $1.25 an hour for overtime."[36] Still, this basically only put the longshoremen back where they had been at the end of 1932 economically and did nothing to improve their job security.[37]

In 1934, the ILA's rank-and-file members met in San Francisco to demand one contract for all of the West Coast ports from San Diego to Seattle,[38] with an "hourly wage of one dollar, a thirty-hour week, a six-hour day and regulation of all hiring through the union hall."[39] The employers rejected these proposals, and on May 9, 1934, almost all of the longshoremen on the West Coast went on strike.[40] Nineteen days later, SFPD Lt. Joseph Mignola ordered his officers to open fire on parading strikers on the Embarcadero, an action his superiors later "defended . . . on the ground that the parade seemed to be led by Communists."[41] At the time, Mignola was even less circumspect. "If the strikers come back for more, you'll find some of them in the morgue after the next time."[42]

To their credit, the board of supervisors passed a resolution asking Mayor Angelo Rossi to appoint a committee to investigate the violence—which Rossi promptly nullified by failing to fill any of the slots on the committee.[43] Meanwhile, when they were not breaking the skulls of striking longshoremen, the SFPD guarded the Waterfront Employers Union's headquarters (where the employers were attempting to hire enough non-union labor to enable them to break the strike).[44] According to Quin, these activities ultimately had to be relocated to Pier 14 and all scabs housed aboard a ship for their own safety during the strike.[45]

On the union side, Teamsters in San Francisco declared that they would not haul any goods to or from the Embarcadero in order to support the longshoremen,[46] and the sailors and seamen soon followed suit and walked off the job as well.[47] Thus, within a few weeks, "some ninety-four vessels were tied up in San Francisco alone, and thousands of tons of cargo, much of it perishable, was congested on the docks."[48]

In retrospect, this seems to have been a golden opportunity for Lanza. He could have thrown his lot in with the strikers and tried to muscle the employers to the table, thereby setting the stage for muscling in on the union and replicating the sweet setup Tough Tony had crafted for himself in Brooklyn. Alternatively, he could have followed the traditional *mafioso* approach and backed the forces of capital, that is, the employers (after all, it is easier to extort money from someone with the resources to pay you) and joined the SFPD's efforts to break the strike. There was, of course, a third—and probably the most Sicilian—option: back *both* sides, and when both were sufficiently weakened, use the influence gathered to control both the ILA *and* the waterfront employers, something even the New York families never quite managed.

It may have been that he or the McDonough Brothers tried to intervene—both SFPD Lt. Mignola and Capt. Arthur DeGuire, who were involved in the May 28 assault on the longshoremen, would ultimately be fired from the department three years later as a result of the 1937 report by Edwin Atherton on police corruption.[49] Or it may have been that Lanza elected to wait and see how the strike would shake out. If so, it did not take long for things to get worse. On June 8, 1934, the tugboat operators struck in sympathy with the longshoremen,[50] making it nearly impossible to move ships to the piers. By late June, the governor of California was threatening to call out the National Guard to "open" the port of San Francisco (although what good that would do without trained longshoremen, tugboat crews, and sailors was never really explained).[51] After more head breaking by the SFPD to aid the employers and the deployment of thousands of California National Guardsmen in full battle gear to the Embarcadero, the union ultimately called a general strike, which began on July 12 and went into full effect on July 16.

As Quin notes in retrospect with a touch of humor "The next day was Friday the 13th. Morning papers announced 'The city's supply of fresh vegetables and greens will be exhausted by nightfall. The supply of fresh and smoked meat on hand in the average butcher shop will last through Monday.'"[52]

Meanwhile, Mayor Rossi—rather than deal with the slight problem that commerce had been shut down in the city he was supposed to be running—preferred to issue threats against a nonexistent communist uprising. In his July 16, 1934 radio broadcast, Rossi bellowed, "[A]s to those in this city who willfully seek to prolong strife, either for their own selfish ends or for the disturbance or overthrow of this government, and of the Government of the United States—all of the forces at my command, all others that may be required will be brought to bear to prevent them from carrying out their plans."[53]

Given that the SFPD *and* the California National Guard had so far proved ineffective at solving the labor strife on the waterfront, one wonders what Rossi had in mind. Indeed, in many ways the union was behaving more responsibly than the elected government, with strike leader (and noted communist) Harry Bridges "recommending [the] establishment of union-controlled food depots throughout the city and committees to prevent profiteering."[54]

Meanwhile, much to the annoyance of the McDonough Brothers and (probably) Lanza, by order of the strikers "All theaters, night clubs and barrooms were shut down. The sale of intoxicating liquors was prohibited by the strike committee as a precaution for preserving order."[55] Yet, the record is remarkably bare of any efforts by the McDonoughs or Lanza to take active measures to rectify the situation, which dragged on to one degree or another until October 1934, when a mediation board awarded the longshoremen "the six-hour day, a thirty-hour week, and time-and-a-half for overtime. The wage was set at 95 cents per hour and $1.40 for overtime"[56] plus additional compensation for handling "difficult or dangerous cargo."[57] The strikers had won almost all of what they had asked for.

But they were not the only victors. As Quin notes, "Harry Bridges, the rank-and-file leader who was decried in the press as a Red, an alien and an agitator was elected to [the] presidency of the San Francisco local of the ILA, and later to [the] presidency of the entire West Coast district."[58] As for the losers, they included Mayor Rossi, who kept getting suckered into needless confrontations with Bridges and—worse for him—kept picking the wrong side.

In March 1935, the Nazi cruiser *Karlsruhe* visited San Francisco on a "goodwill" visit, but managed only to provoke an impromptu strike from San Francisco's longshoremen,[59] who refused to have anything to do with the ship.[60] Meanwhile, Rossi allowed the sailors to travel by motorcade down Market Street for an official welcome at City Hall[61] and had the City pay $2,000 (or half) the cost of the event.[62] This was to cause him trouble in the near future, as we see in Chapter 7.

Despite his awkward fondness for Nazis and Fascists and hatred for communists in general and Bridges in particular, it was during Rossi's time in office that Edwin Atherton was hired to investigate police corruption in San Francisco, leading ultimately to the Atherton Report (which the City tried and failed to suppress) and the downfall of the McDonough Brothers, as we see in the next section.

ATHERTON'S REPORT AND THE END
OF THE McDONOUGHS

Given the nature of his office, San Francisco District Attorney Matthew Brady was involved in some of the more questionable roundups of alleged undesirables by the SFPD at the behest of the employers and Mayor Rossi during the final stages of the waterfront strike, but his contemporaneous comments seem to indicate that he was not happy about it. When the first batch of defendants was brought in, Brady told the court, "Our policy should be to give the Communists little fuel to work with and see that they are given little cause for just complaint. Legal penalties should be imposed on Communists that break the law but *free speech should not be restrained even when they advocate important changes in our political and industrial system*, but those must be made within the framework of our laws"[63] (emphasis added).

Given Mayor Rossi's constant frothing about communists under every bed (and nothing about the portrait of Benito Mussolini in his office, as we see in Chapter 7), Brady's words were particularly brave ones. Then again, Brady had a history of sticking up for the underdog. Shortly after defeating Charles Fickert—who had sent labor activists Thomas Mooney and Warren Billings to prison for their alleged involvement in the 1919 bombing of San Francisco's Preparedness Day parade—Brady asked the governor of California to pardon both men on the ground that they had been wrongly convicted based on questionable evidence.[64] Ironically, Brady would end up having to prosecute Mooney on his retrial in 1933—despite his best efforts to declare a conflict of interest.[65] Ultimately, the court granted the district attorney's motion that a directed verdict of acquittal be entered in Mooney's favor.[66]

As I have spent most of my career as a defense attorney waiting for a prosecutor to say something like this, Brady's deputy William Murphy's comments to the court on this point are worth reproducing. "There is no evidence on behalf of the people to warrant a conviction . . . The defense has nothing to rebut. The charge is not evidence. If the defendant is permitted to produce evidence he is shadow boxing with himself."[67]

Whether because of his experiences with the SFPD during the Mooney imbroglio or just from what he saw and experienced as a lawyer in San Francisco, Brady became concerned that the level of corruption within the City's police force had gotten out of control. So, he turned to Edwin Atherton.

Although it might seem like something out of a 1930s *film noir* for the elected district attorney of San Francisco to turn to a retired FBI agent now working as a private investigator in Los Angeles to clean up the SFPD,[68]

Brady had good reasons for acting as he did. As we see in more detail in Chapter 9, the district attorney's office in San Francisco has historically had limited capabilities to conduct independent investigations, since the office is designed to prosecute cases brought to them *by* the police—and Brady could not very well ask the SFPD to investigate *itself*. So, on November 21, 1935, Atherton went to work.[69] For the next year, he and his partner plumbed the shadowy connections between the underworld and the SFPD with his eyes open. "When we were employed we were informed this investigation was not intended to be a moral crusade in the sense that it should bring about the closing of unlawful businesses, as such a course was contrary to the desires of a great majority of San Franciscans,"[70] wrote Atherton in his final report. "This policy enabled us to gain the confidence of many people in the so-called 'Sporting element' and in the underworld, who 'opened up' and talked frankly to us about the graft situation generally as well as their own individual dealings with police officers and the others who participate in the corrupt system."[71]

As well they should, given the amount of money these operators were paying in protection to the SFPD. According to Atherton's "ultra-conservative" estimate, the police were extorting $27,000 *a month* from the 135 brothels within the City,[72] or approximately $461,987.48 in 2015 dollars.[73] Evidently, those who operated them believed in the first principle of real estate: location, location, location. "In the Central District, within one police beat alone . . . there were 12 houses of prostitution," wrote Atherton. "All of these 12 resorts, plus several others on different streets, were within a radius of three blocks of the Hall of Justice."[74] At the time, the Hall of Justice was located across from Portsmouth Square on Kearny Street just outside of North Beach/Chinatown, where the Hilton San Francisco Financial District Hotel now stands.

Meanwhile, about 150 bookie establishments each month coughed $15,000 *a month* in tribute to the SFPD[75] (or about $256,659.71 in 2015 dollars).[76] At the center of this web—through their effective control of the SFPD—were the McDonough Brothers. "No one can conduct a prostitution or gambling enterprise in San Francisco without the direct or indirect approval of the McDonough Brothers," wrote Atherton. "Anyone engaged in these activities, who incurs the firm's displeasure, is sooner or later forced out of business."[77]

Although the McDonough Brothers focused on those criminal specialties, there was a cornucopia of corruption opportunities in other fields. Not surprisingly, Atherton found that before repeal, "The manufacture and sale of illicit liquor, wine and beer was a succulent source of graft revenue" for the SFPD.[78] This may have explained how the SFPD managed to miss Mike Caldaralla's 500-gallon still under the international hotel (which was a block away from the Hall of Justice) until it exploded, as discussed in Chapter 5. However, even after Prohibition ended, "saloons remaining open past the legally prescribed closing hours and 'speakeasies' were still required to pay for this privilege."[79]

Other scams—nearly four decades before *Roe v. Wade*—included a ring that performed "thousands"[80] of illegal abortions a year, most of which were done by "men and women with no education or license to entitle them to practice medicine or surgery."[81] Not surprisingly, payoffs were needed to keep the cops away both when things were going well and when patients ended up dead after the procedure, either because of a complication or because of the abortionist's sheer incompetence.[82]

Since the SFPD could—and did—issue vagrancy citations to those it considered to be undesirables with little or no oversight, "panderers and other questionable characters in the so-called underworld . . . found it much more to their advantage to pay off [the SFPD]."[83] According to Atherton, bribes flowed upward to "the Captain, and sometimes other superior officers in a [police] district,"[84] but the operators *also* had to "take care" of the beat patrolmen on top of that.[85] All told, Atherton estimated the police were taking in about $1 million in payoffs[86]—or roughly $17.1 million in 2015 dollars[87] every year.

Meanwhile, the feelings of Mayor Rossi and other politicos toward Atherton's investigation ranged from equivocal at best to hostile at worst, such as when Rossi tried to cut Atherton's budget.[88] "His attitude appears to have been that because he approved the appropriations his responsibility ended," wrote Atherton. "I do not agree. As the chief executive of the city, with direct appointive powers over the commissioners who control the police department, he is ultimately responsible for conditions in the department."[89]

Besides the dismissal and indictment of scores of officers and command staff, Atherton recommended that the City formalize its status as a wide-open town by legalizing and regulating both prostitution and gambling. "Statutes which conflict with the laws of human nature are unenforceable and the open flouting of such laws by a large percentage of the people creates disrespect for the law in general," he wrote "Those persons, who think that prostitution and gambling are stopped because of prohibitive legislation, must be likened to the ostrich of popular repute."[90]

Sadly, although Atherton's report and the subsequent grand jury investigation caused the dismissal or resignation of 16 officers and command staff implicated in the scandal, some of whom were later indicted, no one was ultimately convicted as a result of his revelations.[91] Still less did the City take up Atherton's suggestion that only by regulating sex work and gambling could it reduce the ability of the police to demand payoffs from those engaged in those lines of work. This failure set the stage for both the Kefauver Committee in 1950 to make fools of the district attorney and the chief of police, to be followed up by a state report in 1953 that would find SFPD officers "on duty" as *employees* at various gambling establishments, as we see in Chapter 9.

However, the report had one major consequence: it brought down the McDonough empire. As California historian Merritt Barnes points out, "This time the *Examiner's* demand to 'Smash Pete McDonough!' was not only heard but acted upon . . . Figures such as $1 million in police graft and $4-$5 million a year in vice payments shocked people who were individually facing economic oblivion."[92] Ultimately, the state pulled McDonough's insurance license in November 1937, making it impossible for him to operate his bail bond business[93]—and without that, his empire evaporated like a politician's good intentions the day after an election.

However, the economic demise of his rival could bring Francesco Lanza no pleasure, as he had died that June of aplastic anemia.[94] A rare condition that prevents the body from creating sufficient new blood cells, today, aplastic anemia is treated through blood transfusions and in extreme cases, bone marrow transplants.[95] Given that doctors would not be able to perform a successful bone marrow transplant until nearly the 1960s, it is not surprising that Francesco succumbed to the disease. Ironically, this made him the only boss around during the Booze Wars who died because his blood stayed in his body rather than being splattered all over the pavement.

With Francesco gone to his reward and James Lanza apparently deemed too young, control over the family passed to Tony Lima—who had only a few years of peace left before World War II would transform San Francisco beyond recognition, as we see in Chapter 7.

Chapter 7

Marone, We Can't Use the Wharf No More?

CHANGING OF THE GUARD

Following the lead of the late Francesco Lanza, Tony Lima did his best to stay out of the papers—and largely succeeded until getting wrapped up in the Nick DeJohn murder in 1948, as we see in Chapter 8. Born in October 1905 in Johnstown, Pennsylvania,[1] about a year after Francesco made landfall in New York City, Lima represented the gradual changing of the guard in the American Mafia from leaders with Sicilian experience like Francesco to men who were born in the United States and who played the game by U.S., rather than Italian, rules. When he was 23, Lima was indicted for the murder of George C. Cupp,[2] who was whacked on his porch in October 1928.[3] Evidently, Lima, who like Francesco was a produce dealer, allegedly warned Cupp to stop selling bananas wholesale, and the latter said no.[4]

During this period, the United Fruit Company had an effective monopoly on the import of bananas into the U.S. market,[5] so fruit dealers like Lima had a strong incentive to eliminate lateral competitors like Cupp if they wanted to maximize their profits, given that their leverage over the United Fruit Company was minimal. Fortunately for Lima, the jury acquitted him after less than two hours of deliberation.[6] It would be proven to be Lima's last high-profile brush with the law until 1948.

Leaving aside his motivation to stay under the radar stemming from his record and the late Francesco's example, Lima probably had a much easier time of remaining invisible than his predecessor, given that the short attention span of the San Francisco media (who, seemingly as a matter of principle, tended to avoid covering the Mafia if bodies were not showing up in the streets) was already distracted by events in Europe and Asia.

Three years after taking over the San Francisco Family, those foreign distractions would come home in a way that neither Lima nor anyone else could ignore.

PEARL HARBOR BURNS AND FISHERMAN'S WHARF TREMBLES

More than 3,000 nautical miles separate San Francisco from the dock-yards of Pearl Harbor.[7] However, on December 7, 1941, when the planes of Vice Admiral Chuichi Nagumo took off from the *Akagi*, *Kaga*, *Soryu*, *Hiryu*, *Shokaku*, and *Zuikaku* and turned America's Pacific Fleet into a nautical charnel house,[8] distances quickly became irrelevant. This was particularly true for members of San Francisco's Italian American community. Although Benito Mussolini would not declare war on the United States until December 11, 1941,[9] "on the night of December 7, several hundred Japanese, German and Italian Americans whose names were on [FBI and military intelligence's] lists were apprehended nationwide on orders of the attorney general in Washington."[10]

Things got much worse after President Roosevelt signed Executive Order 9066—which gave the military the authority to remove "both citizens and aliens"[11] from specified geographical areas for the first time in American history[12]—on February 19, 1942. As is better known, the executive order allowed the military to uproot nearly 100,000 Californians[13] who also happened to be Japanese Americans and intern them in camps like the Manzanar War Relocation Center.[14] Although the sheer size of the Italian American community (and those of Italian descent) in California and elsewhere in the United States made mass internment (at least on a scale comparable to that inflicted on the Japanese American population),* the military could—and did—inflict substantial economic hardship on San Francisco's Italian American community.

---

*As Rose D. Scherini points out in "Executive Order 9066 and Italian Americans: The San Francisco Story," Lt. Gen. John DeWitt of the Western Defense Command wanted to bar *all* Italian Americans and German Americans from his area of operations in the same way that Japanese Americans were taken out of it, but failed to persuade his superiors of the desirability or practicality of this plan. Scherini, 369.

MAFIA? FUGGETABBOUTIT, WE GOT FOREIGNERS TA WATCH

Beginning in 1936—that is, during the period of time he was ignoring the Mafia and its activities, which gave the organization time to consolidate after the Castellammarese War and its aftermath—FBI Director J. Edgar Hoover started to draft his internal security plans to be used if the United States entered a worldwide conflict.[15] According to a 2001 report by the Department of Justice, "Director Hoover issued orders to make collecting information about any *communist, fascist, or subversive* individuals or organizations the highest priority and emphasized that all information was to be collected from *all sources possible*"[16] (emphasis added).

Hoover's sense of timing is interesting. Although he was blind—whether purposefully or otherwise—to the danger the Mafia posed to the United States during this period, he deserves credit for being ahead of most of the rest of the U.S. government, as well as their counterparts in Britain and France regarding sympathizers of Benito Mussolini.

As inconceivable as it seems, in 1936, Mussolini and his Fascist government were still seen as an eventual potential *ally* by some in Britain and France against Nazi Germany. At that point, it was clear to anyone who took a serious look at Mussolini's regime that "[T]he essence of *Fascism* is the complete elimination of democratic institutions, principles and procedures and the establishment of a disciplined minority under a strong totalitarian dictatorship," as a 1943 report to the California Legislature would point out.[17] Even so, that did not stop France, Britain, and Italy from joining in a formal pact in 1935—the so-called Stresa Front, named for the villa where the discussions took place—to keep Hitler out of Austria.[18]

Although Italy's subsequent invasion of Ethiopia in 1935 and the imposition of sanctions against Rome by the League of Nations lengthened the odds against Italy joining a revived Allied coalition,[19] by 1936 it was far from certain that neither Italy nor the United States would be a belligerent in any future European or world conflict, much less that they would be on opposite sides.

Indeed, in 1931, the United States issued a formal apology to *Il Duce,* after U.S. Marine Gen. Smedley D. Butler had the temerity to hurt the dictator's feelings in a Philadelphia speech.[20] Butler was initially subjected to a court-martial for his speech, although charges were ultimately dropped after he released his own statement of regret.[21] In 1933, Franklin Delano Roosevelt referred to Mussolini as "that admirable Italian gentleman."[22] Furthermore, as Noam Chomsky points out, when Mussolini claimed to have won 99 percent of the vote in a 1934 election, the U.S. State Department believed this "demonstrate[d] incontestably the popularity of the Fascist regime."[23]

Given that some of the sharpest minds in Washington D.C.—who had access to the information-gathering resources of the federal government unavailable to the general public—could not make up their minds about whether Mussolini was a friend or a foe, it is not surprising that many of the fishermen, shopkeepers, and others, who made up the Italian American community in San Francisco were equally ambivalent. The difference, of course, is that after Mussolini—jumping the gun on Adolf Hitler in the process—declared war on the United States on December 11, 1941,[24] it was not the analysts from Foggy Bottom or the president of the United States who were rounded up by Hoover's G-men, saddled with restrictions, or removed from California entirely, but Italian Americans.

FASCISTS IN NORTH BEACH?

Some historians—notably Dr. Rose D. Scherini and Lawrence DiStasi—have pointed out that the government's response to concerns about Fascist agents among the Italian American community was both disproportional to the threat posed and manifestly unjust to the mass of people who were longstanding residents of San Francisco. Indeed, DiStasi was one of the first to address the subject in his *Una Storia Segreta: The Secret History of Italian American Evacuation and Internment During World War II*. Both DiStasi's book and his successful lobbying of Congress to require the Department of Justice to account for what was done to Italian Americans during the war were a real public service for historians, as he caused the government to collate and release records in one place, which had been hidden or difficult to access for years.[25]

I agree with Scherini and DiStasi's general thesis that (a) the military, particularly the Army and Coast Guard, imposed a plethora of restrictions across the board on Italian Americans without considering each individual's particular circumstance and (b) these restrictions imposed serious—and in some cases, grievous—harm on loyal Americans. However, to the extent that they or any other historian argues that there were *no* Fascist agents or fellow-travelers in San Francisco in the 1930s and at the start of World War II among the Italian American community, I must respectfully dissent, because contemporaneous sources support the idea that Hoover's paranoia was not completely unjustified. To put it another way, as Golda Meir is reported to have responded to Henry Kissinger after he called her "paranoid" during the talks after the Yom Kippur War, "even paranoids have enemies."[26]

Given the size of San Francisco's Italian American community and the City's status as a major military center and port, it would have been shocking (and a major strategic error) if Mussolini *had not* tried to spread Fascist propaganda here. According to a 1943 report[27] by the Joint Fact-Finding Committee on Un-American Activities in California (also known as the Tenney Committee after its chair, state Sen. Jack B. Tenney of Los Angeles), that is exactly what the Italian dictator did.

At the outset, it is hard to read Tenney's findings in that report today without a sense of dark foreshadowing of his future career. Today, Tenney is probably best known for unsuccessfully trying to require employees of the University of California to sign oaths attesting that they were not members of the Communist Party,[28] for running for vice president (although still technically a Republican) on the Christian Nationalist Party ticket in 1952,[29] and in 1954 for authoring the infamous *Zion's Trojan Horse*, an anti-Semitic book that (among other things) claimed that the creation of Marxism and *both* World Wars were somehow part of a vast Jewish conspiracy.[30]

Tenney's 1943 report goes out of its way to avoid the insanity that would later characterize much of his work. Indeed, he notes that "Anti-Semitism does not appear to have been an important plank in the Fascist platform at the beginning"[31] (as compared with his claim in 1954's *Zion* that anti-Semitism did not exist as a concept) and that his committee "has not found the Italian people in California associating with subversive groups to the same extent as have German-Americans."[32] Having said that, his committee did hear testimony in San Francisco from multiple leading members of the Italian American community in 1942 and 1943 who said not all of Mussolini's words had fallen on deaf ears.

As Tenney noted, Carmelo Zito—then the editor and publisher of *Il Corriere del Popolo*, a local Italian paper—testified that "most of the Italian businessmen in the area depended on the import trade from Italy and, therefore were economically obligated to preserve good relations with the official Italian government."[33] As a result, Zito's paper was the frequent target of boycotts.[34] According to Zito (and as recounted by Tenney), the "most important pro-Fascist publications" were *L'Italia* and *La Voce del Popolo* (both of which were edited by Ettore Patrizi), *Il Leone* (the house organ of the Sons of Italy), and *La Rassegna Commerciale* (which was published by the Italian Chamber of Commerce).[35]

Besides the written word, Zito accused Patrizi of spreading Fascist propaganda through the *La Voce del Italia* show on KROW radio, including declaring on one occasion that "Mussolini was ruling Italy with an 'injection of love.'"[36] Zito also raised concerns about local Italian language schools, which he accused of indoctrinating children with Fascist ideas.[37]

"He told the committee of excursions for Italian-American children to Italy from San Francisco and stated that these trips had been financed by the Italian government," noted Tenney. "The best children in the Italian language schools were selected and upon arrival in Italy immediately swore allegiance to Mussolini."[38]

Another witness, A.M. Cogliandro, narrowly missed an assassin's bullet three days before Pearl Harbor and went on to face successive death threats since, according to the committee.[39] "Cogliandro stated that before an Italian-American might secure permission to visit Italy, he had to prove to the [Italian] Consul that he was, in fact, a Fascist. This situation had existed for 10 years."[40] Moreover, Cogliandro testified that the "Italian consul maintained a number of Fascist spies in the San Francisco Bay Area."[41]

According to the Tenney Committee's report, Zito testified that before Mussolini's march on Rome and seizure of power in 1922, "only one Italian language school had existed in San Francisco."[42] Over the ensuing two decades, "this one school then branched out and 36 units existed throughout the State of California"[43] with the Italian consulate providing teachers on diplomatic passports and free textbooks.[44] Also, according to the committee, Zito advised San Francisco Mayor Angelo J. Rossi of his concerns about the schools in 1936, but was ignored.[45] Then again, this may not have come as a big surprise, since Zito "emphatically declared that he had personally seen Mayor Angelo J. Rossi give the stiff-armed Fascist salute in public in the Scottish Rite Auditorium and that, because of this conduct on the part of the Mayor, Fascism had received a 'sort of official blessing,' and the Italians in San Francisco accepted it."[46]

For his part, when Patrizi appeared before the committee, he claimed he had been misquoted in a 1941 newspaper interview when he said Italian Americans would never fight against Italy.[47] However, Patrizi reportedly admitted he "did not believe that the United States Government should force American-Italians into a branch of service where they would have to fight against Italy."[48]

Patrizi was not against war as a concept—in February 1917 on *L'Italia's* editorial page, he strongly supported President Wilson's decision to break off relations with Germany after the Kaiser announced the beginning of unrestricted submarine warfare.[49] Of course, at that point, Italy was fighting alongside Britain and France against the Central Powers of Germany and Austria-Hungary and the Ottoman Empire—and a far different set of facts were in place in 1942.

Patrizi admitted that he had written a letter to Mussolini where he told the dictator, "I put myself at your disposal, if I can help you in any mission, any work bound for the welfare of the mother country."[50] He also admitted that he had never opposed Fascism in the pages of *L'Italia,* and that in his view, "Mussolini had 'worked for the restoration of Italy.' "[51]

The Tenney Committee also heard from Harry Bridges, president of the International Longshoremen's and Warehousemen's Union—and one of the key figures of "The Big Strike" in the 1930s that shut down the waterfront. According to Tenney's summary of Bridges's voluntary testimony, Bridges said his longshoremen had refused to load scrap metal collected for Fascist Italy in San Francisco in 1935 after Mussolini had invaded Ethiopia and had maintained this blockade for two months. Then, according to the committee, "The Italian Consul visited Bridges and told him that Mayor Angelo Rossi had ordered the longshoremen to load the scrap metal and stated that if the longshoremen refused to do so that the police would be ordered to break the resistance."[52] Bridges testified that "he told the mayor that his men would not load the metal and the mayor informed him that he would find men who would load it and give them police protection."[53]

Tenney also recounted that Bridges pointed out that Mayor Rossi had attended a rally held in October 1938 by Baron Von Killinger, then Nazi Germany's consul general in San Francisco. According to Tenney's summary of Bridges's testimony, "800 to 1,000 people gathered to protest the meeting and particularly protested the presence of Mayor Rossi."[54] Twelve anti-Nazi demonstrators—seven men and five women, a composition that was apparently unusual enough in that era to warrant notice in contemporary media accounts—were arrested in the fracas.[55] At the time, the United Press reported that Von Killinger said, "the pickets outside are not Germans nor Americans, but international Communist hoodlums,"[56] and that he encouraged the crowd to give the Nazi salute in "honor" of President Roosevelt.[57]

According to Tenney's report, Bridges testified that the meeting was to celebrate Germany's annexation of the Sudetenland from Czechoslovakia[58] and that Bridges and the Maritime Federation condemned the SFPD for "brutally attack[ing]" the demonstrators, and Mayor Rossi (on general principles) for associating with Nazi diplomatic representatives.[59] To be fair, Rossi lacked complete freedom of action. Elected in 1931 after "Sunny Jim" Rolph became governor of California, one could argue that he was obligated by virtue of his position as mayor to cross paths with foreign diplomats like Von Killinger, no matter how odious the regimes they represented were. After all, the United States did not close the consulates of Nazi Germany and Fascist Italy until less than six months before Pearl Harbor[60]—and the embassies of both Italy[61] and Germany[62] in Washington, D.C. remained open until they declared war on the United States on December 11, 1941.

Even so, it is hard to avoid the conclusion that Rossi was not that bothered by the prospect of consorting with either Nazis or Fascists, as long as it did not hurt him politically. In *Mussolini and Fascism: The View From America*, John Patrick Diggins notes that Patrizi's *L'Italia* newspaper was one of the two "most influential [Italian] newspapers" in the United States at the time and that Patrizi was politically close to Rossi.[63]

In May 1937, Rossi refused to remove Nazi flags that had been erected on Market Street in preparations for the inauguration of the Golden Gate Bridge—and Bridges's unionists declared they would refuse to march down any street where the swastika flew.[64] After someone else tore down a Nazi flag outside of the German Consulate on Market Street, Rossi issued an official apology.[65] Another witness—George T. Baker of the Citizens No Foreign Wars Coalition—testified that he saw Rossi give the Hitler salute with Von Killinger at a German Day celebration.[66] Both Baker and the coalition were notorious isolationists—and thanks to his testimony, the Tenney Committee declared the coalition to be both anti-Semitic and to have had a "close association with Fascist and Nazi organizations."[67]

As we saw in Chapter 6, Rossi and Bridges had been adversaries in "The Big Strike," which had closed the San Francisco waterfront for weeks and which—thanks to Rossi's demand for the National Guard's intervention—turned violent at several points. Whether, as a result of that, he harbored a secret admiration for the way Adolf Hitler and Benito Mussolini were able to deal with troublesome unionists like Bridges (i.e., by shooting them or interning them) is difficult to say. Maybe his hatred for communists like Bridges was greater than his distaste for Nazism and Fascism. Or maybe he was one of those Italian Americans of his era who bought into the myth of Mussolini as the modern Caesar Italy needed to restore its place in the world.

What is clear, however, is that other American politicians in similar positions made far different choices, although it was not always easy. As Salvatore John LaGumina points out in *The Humble and the Heroic: Wartime Italian Americans*, "Some politicians, such as East Harlem Congressman Vito Marcantonio . . . came to pay a heavy price for his conspicuous denunciations of Fascism. In August 1935, as tension over Ethiopia mounted, he was one of only a few leading Italian-American[s] . . . to participate in an anti-Fascist rally in Madison Square Garden, an action that led to the burning in effigy of Halie Selassie in front of his house."[68] He also lost his seat in Congress a year later.[69]

Others have pointed out that even Fiorello H. La Guardia, who was never known for keeping his mouth shut on any subject when he was mayor of New York, was "circumspect" on the issue of Mussolini and Italian Fascism in general when he was in Congress.[70] As Howard Zinn notes, "It was hard to believe he was not sensitive to the extent of pro-Mussolini feeling among New York Italians and aware of how many votes he stood to lose by openly attacking the Fascist regime."[71] Still, no one has ever accused La Guardia of being a Nazi today. Indeed, in March 1937, he caused an international incident by suggesting that the 1939 World's Fair in Flushing Meadow Park contains a "chamber of horrors," with the climax being "a figure of that brown-shirted fanatic [Hitler] who is now menacing the peace of the world."[72]

Predictably, Hitler's press responded by naming La Guardia "New York's gangster-in-chief,"[73] which was evidently meant to be uncomplimentary. Following what was then Roosevelt's *modus operandi* with the dictators, Secretary of State Cordell Hull apologized to the Nazis for the affair a few days later.

Since La Guardia and Marcantonio showed that it *was* possible for an Italian American politician to oppose Germany and Italy if they were willing to pay the price for doing so, we can only conclude that Rossi chose *not* to do so. In any case, he had an unpleasant time before the Tenney Committee. As their report noted, "It was well established that [Rossi] was an old friend of both Sylvester Andriano and Ettore Patrizi . . . The evidence before the committee was overwhelming as to Fascist propaganda and indoctrination in the Italian colony in San Francisco."[74] Thus, according to the committee, "The main purpose in examining Angelo Rossi under oath was to determine what he had done to remedy the Fascist situation, widely publicized as a result of the committee's hearing; to learn whether or not the mayor was cognizant of the facts concerning the matters described to the committee by witnesses at that hearing."[75]

Alas, things did not quite go according to plan. In his testimony, Rossi "[P]roclaimed his 100 per cent loyalty to the United States of America . . . denounced the testimony of the witnesses and accused the committee of holding 'star chamber' sessions. He declared that he had cooperated with Federal authorities 100 per cent and that he believed the investigation of the committee was a 'smear campaign' against him."[76] Not surprisingly, this did not go over well with Tenney or his committee, especially after Rossi "[A]dmitted that he had an autographed picture of Mussolini in his office and stated that it had been presented to him in 1933 when Senator Marconi had visited San Francisco."[77]

Evidently, isolationism ran in the family. The committee also subpoenaed Eleanor Morris, Rossi's daughter, about her work with the National Legion of Mothers of America[78] as well as with the America First Committee.[79] Both groups opposed U.S. involvement in Europe, but elements of the legion, particularly those on the East Coast, got progressively more anti-Semitic and anti-Roosevelt in the months before Pearl Harbor.[80]

To Tenney, "It was amazing, if not actually alarming, that the Mayor of the City of San Francisco could testify that he was absolutely unaware of Fascist activities."[81] But then again, as Tenney noted, Rossi was not the only one who claimed ignorance. "It is rather significant that many witnesses examined in San Francisco who had been directly accused by many people of being pro-Fascist, *and, from their own testimony involved in Fascist activities*, denied having *any knowledge whatsoever* of Fascism or Fascist propaganda in the city"[82] (emphasis added). For example, although Patrizi claimed to know nothing about a *fascio*, or cell of Fascist adherents, in San Francisco, "in an article which appeared in *La Rassegna Commerciale* for July 1940, Patrizi himself stated that the *Fascio* had been formed throughout the world and that a unit was established in San Francisco."[83]

Tenney left some interesting tidbits out of his report, which seem especially ironic given his later focus—or obsession, depending on your perspective—on rooting out supposed communist conspiracies. First, as Scherini points out, Zito's paper was avowedly socialist in outlook,[84] and second, Zito *himself* had been listed on the FBI's Custodial Detention List and declared "prematurely antifascist" by Hoover's G-men.[85]

As Gen. Butler learned to his cost several years previously, evidently picking the correct moment to condemn Mussolini was everything in the eyes of the federal government. Too soon, and one got court-martialed for insulting a foreign leader (or ended up on the FBI's roundup list). Too late, and one ended up as a target for the Tenney Committee and Lt. Gen. DeWitt's exclusion fetish. Evidently, there were more in the latter group in San Francisco and elsewhere in California than the former. By 1942, according to Zito's testimony before the Tenney Committee, "most of the Italians and the Italian associations in San Francisco now state they are for the war and want the United States to win, but that they don't want to commit themselves as 'anti-anything.' "[86]

Rossi's tolerance or enabling (depending on your perspective) of Fascist propaganda in San Francisco by Patrizi and others, as well as the boycotts that Zito said he suffered[87] as a consequence of his anti-Fascist activity, had apparently done the job they were intended to do. Moreover, by then the United States had given the Italian American community in San Francisco new reasons to be annoyed with Washington, D.C.

OF SARDINES AND SUBMARINES

As Lawrence DiStasi points out in *Una Storia Segreta: The Secret History of Italian American Evacuation and Internment During World War II*, local Italian American fishermen started to pay the price for the nation's failure to contain Japan, Germany, and Italy even before Pearl Harbor.[88] In July 1941, the navy had begun construction of a net to keep Axis submarines out of the San Francisco Bay, which—combined with the navy's other antisubmarine activity—ended the harvest of sardines by San Francisco mariners.[89]

After Pearl Harbor, the military issued a slew of restrictions on the so-called enemy aliens, such as "a ban on the ownership of guns, cameras and short-wave radios"[90] an 8 p.m. to 6 a.m. curfew and a ban on traveling more than five miles from their home.[91] As a result, according to Scherini, "Large groups of Italian Americans in the San Francisco area, especially fishermen, restaurant workers and janitors, lost their employment because of the curfew and travel restrictions."[92]

Things were particularly rough for the Italian Americans who made up most of the crab and fishing fleet at Fisherman's Wharf. A February 10, 1942, confidential letter from Capt. R.P. McCullough, the navy's district intelligence officer, and Lt. Cmdr. R.E. Lawrance to FBI Special Agent in Charge N.J.L. Pieper listed 55 vessels, "all Crab-type fishing boats" in San Francisco, which were owned by Italians as of September 1941.[93]

Like the crabs they hunted, a trap was about to spring shut around the owners of these vessels. Beginning in May 1942, the Coast Guard required that each vessel that left the Bay be captained by an American citizen, "unless over 50% of the vessel's personnel complement are American citizens."[94] Furthermore, all enemy aliens (i.e., non-naturalized Italians, Germans, and Japanese) were banned from boarding ships at all, unless the ship in question was intended to carry paying passengers.[95] In *Crab Is King*, Bernard Averbuch recalled the edict's impact.

Antone Sabella . . . had tears in his eyes as he talked of "Papa." Papa was Luciano Sabella, then 71, who had been fishing at Fisherman's Wharf for more than 50 years. "He is a good American," said Sabella. "This is a good government. They will help. We all have hope and faith in America."[96]

Worse was to come for those Italian Americans who had not become American citizens. As DiStasi recalls, "not even the father of the great Joe DiMaggio could get within blocks of Fisherman's Wharf, not even to look in on his son's San Francisco restaurant."[97]

On October 12, 1942, Lt. Gen. DeWitt issued a West Coast exclusion order for Patrizi, Sylvester Andriano (who, besides being chair of the board of directors for the Italian language schools,[98] was ironically chair of the San Francisco draft board) and Renzo Turco, a local lawyer, as well as 43 others.[99] Neither Lima nor James Lanza was among them.

Although it is hard to feel sorry for Patrizi or Andriano, given what
they told the Tenney Committee in hearings conducted before the exclusion order was issued, it does seem that innocents like Sabella and DiMaggio's father were made to pay the bill for a Fascist meal they had no role
in ordering. It is also worth noting that the only consequence Rossi
apparently suffered for being (at best) willfully blind to Patrizi and Andriano's shenanigans (and at worst, for being a public supporter of Fascism
and Nazism) was losing the 1943 mayoral election to political neophyte
Roger P. Lapham.[100] Rossi died in 1948.

Despite the mayor's reputed partiality to Nazi and Fascist salutes and
closeness to Mussolini's alleged agents in San Francisco (as alleged by
multiple witnesses before the Tenney Committee), the City later named a
playground[101] and avenue after Rossi. Both are in the Inner Richmond.

Meanwhile, things slowly got better for those Italian Americans who
had somehow navigated between Scylla of the Tenney Committee and
DeWitt's exclusion orders and the Charybdis of not being able to earn
a living as an enemy alien. As Scherini notes, on Columbus Day, 1942,
Attorney General Francis Biddle announced that "Italian immigrant aliens
were no longer subject to curfew and travel regulations,"[102] which made
life a bit easier for those who were not already excluded or subject to
restrictions specific to them. Luciano Sabella was one of the lucky ones. He
lived to fish again, and his restaurant, Sabella & La Torre, remains operational to this day on Fisherman's Wharf and in the hands of his family.[103]

On September 3, 1943, after the overthrow of Mussolini, the Italian
government surrendered to the Allies and declared war on Germany a
month later.

PURE AS VIRGIN OIL?

While all of this drama was playing out and some of the mightiest names
in the local Italian community like Patrizi and Andriano were being sent
into internal exile by Gen. DeWitt, James Lanza and his brother were
engaging in their favorite pastime: remaining outside of the public eye and
out of the newspapers, let alone the Tenney Committee.

According to some, their business was olive oil. By the late 1950s, the
FBI was hearing from local informants that the Lanzas "had operated in
the black-market in olive oil during World War II."[104] There was ample
motivation for them to do so. The federal government set a maximum
price for olive and other edible oils less than a week after Pearl Harbor.[105]
By December 29 of that year, manufacturers and processors were barred
from holding more than a 90-day inventory to prevent hoarding.[106] Three

months later, the Office of Price Administration (OPA) created the Fats and Oils Branch within its Food Rationing division[107] and began rationing olive oil, as well as "dairy products . . . together with meat and canned fish" on March 29, 1943.[108]

A number of factors drove the decision to ration olive oil. First, Italy's membership in the Axis cut off imported olive oil supplies. Even if Italy had been neutral, Nazi submarines were playing havoc in the North Atlantic during this period and would not be brought under control until mid-1943—and the Allies had higher priority cargoes to devote their limited shipping to than olive oil. Second, by January 1943, the country was experiencing "acute" levels of shortage of butter, fats, edible oils, meat, cheese, and canned fish,[109] and since these products used similar production and distribution channels, it made sense to OPA to ration them as a group,[110] although the agency would live to regret this decision later on.[111]

Of course, rationing coupled with price controls had the same effect they have had throughout history—the creation of a vibrant black market. Although little data exist as to the specific prices charged for black market olive oil, especially those varieties considered "extra virgin" (i.e., those produced without the use of chemicals or machines other than an olive press), by comparing it with the authorized price of inferior varieties, we can get a sense of how lucrative the trade must have been.

By early 1944, "imitation" olive oil cost 40 ration points and $2.64 a gallon[112]—or $35.80 in 2015 dollars[113]—when it *could* be had through legitimate sources. Although more than half of California's olive crop from 1940 through 1945 ended up as olive oil,[114] it was not enough to meet the demand, especially given rationing restrictions on butter and other fats. For this reason, as late as April 1946—almost a year after Germany had surrendered and eight months after Japan laid down her arms—the U.S. Office of Price Administration noted that a "thriving black market in olive oil" remained in place in the United States.[115]

As Robert Weintraub notes in *The Victory Season: The End of World War II and the Birth of Baseball's Golden Age*, "The estimates of goods being resold on the black market were staggering—75 percent of automobiles, 70 percent of lumber, 75 percent of grain, 85 percent of bananas. Clothing, meat, liquor—if it could be sold, it was sold at a markup, accompanied by a muttered 'you looking to buy something?' "[116]

San Francisco was no exception to this trend. On February 18, 1944, OPA investigators discovered ration books for approximately *3 million gallons* of gas were missing from the San Francisco rationing board.[117] On paper, black marketers risked severe criminal and civil penalties if they were caught, but as with Prohibition, the reality was quite different.

The OPA only sought criminal sanctions in 6 percent of its enforcement actions, despite the fact 1 in 15 American businesses had been accused of running afoul of the regulations in one way or another.[118]

For all of these reasons, the olive oil trade was a fine racket. Thanks to the fact that price controls remained in place on olive oil until October 24, 1946[119]—13.5 months after the Japanese government signed the instruments of surrender aboard the USS *Missouri* in Tokyo Bay—the government effectively, although inadvertently, provided organized crime with an opportunity to maximize their returns, while minimizing their risks for years on end.

Lanza had reportedly been in the business since 1931,[120] as a side venture to his wine business. In May 1942, he and his brother Anthony, along with Leon DeSimone[121] (who was Anthony's brother-in-law), and the "A. Bennati Co."[122] each purchased a one-fourth interest in the Lucca Olive Oil Company in Lindsay, California.[123] This was an interesting family connection in both senses of the word. Anthony's wife Tonina was a cousin[124] of Frank DeSimone, who would transition from being a lawyer for mobsters and others to being the boss of the Los Angeles Mafia Family for a time.[125] Frank's father, Rosario, had run the family in L.A. for a brief period during the 1920s but failed miserably at passing on either the knowledge or the skills needed to be a boss to Frank, during whose time the Los Angeles Family was derided as the "Mickey-Mouse Mafia."[126]

A few years later, as we see in Chapter 10, Frank DeSimone and James Lanza, along with Joseph Cerrito of the San Jose Family, would end up at the Hotel Casey together in Scranton, Pa., on November 13, 1957—24 hours before the Mafia's aborted meeting at Apalachin, New York—with their bills being paid by Russell Bufalino,[127] who was believed by some to be the underboss of the Barbara Family.[128] Scranton, of course, was less than two hour's drive from Joseph Barbara's ranch, where the meeting was held. Although Lanza would deny to his deathbed that he was at Apalachin, based on hotel records and other evidence, most observers believe he was there in his capacity as underboss for the San Francisco Family.[129]

But all that was in the future. At this point, Lanza listed the Lucca Olive Oil Company's "principal place of business" for credit reporting purposes as 153 North Virginia Street, Reno, Nevada[130]—nearly 400 miles away from the firm's olive groves in Lindsay. He would have had two obvious reasons for doing so. First, at the time, Nevada did not charge a gross receipts tax on nongaming businesses. Second, keeping the business's headquarters in a different state from where its operations were located would have made it more difficult for any nosy investigators from the OPA to keep tabs on what he was doing. The Lanzas, displaying their usual good sense of timing, sold their interest in 1946—right around the time rationing restrictions were lifted.[131]

By that time, the family had more pressing concerns closer to home, thanks to a dope peddler from Chicago named Nick DeJohn, but that would be mostly Lima's problem, as we see in Chapter 8.

Chapter 8

DeJohn Takes the Big Sleep

As San Francisco adjusted to peacetime—or more accurately, the not-quite-peace of the Cold War—the City appeared determined to stick to the tried and true ways of managed graft.

In 1948, the City would elect Elmer Robinson—a former judge—as mayor. He would go on to be remembered as "'a professional politician of the smoke-filled room school' who 'didn't do the town any harm, [but] didn't do it much good either.'"[1] As with Rossi, much of Robinson's power was thought to stem from his reported practice of "closely supervising (and some charged benefitting from) the city's vice interests."[2] In other words, not much had changed since the days of the Atherton Report, but even Edwin Atherton recognized that there never was a large constituency in San Francisco for the enforcement of laws against gambling and prostitution inflicted on the state by Sacramento bluenoses, which is why he had recommended both be legalized, as we saw in Chapter 6.

Sadly, the strongest argument in favor of Atherton's proposal—that is, that regulation would end *most** official corruption—was to politicians

---

*As we learned in Chapter 6, the Atherton Report uncovered multiple examples of the SFPD extorting businesses with a legal right to operate, such as bars (after repeal) that wanted to stay open past closing time. Presumably, if gambling and prostitution operations had been decriminalized, the SFPD would have continued to prey on them in a similar fashion, although to a lesser degree than was taking place in an environment where gambling and sex work were *per se* illegal.

also the strongest argument *against* it. The police and the mayor did not exactly want to kill the goose that laid the golden eggs of graft, but neither did they want to let it run free. Besides, there were lots of other activities for politicians to exercise patronage and pay off old scores or debts. The San Francisco Redevelopment Agency was formed in 1948 on Robinson's watch and—thanks to 1949 federal legislation—would go on to be an important conduit of funds from Washington to the City by the Bay.[3] It is probably not surprising that Robinson made a number of questionable appointments to the Redevelopment Agency's board, including a political opponent who was an optometrist and another individual who was a private detective.[4]

In some ways, it was as if San Francisco was stuck in the 1930s rather than at the end of the 1940s. However, there was one major player who was no longer on the chessboard. The McDonough Brothers and—to a lesser degree—Jerry Ferri, Gennaro Broccolo, and Luigi Malvese, as we saw in Chapter 5—had managed to keep the Chicago Outfit out of San Francisco (Capone was quoted as saying "the more lucrative forms of crime were so highly organized and well protected that outsiders couldn't break into San Francisco")[5] through the end of World War II.

The end of the war brought a new set of facts on the ground. By 1947, the McDonough organization was virtually defunct and Ferri, Broccolo, and Malvese were pushing up daisies. Tony Lima was around and active, but trying to keep his moves as obscure as the City's fog. The circumstances seemed primed for an Outfit bookie and dope dealer named Nick DeJohn to try his luck in the City by the Bay. In reality—and as DeJohn would learn to his ultimate cost—they were anything but.

OF CHEESE AND MEN

Born on August 15, 1909, Nicholas DeJohn first came to prominence in February 1936, when he was brought in for questioning after the killing of Jack "Machine Gun" McGurn, who was once one of Al Capone's main gunsels.[6] True, McGurn was long past his prime when the reapers came for him and DeJohn was probably insulted by being referred to as "minor gangste[r],"[7] but publicity *is* publicity.

According to later accounts "DeJohn had dabbled in alcohol during the Prohibition era and later graduated to bookmaking and the Italian cheese market."[8] Unfortunately, his plan to seize control over the latter brought him into direct conflict with Jake "Greasy Thumb" Guzik, Capone's former bagman and advisor and a gambling power in his own right.[9]

On December 6, 1943, two gunmen blasted Thomas Oneglia's (also referred to as Thomas O'Neglia in some accounts) brains over a North

Side of Chicago barber shop.[10] Oneglia had been one of the principal stockholders of the Grande Cheese Co. of Chicago.[11] Shortly thereafter, Chicago police found the "battered and bound" body of James DeAngelo in the trunk of his wife's car[12] and searched for nearly a year before finding the corpse of DeAngelo's friend, Onofrio Vitale, in Chicago sewer.[13] Like Oneglia, Vitale and DeAngelo had also had stakes in the Grande Cheese Co., before they took their respective last rides.[14]

What was so special about the Grande Cheese Co., which made it worth the lives of at least three men? First, as we saw in Chapter 7, during the last few years of World War II, cheese was rationed—so controlling a cheese company meant being able to make money off of both legitimate and black-market sales. Second, the infrastructure needed to move consumer goods like cheese and olive oil around the country can easily be adapted to move contraband like drugs as well. As Frederic Sondern Jr. pointed out in *Brotherhood of Evil: The Mafia*, "It is not a coincidence that many members of the brotherhood who are known to be active in the narcotics traffic also . . . have interests in trucking companies, import-export houses, and the wholesaling of cheese, olive oil and other imported produce. This means that a kilo of heroin (about 33 ounces) placed in a barrel of olive oil or a wheel of cheese before shipment will be in 'safe' hands from the time it reaches dockside in the United States until it is delivered to the buyer."[15] Third, a food wholesale business can be an admirable vehicle to provide an "official" job to family members attempting to justify their expenditures (and thus ideally deter a criminal or IRS investigation) or to take care of those associates who need a legitimate job in order to remain in the good graces of their parole officer.

Of course, to gain any of those benefits, it is necessary to *win* control over the enterprise—and the Grande Cheese Co. was apparently too big a morsel for DeJohn to digest without the permission of Guzik or rest of the Chicago Outfit, which DeJohn obviously did not have. After DeJohn's uncle was murdered,[16] Nick evidently decided flight was the better part of valor and left for Santa Rosa, California (about 55 miles north of San Francisco) sometime in 1946, where he assumed the name of Vincent Rossi.[17]

Gone from Chicago he may have been, but in the game he remained— and he was about to pay the ultimate price.

DEJOHN'S LAST RIDE

The designers of the *San Francisco Chronicle*'s front page must have felt they had time-warped back to the 1920s. The paper's May 10, 1947, issue carried the headline—in near end-of-the-world-type seven columns across the front page—"RIVAL OF CAPONE GANG STRANGLED IN CAR HERE!"[18]

It was the highest profile Mafia killing in San Francisco since the death of Luigi Malvese 15 years earlier, even if the technique (garroting DeJohn and leaving his body in the trunk of a car) was closer to the murder of Frank Boca in 1929, as we saw in Chapter 5. DeJohn's body was discovered on Friday, May 9, on Laguna Street after a resident called the San Francisco Police Department (SFPD) because he believed the car was stolen, as it had not been moved since the previous Thursday morning.[19]

DeJohn's "big diamond ring was gone" reported the *Chronicle*. "There was only 77 cents in the pockets of his tailored trousers."[20] Regrettably for posterity, those who killed DeJohn did not leave an insulting note on the body as McGurn's assassins did—either their operational security was better, they felt DeJohn was not worth the trouble, or they felt the manner of DeJohn's death sent the message they needed to without additional embellishments.

Three days later, the SFPD's typical response to these incidents—that is, roust the usual suspects and arrest them as $1,000 vagrants and generally make the Tenderloin a miserable place to do illegal business—was in full effect.[21] This was in many ways an echo of what the SFPD did in the 1920s and 1930s after the killings of Ferri, Boca, and Malvese, as if to comfort the citizenry that although the players had changed, the play itself remained the same.

Then, the civil grand jury decided to flip the script. On Wednesday May 14, 1947, Foreman Carroll Newburgh declared, "The Grand Jury wishes to go on record as being intensely interested and investigating subversive activity in the City and County of San Francisco . . . [h]owever, the Grand Jury is more interested in the present crime situation in San Francisco and is inviting the Mayor, the Police Commission, the Chief of Police and the District Attorney to appear before them immediately."[22] Translation: actual dead gangsters are far more interesting than imaginary communist conspiracies and how many times can we *really* talk to our favorite local communist, Harry Bridges, of the International Longshoremen's Association, anyway?

Evidently, the thought of their brass being hauled before a civil grand jury spurred the SFPD to greater than usual efforts. For the first time since the slaying of "Don Broccolo the Magnificent" (which did not really count, since in that case the police walked in and *saw* the shooter holding the still-smoking gun), the SFPD was actually *trying* to arrest a living suspect for DeJohn's murder. This was new territory for both the police and their usual paymasters and current adversaries in organized crime.

NO CITY FOR POODLE DOGS

On May 17, Captain of Inspectors Bernard McDonald told the *Chronicle* that the police had questioned several "suspects" without arresting them—which the paper concluded "were apparently local figures known to have been associates of DeJohn and *said to be connected with the Mafia in narcotics and black market operations*"[23] (emphasis added). By May 22, the SFPD had arrested Leonard Calamia—who, like DeJohn, had Chicago connections—and John Passantino for questioning in the case.[24]

Although Passantino was a local of no real fame, Calamia's record was far more interesting. He did two 90-day stretches in jail in Chicago for dope peddling in 1930 and two years later "shot and killed Ralph Ferrara, a boy friend of his sister, in Chicago. He was charged but released when his sister refused to testify."[25] By the mid-1930s, he had graduated to doing federal time for violating the narcotics laws, including a stretch at Leavenworth.[26]

One day later, Daniel T. Capece, one of the owners of the Poodle Dog Restaurant, a favorite underworld hangout on 1121 Polk Street, joined Calamia in the lockup[27] for the "crime" of being simultaneously one of the last people to have seen DeJohn alive and being unable to explain himself to the SFPD's satisfaction. Meanwhile, the SFPD hunted Jimmy Franzone, whom the *Chronicle* declared was a "Chicago hoodlum contemporary with DeJohn"[28] and more interestingly had a piece of the Poodle Dog and a local olive oil firm that Calamia was associated with.[29]

Things got more interesting by the time the May 24th edition of the *Chronicle* hit the streets. At that point, Capece's lawyer announced his client was "co-operating with the police."[30] Furthermore, the paper reported Franzone "was associated with an olive oil firm which has been accused of adulterating its product. One of his associates in the business was Frank Scappatura, whose auto Calamia was driving when first arrested."[31]

Scappatura's criminal adventures began in 1931, including a May 1935 bust for passing counterfeit currency in Buffalo, N.Y.[32] Although the Federal Bureau of Narcotics[†] suspected him of involvement in narcotics trafficking, they failed to make a case against him on it before his death.[33]

[†]Although James Lanza's FBI file mentions the Bureau of Narcotics' suspicions about Scappatura, Scappatura is not listed in the Bureau's original organized crime file (which does include James Lanza and other members of the San Francisco family), which was later codified and published as *Mafia: The Government's Secret File on Organized Crime*. This may have been because Scappatura was not considered to have been enough of a senior-level mobster to merit inclusion.

However, in 1945 the feds *did* manage to bust Scappartura for selling cottonseed oil as olive oil across state lines.[34] As we saw in Chapter 7, supply and transport dislocations caused by World War II and its aftermath caused olive oil to remain on the ration list until 1946, thereby giving Scappatura and others an incentive to push cottonseed oil as "olive oil."

On the 24th, the SFPD finally charged Calamia with the murder of DeJohn, notwithstanding the fact that the Captain of Inspectors Bernard J. McDonald admittedly did not know "'whether Calamia is one of the killers or an accomplice who 'fingered' DeJohn for the men who did the job."[35] They also released Capece, thereby doubtlessly improving operations at the Poodle Dog, as Franzone remained on the run.[36] More substantively, the next day the *Chronicle* reported that federal narcotics agents had linked the Poodle Dog to the "Star Dust narcotics gang," which the paper claimed had been "a million-dollar drug ring which smuggled narcotics into San Francisco from Mexico."[37] Strangely, although the said ring had supposedly been previously smashed by federal agents, there was no mention of the gang in the *Chronicle* before DeJohn's murder.

On May 26, the public learned from Calamia's attorney that "DeJohn and Calamia were at Capece's cafe until about 8 o'clock on May 7, the supposed night of the murder . . . Then, I am told, DeJohn and Calamia went to LaRocca's bar on Broadway, where they separated."[38]

Although the police disputed this story, this was the first time DeJohn's movements would be traced to LaRocca's Corner in North Beach, a detail that would become of greater significance in the coming weeks and months, because the hammer was about to fall closer to home.

LIMA ARRESTED AND THE LAROCCAS
IN CUSTODY—BRIEFLY

On May 26, 1947, the SFPD arrested Tony Lima (who the *Chronicle* identified as a "Lodi fruit packer."[39] Although Lima *did* have agricultural interests in Lodi, which is nearly a 100 miles northeast of San Francisco, they did not want to query him about tomatoes. Instead, they were trying to draw a link between the March 1947 slaying of Tom Buffa, who the *Chronicle* identified as a "60-year-old tavern keeper" in Lodi,[40] and that of DeJohn.

As with Lima and DeJohn, there was more to Buffa than met the eye. As Daniel Waugh points out in *The Gangs of St. Louis: Men of Respect*, "Tom Buffa was the most powerful Mafia boss in St. Louis in 1940, having eliminated just about all threats to his power and becoming one of the top narcotics distributors in the Midwest."[41] A few years later, Buffa fell from power after attracting federal heat for his narcotics work[42] and—like DeJohn—apparently figured northern California was a great place for deposed or hunted mobsters to hide. Indeed, it may have been—until both paid the ultimate price for that mistake.

Although the SFPD tried to connect the dots between Lima, DeJohn, and Buffa, they continued to make life uncomfortable for the eating and drinking establishments that served the family. The same day they arrested Lima, police took Leo and Alphonse LaRocca—proprietors of LaRocca's Corner—into custody for a day's worth of interrogation.[43] Evidently, they held their mud, as the *Chronicle* reported that "police were bringing in witnesses 'who might refresh the boys' memory.' "[44] Alas for the SFPD, they were "[u]nable to locate those witnesses, [so] they ordered the brothers released."[45]

It is rare today to see a suspect in police custody to have the intestinal fortitude to call the cops' bluff in the way the LaRoccas apparently did. Given that the "acceptable" range of behaviors police could (and frequently did) inflict on prisoners at that time was far greater in the late 1940s (including but not limited to physical beatings and what we would consider to be torture) than it is now, the LaRoccas' steel is doubly impressive. Alternatively, they may have been more concerned about what *would* have happened to them if they did talk rather than what *could* happen to them if they did not.

By the evening of May 28, the district attorney was presenting the case to a criminal grand jury, with Lima, Scappatura, and Mike Abati (whom the *Chronicle* misidentified as "Mike Abata") as the first witnesses.[46] Meanwhile, Chief of Police Charles W. Dullea demanded his officers get even *more* aggressive with the use of California's vagrancy statute—the same statute that had been so strongly criticized by Edwin Atherton for abuse in his report, as we saw in Chapter 6. But, Dullea had a different view. "The vagrancy statutes have been valuable in the past of ridding San Francisco of the criminal scum," he wrote in a written order to his officers "and if more serious charges cannot be placed against the gangster, then the vagrancy statutes should be applied."[47]

Although Dullea's conclusion that San Francisco had *ever* been rid of "criminal scum" is somewhat dubious, he was probably right in his implicit statement that the vagrancy law was an admirable tool to keep criminals—at least those the police were not paid or otherwise ordered to tolerate—out of the City when the cops lacked the annoying constitutional requirement of having evidence against somebody they wanted to lock up.

Still, not everyone was fooled. That same day, Herb Caen—the *Chronicle*'s columnist who seemed better informed than the papers' police beat reporters—declared, "You could do worse than make a slight bet that Leonard Calamia, the ex-con charged with murder in the de John Nick-tie party, will be freed for lack of evidence."[48] Caen also pointed out that he supposed "the coppers know that Jimmy Franzone, mucho wanted for 'questioning,' is walking around Chicago, fit as a fiddle and not at all unstrung"[49] and that he placed 2-1 odds on Franzone being the string-puller behind DeJohn's murder.[50]

Caen was far closer to the truth than he knew. Almost four decades later in *The Last Mafioso: The Treacherous World of Jimmy ("the Weasel") Fratianno*, veteran crime reporter Ovid Demaris said that Franzone had been an Outfit *caporegime*, or crew leader, who had dispatched soldier Dominic Galiano to kill DeJohn in San Francisco.[51] Galiano, of course, was never charged in San Francisco with the killing. Of course, lacking that knowledge the SFPD focused on following up the leads they had—and struck gold, or so they thought. By May 28, they made a discovery that was sure to cause the LaRoccas even more *agita*, as the location where DeJohn was met the business end of a garrote was apparently "the basement of a Taylor Street apartment house half a block from La Rocca's Tavern at 957 Columbus Avenue."[52] This was also the moment state liquor officials started proceedings to suspend or cancel the Poodle Dog's liquor license, purportedly on the ground that the other owners had forgotten to mention Franzone's interest in the business when they got the license in the first place.[53] By May 31, they had something approximating a motive. That day's *Chronicle* reported, "For some reason, DeJohn's killers did not want it known in North Beach that he was rubbed out in a business deal. A killing over a girl was all right."[54]

This called for a little impromptu theater at the house party DeJohn went to after leaving LaRocca's. According to the *Chronicle* "One of the men accused DeJohn of taking his girl. The argument was noisy and hot. In the eyes of everybody in the place, it was established as a grudge."[55]

More substantively, the SFPD also had Joseph Curreri, also known as Phil Ruggero, under guard at a San Francisco hospital. Curreri had an energetic record going back to the 1920s involving crimes in both the United States *and* Canada, including murder allegations in both Quebec and Ontario,[56] but he was also connected to the same Sunland Olive Oil firm that linked all the other players to this drama.

On June 1, Caen's prediction came true when the court granted Calamia's petition for a writ of habeas corpus[57] (based on the people's failure to present any evidence against him) and he walked out of court a free man. Two days later, IRS officials were trying to determine how Sunland managed to have an income "of $500,000 a year strictly from sales of olive oil and cheese."[58] Given that this would amount to more than $4.92 *million* in 2015 dollars,[59] the government's skepticism was understandable, especially given its past experience with other food companies being used as fronts for contraband traffic. Although not much would come from this inquiry in the short term, Sunland would come back to haunt the Lanzas and others for decades, as we see later.

Meanwhile, when the matter of DeJohn's death went to the Coroner's Jury on June 4, the proceedings were less memorable for the verdict—"death at the hands of a party or parties unknown"[60] (after all, garroting oneself would take a memorable level of skill, even for a gangster of DeJohn's standing)—than for the way District Attorney Edmund G. "Pat" Brown treated DeJohn's widow afterward. According to the *Chronicle*, Brown needled Lena DeJohn if she was not "interested in getting back the $9,000 [wedding] ring"[61] that DeJohn had worn when he was last seen alive. Following in the tradition of Naana Wortova and Ramona Crawford, as we saw in Chapter 5, Lena DeJohn cut the lawman dead. "I'm more interested in getting beyond the ring than the ring itself," she said.[62] Then again, she had already driven Brown and his chief deputy Tom Lynch to distraction during the hearing by (like Wortova and Crawford) proclaiming her complete ignorance of DeJohn's business activities despite being married to him for two decades, other than to proclaim that he "never had an enemy."[63]

The investigation proceeded in fits and starts, with Sebastiano Nani and Ciro Gallo testifying before the grand jury on June 18,[64] their first substantive appearance in the case. It would take another 17 months—or until November 1948—for the SFPD to declare the case "solved."[65]

WHY PAWNING EVIDENCE IS A BAD IDEA

On November 21, 1948, the *Chronicle* reported that Nani and Abati had been charged with murdering DeJohn.[66] The next day, the police announced that they had also charged—but could not find—Calamia, Lima, Scappatura, and Leonard Bruno with involvement in DeJohn's killing.[67]

Nani's strongest link to the crime was through an act of remarkable (and, given his prior and later record, uncharacteristic) stupidity on his part. Thanks to Nani having several pawn shop tickets on him when he was arrested made out to a "J.V. Lucci" and "B. Nani," it was a simple matter for the SFPD to trace the items back to a Brooklyn pawn shop, where they located DeJohn's famous wedding ring and watch.[68] It may have been that DeJohn's ring (valued at between $8,000 and $9,000 in the late 1940s, it would be worth over $85,000 in 2015 dollars even at the more conservative estimate)[69] was too big for Nani's usual fencing contacts to handle, or he may have assumed the SFPD would never try to track down the items all the way to Brooklyn. In any case, it would prove to be a costly mistake, at least in the short term.

Given that nearly everyone involved with the case seemed to have a tie to Sunland in one way or another, it is not surprising the SFPD had the company under a microscope, revealing in late November 1948 that they had found records of shipments of olive oil cans from Sunland to Joe Ingoglia,‡ who the *Chronicle* described as "a big-time narcotics dealer who was arrested by Federal agents in Oakland a few weeks ago."[70]

As for Lima, he apparently really *had* been on a trip to sell grapes to customers in Pennsylvania when the charges came down, but by early December his wife resignedly told the *Chronicle* "I don't think Tony'll be home for Christmas after all."[71] At that point, the police had adopted the story that DeJohn was killed because he was trying to muscle in on Sunland, which—given DeJohn's past connections with both narcotics and the Grande Cheese Co., in Illinois—doubtlessly seemed plausible.

More intriguingly, the SFPD now admitted their primary source of the story about the alleged conspiracy between the defendants to kill DeJohn came from Anita Rocchia Venza, who was then under investigation for suspected involvement in an abortion ring.[72] When the case came to trial, the prosecution probably wished Venza *had* been an abortionist, as that would not have hurt her credibility as much as the list of her prior convictions would.

Meanwhile, by Christmas Eve of 1948, the FBI had run Calamia to ground in Albuquerque, New Mexico, where he had been working (as "Leonard Tallone") for the New Mexico Bureau of Revenue processing driver's license applications.[73] He was soon extradited back to San Francisco.

CALAMIA, ABATI, AND NANI IN THE DOCK

With no sign of Lima or the other fugitives and not being able to delay the case indefinitely, Brown decided to put Calamia, Abati, and Nani on trial for DeJohn's murder by themselves in early 1949. Although he may not have had any alternative, doing so was risky, as it gave defense counsel a perfect opportunity to engage in an "empty chair" defense—that is, blame the crime on the people who were not there to defend themselves, rather than the three men in the courtroom. To make matters worse, the background of many of the key witnesses relied on by Brown and his

‡This may have been a misidentification of *Andrew* Ingoglia, who ran a heroin ring in Oakland before ending up on the wrong side of the Federal Bureau of Narcotics.

chief deputy Thomas C. Lynch to make their case against Calamia, Abati, and Nani was hardly stellar.

In retrospect, what is most surprising is that Brown did not try to "flip" Calamia by offering him a plea to a lesser charge and/or offering consideration at sentencing in exchange for Calamia's testimony against Abati and Nani (and Lima and the other fugitives, if it came to that).

Ironically, it did seem like Calamia's thoughts were leaning toward cooperation at an early stage of the case. When he was initially arrested in the case in 1947, he sang a virtual aria of disclosures to the SFPD, which the police—uncharacteristically—kept secret from the media until the case came to trial. On February 17, 1949, the prosecution dropped their bomb by calling SFPD Homicide Inspector Frank Ahern to the stand, who in turn "uncorked a lengthy statement and two crude maps" given to the SFPD by Calamia back in 1947 when he was first arrested.[74]

Normally, out-of-court statements presented for their truth—in this case, Calamia placing Lima, Nani, Abati, and Scappatura in LaRocca's Corner and meeting with DeJohn the last night he was seen alive[75]—are considered to be hearsay and, therefore, inadmissible in a criminal trial. However, there is an exception for out-of-court statements made by a party to the case, like Calamia. After a slew of objections from Ferriter, who represented Nani and Abati, the court instructed the jury that the Calamia disclosures could only be used against him, not his codefendants. Still, as Ferriter ruefully noted, "you can't unring a bell or unscramble an egg."[76]

Besides, Nani ended up doing similar damage to himself after the prosecution presented the transcript of his testimony to the 1947 grand jury investigating DeJohn's death, where he said he delivered two dresses to Pasquale LaRocca on May 6, 1947.[77] Although this might seem innocuous on its face, it had the unfortunate effect of partially corroborating the testimony from Venza, who claimed she overheard the defendants plotting the death of DeJohn on that date.[78]

Still, Ferriter—as one would expect—hammered Venza hard on her past convictions for passing bad checks, as well as one for grand theft.[79] Although any felony conviction can negatively affect a witness's credibility, the so-called moral turpitude offenses—like theft and fraud—are considered even more damaging to the jury's judgment of a witness's character. Venza probably did not do herself any favors in this area by answering, in responses to Ferriter's queries "I plead guilty to something. I don't know whether [it] is felony or misdemeanor,"[80] even if Ferriter's attempts to get her to admit to attempting to open a (legal) brothel in Virginia City, Nevada went nowhere.[81]

Calamia's attorney James Purcell did better, not only getting Venza to admit that Calamia was not one of the murder plotters she allegedly overheard but also that Venza had previously helped the state prosecute an abortionist for whom she had worked as a housekeeper,[82] which made her look like a professional snitch.

Meanwhile, given that the state's two other key witnesses—Frank Tornabene and John Passantino—backtracked on earlier testimony they gave the grand jury when it came time to testify at trial,[83] the defense had reason to be confident when they opened their case on February 23, 1949.[84]

THE DEFENSE RESTS AND THE PROSECUTION SURRENDERS

After two weeks of the defense's case, the court placed the fate of Calamia, Nani, and Abati in the jury's hands on March 7, 1949. In theory, the three men face a potential capital sentence if they were convicted, but in practice there seemed little chance of that happening. Beyond the circumstantial nature of the case against the trio and the issues with Venza's background, the court told the jury they could only consider first-degree murder charges against the defendants, which made the prosecution's already high burden even tougher to meet.[85]

After a day of deliberation and three ballots, the jury was 7-5 for acquittal by the evening of March 8, 1949—when suddenly Brown folded.[86] Without prior notice to the police or his trial team, he ordered Lynch to move to dismiss the case. To call this unusual or remarkable would be to engage in criminal understatement. In more than 10 years of practice as a criminal defense attorney, I have never seen a case where a prosecutor would attempt to dismiss a case *after* it went to the jury unless the parties had reached a plea bargain. After all, if the jury ultimately reported they were hopelessly deadlocked and could not reach a verdict, the court would declare a mistrial and the state would be free to retry the case (or not, as it determined), since the constitutional prohibition on placing defendants in double jeopardy does not apply if the jury cannot make a decision.

Although Brown may have worried the five holdouts for conviction might ultimately change their votes to go with the majority and acquit the three men, that is the risk the prosecution takes when it brings a case to trial and lets it go to the jury. After all, even if Calamia, Nani, and Abati *were* acquitted (and there is no sign Brown was aware of Abati's role in the local family, much less expect he should go on to succeed Lima as boss), Brown *still* could pursue his fugitive defendants and bring them to trial.

Criminal defense lawyers like to say there are three certainties in this life: death, taxes, and people in warrant will eventually be found. By definition, professional criminals are going to engage in activities that are statistically certain to bring them to the attention of law enforcement if they keep at them long enough and are not bumped off by somebody else, so the risk of Lima and his colleagues remaining on the run for decades was minimal at best. As an experienced prosecutor, Brown presumably knew this. On the other side of the ledger was Brown's political ambition to be attorney general and governor. Even so, although an acquittal in the DeJohn trial would have hurt him, but would hardly have been fatal, since he could fairly blame that outcome on the jury.

In contrast, responsibility for the course of action Brown ultimately chose could only be left with him, which begs the question of why he chose it. Although it would be tempting to draw the inference that Brown was persuaded to sink the case by friends of the defendants through one means or another, so far no credible evidence has yet come to light to support that conclusion. Among other things, if Nani or his cronies had swung the payoff, we would expect to pick up chatter of them talking about it to other family members—and of that chatter to be picked up on FBI wiretaps, whether legal or otherwise, as we see in Chapter 11 and 12.

So far, that evidence is not publicly extant. Still, many observers at the time and today believe that Brown's decision was spectacularly inappropriate and that it severely irritated his relations with the SFPD, as we see in Chapter 9.

AFTERMATH

Ultimately, although Brown abandoned his efforts to hold any of the defendants responsible for DeJohn's murder—even those who he had not managed to bring to trial—on April 11, 1949 when he dismissed the charges against all of them,[87] few escaped scot-free.

The Grande Cheese Co.—the botched takeover of which appears to have been the catalyst that encouraged DeJohn to head west to his eventual doom—continued to be associated with the Mafia. In 1949, the company moved its headquarters from Chicago to Fond du Lac, Wisconsin, where it was managed by Giovanni Vincent DiBella, aka John DiBella,[88] one of the late Francesco Lanza's old associates from their New York days.[89] DiBella was close to Joe "Joe Bananas" Bonanno, who sat on the Mafia's commission until he ended up having to flee both law enforcement *and* his colleagues simultaneously, thereby putting James Lanza in a very awkward position, as we see later. Bonanno's wife Faye was also a stockholder in the firm.[90]

Despite his loose lips to the SFPD, Calamia managed to remain active in Chicago Outfit circles as a reported hitman and drug dealer into the

1960s.[91] Although Scappatura beat the DeJohn murder rap, he could not outrun a lung tumor that killed him on November 28, 1952.[92] Ironically, he had collapsed earlier while riding in a car with Abati *and* James Lanza.[93]

Meanwhile, in 1954, Nani was convicted by the feds of narcotics trafficking. Although at the time this meant a relatively minimal sentence (three years, in Nani's case), the felony conviction together with his concurrent charge of attempting to bribe a federal agent placed him in the federal government's crosshairs for deportation.[94] Nani held off the inevitable for a time through multiple legal challenges, but he was sent back to Italy in February 1958.[95]

As for Lima, he ended up in trouble long before that. In November 1951, he was arrested in San Joaquin County for allegedly ripping off the Italian-Swiss Wine Company.[96] As silly as the caper—which involved falsifying bills of sale and altering scales used in grape purchases—seemed in comparison to Lima's other activities, it turned out to be the one that sent him to prison. The prosecution opened its case on March 2, 1953, against Lima and two other men,[97] and the subsequent conviction they obtained doubtlessly reinforced Lima's belief that it was best to remain a fugitive when facing criminal charges, as he did in the DeJohn case. After Lima was paroled in 1956, he returned to San Francisco, where he worked at his brother Dominick's fruit stand at 1676 Market Street—at least officially.[98] Still, conviction cost Lima both his freedom (although briefly) and his spot as boss of the San Francisco family, where he was succeeded by Mike Abati.

Since this meant Abati was at the helm when the biggest disaster to hit the modern U.S. Mafia hit in 1957, he probably regretted that achievement, as we see in Chapter 10.

Chapter 9

The Kefauver Show

Several days before Thanksgiving Day of 1950, the traveling circus known as the Special Committee to Investigate Organized Crime in Interstate Commerce and its Chairman, Sen. Estes Kefauver, finally came to San Francisco. The committee had been established in May 1950 by Senate Resolution 202, after a request by the American Municipal Association (which represented local governments), asking Congress to examine the power of organized crime in postwar America.[1] Over the following 15 months, the committee took testimony in 14 cities.[2] About 30 million Americans[3] watched the hearings on television (or about *one-fifth* of the entire country, given the continental United States' estimated population was just more than 151 million in 1951).[4]

Alas, in San Francisco, it was local law enforcement that came out looking like clowns—or turkeys—depending on what metaphor you prefer. In short order, the committee was treated to the spectacle of the district attorney (and attorney general-elect), declaring that he did not think it was his job to "be a policeman"; a local businessperson who cleared what would be the equivalent of hundreds of thousands of dollars today, simply by matching up gamblers with those who would take their action; and the chief of police admitting he was aware of the said businessperson but that he was powerless to do anything about it because his patrol officers failed to bring him any citations for violations. As a sort of maraschino cherry on this sundae of arrogance, the San Francisco Police Department (SFPD) also declared that the Mafia had been "exterminated" in San Francisco in 1948, based—apparently—on a murder they failed to solve.

THE KANSAS CITY PROLOGUE

As we saw in Chapter 8 the biggest recent Mafia-related news in San Francisco was the unsolved garroting of Chicago Outfit associate and alleged drug trafficker Nick DeJohn in 1948, whom the SFPD discovered in a trunk of a car two days after he was last seen alive at a North Beach bar. Appropriately enough, the Kefauver Committee got a taste of what they would face in San Francisco at an earlier hearing in Kansas City on September 28, 1950, when Bureau of Narcotics Agent Claude A. Follmer testified about a mob-run narcotics chain operating during the 1940s that DeJohn was connected to. "Early in 1940, Louis and Patsy Ventola were arrested by Federal narcotic agents and police detectives at Kansas City for making numerous small sales of narcotic drugs to a government agent and a supply of heroin having a wholesale value of $3,000 was seized,"[5] Follmer testified.

This may not sound exciting until you realize that this equals $50,857.71[6] in 2015 dollars.

Follmer continued:

The drugs were contained in a brief case belonging to Pete Di Giovanni. It was learned the Ventolas were employed as retail salesmen of heroin by Charles Bengimina, alias Red Brick, and that Bengimina, in turn was a distributor for one Carl Carramusa. Carramusa was a minor member of the Mafia and the "front man" of the Kansas City narcotics syndicate, *owned and operated by the local Mafia*.[7] (Emphasis added)

The last sentence is emphasized for two reasons. First, it illustrates that just nine years after the founding of the commission and its supposed ban on drug dealing, the Mafia was knee deep in the trade. Second, it is an example of how Bureau of Narcotics Director Harry Anslinger—unlike the FBI's J. Edgar Hoover—*did* believe in the Mafia.

In any event, "In 1942 it was determined one of the sources of supply for the Kansas City group was a Mafia organization in Tampa, Fla., who in turn received drugs smuggled from Marseilles, France via Havana, Cuba,"[8] said Follmer. Thus, the Mafia was moving narcotics from Vichy, France, through the Nazi U-boat packs prowling the Atlantic Ocean and Caribbean Sea, to Havana, and ultimately Tampa. "The traveling representative who brought the drugs to Kansas City was James DeSimone," said Follmer. "It was also indicated that Sebastino Nani, one-time

Brooklyn Mafia hoodlum now established in California, had furnished several large shipments of drugs to the Kansas City syndicate from New York."[9] This would be the same Nani who would go on to be involved in the DeJohn case, as we saw in Chapter 8.

Ultimately, Follmer said the Bureau of Narcotics brought a 155-count indictment against 14 individuals involved in the conspiracy, aided by Carl Carramusa's decision to switch sides and testify for the government. Carramusa probably regretted that decision. None of the defendants received a sentence of more than six years—and some received only a day in jail. Carrumusa, however, received the traditional punishment for informers administered by his former colleagues—death. According to Follmer:

In addition to the murders of Carramusa, Ignatious Antinori and Tom Buffa, some of the other murders relating to this case in recent years are those of *Nick DeJohn, a Chicago narcotic peddler, at San Francisco, in which Sebastino Nani is still a primary suspect,* and the recent murder at Tampa Fla of James Lumia, Antinori associate and suspect in the Carramusa killing . . . [10] (Emphasis added)

When the committee's chief counsel Rudolph Halley asked whether he knew who was responsible for narcotics entering the United States at New York, Follmer quickly responded, "Sebastino Nani."[11]

GANGSTER'S PARADISE BY THE BAY?

When the committee got to San Francisco, appropriately one of the first witnesses was Joseph L. Alioto, Esq., future mayor of San Francisco, relative[12] of Giovanni "John" Alioto, who would be named boss of the Milwaukee family two years later, and then, current tax attorney for local bookie Mario Cambo Georgetti, who mysteriously failed to show up.[13]

Then the real show began with Attorney General-Elect Edmund G. Brown. During his seven years as district attorney, he said he learned, "Of course, the rackets will grow out of, No. 1, gambling; No. 2, prostitution; No. 3, narcotics; No. 4, abortions;[14] No. 5, probably extortion upon legitimate business. I believe that embraced all of the sources of rackets or racketeers."[15]

In terms of San Francisco's situation, "There unquestionably is gambling. There must be prostitution," said Brown. "Narcotics are a real problem. I do believe we have cleaned up the abortion situation in our city, and I know of no extortion upon legitimate business in our city. I have had no reports whatsoever." Since—by his own estimation—San Francisco had a problem with three of the five types of crime from which the Mafia drew most of its power, one would assume San Francisco had a substantial Mafia presence, right?

Wrong. "I do not believe that there is in San Francisco any organized crime," said Brown. Of course, Brown's assessment might have been influenced by his sources of information—or more properly—the lack thereof. According to Brown:

I might say that all of my information with respect to gambling is gained from *one undercover agent* that I employ under a secret fund that I have. Other than that I must rely on newspaper reports that I get from citizens advising me, which reports I pass on to the police department. In the event that they do not act, I have been compelled, very frankly, to use the power of public opinion in most of these cases and oftentimes I suppose I have been considered rather a publicity seeker, but it is the only way I have been able to accomplish the results without the investigators.[16] (Emphasis added)

In 1950, San Francisco had fewer residents (775,357)[17] than it does today (825,000),[18] but had four English-language newspapers that actually competed with each other,[19] as well as (last but not least) 1,710 police officers[20] compared with around 2,207 police officers in 2013.[21] Even so, their combined efforts (along with Brown's secret investigator) were apparently not sufficient to advise the City's top prosecutor of where the gambling dens were. "I think that the bookies, if they are operating, are operating covertly and under cover," he said. "Unquestionably there are telephone bookies. But I couldn't tell you where they are at the present moment."[22]

Similarly, although he testified that there "must" be prostitution in San Francisco, Brown proclaimed himself ignorant of where it was taking place. "With respect to prostitution, I do not believe that there are any houses of prostitution unless they are in the Negro district," Brown said. "Probably there are houses of prostitution in the Negro district, but I know of no addresses at the present time."[23]

In contrast to Brown's admitted ignorance before the Kefauver Committee, three years later, the final report of the state of California's Special Crime Study Commission on Organized Crime would note that it had previously found five bookmaking joints in operation during this period, one of which—the Merchants Club at 84 Ellis Street—reportedly had San Francisco Police Inspector Pat Wafter (or Wafer) on duty as an *employee* at the time the commission's investigator visited.[24] The commission also found a plethora of illegal dice games proliferating throughout the City with little or no interference from law enforcement, including, but not limited to, "dice boards" at the Bimbos 365 Club,[25] whose owner Agostino "Bimbo" Giuntoli wisely declined to testify before the commission.

With regard to prostitution, the commission found "Houses of prostitution have been openly tolerated in the City and County of San Francisco for many years. They have been generally well known to the public and in spite of 'regular' raids, evidence secured by this Commission indicates that conditions have not changed."[26]

During this period, the commission found that:

The man on the street is familiar with call-houses and houses of prostitution in San Francisco and it is difficult to understand how their operations, which are not conducted in secret, can for so long escape the knowledge of the police in the City and County of San Francisco, or if they have been brought to the attention of the police, why no action was taken to stop their operations. Testimony received by the Commission indicates that taxicab drivers who participate in a call-house prostitution operation . . . receive approximately 40 percent of the payment made by the customer to the madame or the prostitute and in addition often receive a bonus from the customer at the time the cabby completes the arrangements. Testimony was to the effect that some taxi drivers have earnings in excess of $400 weekly on their percentage of this traffic in women.[27]

In 1949, the median family household income in San Francisco was $3,923 annually.[28] Assuming a taxi driver made $400 a week extra on average and took a two-week vacation each year, they should be looking at an additional $20,000 in untaxed income—or $199,442.02 in 2015 dollars.[29] Not a bad haul for simply putting together providers and consumers of commercial sex.

DEJOHN TAKES THE BIG SLEEP

With regard to the DeJohn murder, Brown claimed that: "In Chicago he was reputed to be a bookie. Mr. Lynch and I went back there. He was supposed to have 10 or 12 bookies under his jurisdiction."[30] After moving to the Bay Area, Brown said that DeJohn lived in Alameda County before buying a house in Santa Rosa.[31] It is curious that Brown never mentioned any of this to the public when he was trying a trio of men for allegedly murdering DeJohn, as we saw in Chapter 8. "He was found dead in an automobile on May 7," said Brown. "[DeJohn] was found in the back of an automobile with a wire—we were never able to find the rope or wire that killed him—that was taken off. But he was garroted, choked to death, died of asphyxiation."[32]

DeJohn was found in his own car on Lombard Street on May 9 and had been dead for two days.[33] In the light of an earlier testimony by Agent Follmer and Brown's own belief that narcotics was a problem in San Francisco, it is notable that Brown did not mention DeJohn's apparent connections with the heroin trade to the committee, especially since he had spun a completely different story to the San Francisco papers and to the court during the trial of three of DeJohn's alleged killers.

Chief Assistant District Attorney Thomas C. Lynch, who would go on to succeed Brown both as district attorney and attorney general, elaborated, "on the last day [DeJohn] was known to be alive, he toured San Francisco in company with Leonard Calamia."[34]

"Leonard Calamia is a well-known police character," said Lynch. "He comes out of the Chicago area. He has been known as an aide to gangsters rather than a top-flight gangster himself. He is reputed to have been mixed up in the killing of Caramusa in Chicago."[35]

Despite being corrected by Halley, the committee's general counsel, that Calamia came out of Kansas City, not Chicago, Lynch pressed on.[36] "It also developed that he was with a large number of characters on that day in a bar known as LaRocca's Tavern[37] on Columbus Avenue, *which obviously, because it has been known to the Federal Bureau of Investigation, and to some extent the police department, as a rendezvous for the Mafia*," said Lynch (emphasis added).

Given that this was seven years before the debacle at Apalachin, where the widespread arrests of Mafia bosses (some of whom were caught running away in the woods)—on extremely dubious or nonexistent charges—finally forced J. Edgar Hoover to concede that the Mafia did, in fact, exist, as we see in Chapter 10, itis interesting that no one called Lynch out for speaking out of school. It also reinforces his credibility on this point. "There were also present one Sebastian Nani . . . a gangster out of Brooklyn, and a man who was at least known as a narcotics peddler, if he had not been convicted of it; and another man present at that time was Ciro Gallo," said Lynch.[38]

As we saw in Chapter 8, Lynch and Brown convinced Calamia to snitch out everyone else who was at the bar that fateful night. At the end of the day, this did him little good, as Calamia was prosecuted anyway. "He was charged with murder himself, on the testimony of a woman who claimed to have overheard a conversation," Brown said. However, "the jury was out for 28 hours, when I walked before the court and told the judge, after the jury was out for 28 hours, I would ask that the jury be dismissed because I disbelieved the principal witness, the witness upon whom we had to rely."[39]

This would have been convicted fraudster Anita Rocchia Venza, whom—as we saw in Chapter 8—Brown apparently believed *was* credible, until the jury was heading toward an acquittal. According to Brown "The police department disagreed with me. They felt she was telling the truth. But Mr. Lynch, who tried the case, myself and Judge Devine felt that she was not telling the truth."[40] Given contemporaneous press reports at the time to the contrary, that must have been news to Lynch.

Brown did not elaborate to the committee how or why he came to this epiphany after the jury had been deliberating for more than a day. Still, he did admit that the Mafia existed, as did Lynch. "[DeJohn's] case illustrated at least to us in this area how this particular underworld group, loosely called the Mafia, do operate in various parts of the country," said Lynch. *"There is no question in my mind they had been established in some type of racket, and probably connected with the sale of olive oil, and also engaged in terrorizing some of the Italian merchants"*[41] (emphasis added).

Noting that in San Francisco "being a metropolitan area, a county line is only an imaginary thing," Lynch said there was "no question" the Mafia "were terrorizing some of the merchants in places like Lodi, Fruit-vale, Emeryville, and other places where people have their places of business."[42]

Even so, said Brown:

[I]n frankness we have never been able to get anybody to sustain that. As a matter of fact, Mr. Lynch and myself supplemented the work of the police department by going to every known or unknown racketeer we would think of in San Francisco to try and find out whether DeJohn, the man who was murdered, or any of those Italians had ever tried to muscle in on bookies, gambling, prostitution or narcotics.[43]

Amazingly, no "known or unknown racketeers" appeared to be willing to unburden their soul on this subject to either Brown or Lynch, whose job it was after all—technically, anyway—to put bookies, gamblers, pimps, prostitutes, and narcotics dealers in prison. Thus, "It is my opinion the murder of DeJohn grew out of nothing local," said Brown. "I think it was something growing out of the Chicago bookies of some kind, nature or description. That is my opinion."[44]

After enlightening the committee with war stories involving the pursuit of back-alley abortionists, Brown returned to his main theme. "In San Francisco—I want you to fully understand my function," he said. *"The thing I tried to do as district attorney was not to be a policeman"*[45] (emphasis added).

In line with this somewhat surprising perspective from the City and county's chief law enforcement officer, Brown declared a city ordinance that legalized the playing of "26," a dice game played at cigar stores and other locations where the winners were paid off in merchandise or cash.

The story of "26" is an abject lesson at how relatively quickly gambling fashions can change. According to a 1986 article of the *Chicago*

Tribune[46] lamenting the death of the game in the Windy City in 1962, "The customer would choose a number—'shooting sixes,' for example—and roll 10 dice out of the cup 13 times. To win, the chosen number had to come up 26 times or more in the 13 rolls. The payoff for a quarter bet would be in chips or coupons worth $1 in drinks, which in those days usually meant three rounds."[47]

Nearly a half century later, "26" has been mostly forgotten. But in the 1950s, Brown admitted that the game "probably constitutes a [illegal] lottery under the State laws of the State of California, but I have never tested it. I will be perfectly frank."[48]

In fact, a simple perusal of Penal Code 319, which has not been amended since it was enacted in 1872, would reveal that "26" *did* qualify as an illegal lottery. Under the statute:

A lottery is any scheme for the disposal or distribution of property by chance, among persons who have paid or promised to pay any valuable consideration for the chance of obtaining such property or a portion of it, or for any share or any interest in such property, upon any agreement, understanding, or expectation that it is to be distributed or disposed of by lot or chance, whether called a lottery, raffle, or gift enterprise, or by whatever name the same may be known.[49]

Thus, whether "26" was played for merchandise or cash, it constituted a lottery under Penal Code 319.[50] And San Francisco's laws to the contrary be damned, at least in the eyes of the California Supreme Court.

Back in 1942 in *In re Portnoy*,[51] the court determined, pursuant to Article XI, Section 11 of the California Constitution that, "The control of gambling activities is a matter concerning which local governments possess power to enact and enforce local regulations not in conflict with general laws, *for the purpose of supplementing those laws . . .*" (emphasis added). Stripped of legalese, the *Portnoy* Court held that although local legislatures like the San Francisco Board of Supervisors could *add* regulations to accomplish the goal of the antigambling statute, they could not permit behaviors the statute declared to be illegal, or conversely, forbid activities banned by the statute but proscribe a different punishment.

Fortunately for the "26" operators and players, "whether or not this '26' game is illegal or not I have never checked the law," said Brown.[52] Instead, he would only get involved if he received evidence of a payoff to the police, because "as District Attorney I have left it to the police department to handle that situation in the absence of corruption."[53]

There may have been more to Brown's efforts to maintain his official ignorance of gambling activity. From 1872 through the present, California's Penal Code Section 335 has provided the following: "Every *district attorney, sheriff, or police officer* must inform against and diligently prosecute persons whom they have reasonable cause to believe offenders against the provisions of this chapter,[54] *and every officer refusing or neglecting so to do, is guilty of a misdemeanor*" (emphasis added). However, the statute says nothing about a "duty to inform" when one lacks "reasonable cause" to believe gambling is going on. That is a strong motivation for cops and prosecutors to maintain their purposeful ignorance—in much the same way Captain Renault in "Casablanca" cried that he was "shocked!" at reports of gambling in his jurisdiction.

Meanwhile, both Lynch and Brown denied the existence of syndicated gamblers in the City, despite bookmakers like the Film Row Club that had documented connections to Los Angeles and Las Vegas gamblers.[55] Moreover, Brown openly admitted that the SFPD had "a small Chinatown squad of 9 of 10 people who are supposed to police Chinatown. We recommended to the Police Commission that it be eliminated so that it would be policed by all the police department, but they have never done it."[56] Thus, with regard to the pai gow and lottery operations in Chinatown, "Any time anything exists over a long period of time that is illegal, somebody is being paid off," Brown said. "There is no question about it whatsoever."[57]

From the transcripts, one can almost sense the exasperation in the next question from Halley, the committee's chief counsel. "How do you hope to cope with this public-opinion problem so long as gambling with dice is condoned and, in fact, legal and encouraged in cigarette stores all over the City and some bars?"[58] he said. Brown protested that he had avoided "instantaneous" arrests (whatever that meant), but that over the past seven years "we have prosecuted the bookies. We have stopped the abortionists. We have pulled the wire service. We have closed the poker clubs."[59] In other words, Brown seemed to be saying, I prosecuted some bookies who were too dumb not to get caught by a police department not looking for them, pressured back-alley abortionists to leave and told Bugsy Siegel and his wire to go away. What more do you want from the top law enforcement officer in one of California's largest cities? Consistent enforcement of California's laws against gambling? Don't be *ridiculous*.

I'M A COMMISSIONER OF ODDS, NOT A BOOKIE!

During its hearings in San Francisco and elsewhere, the committee had extensive experience with alleged organized crime figures asserting their Fifth Amendment right against self-incrimination, as well as some witnesses—like Willie Moretti—who unwisely blabbed more than they should and paid the ultimate price later. But the appearance of Floyd Russell was in a class of its own.

First, Russell showed up with his attorney, James T. Davis. Normally, when an attorney appears with a client in an adversarial proceeding like this, their purpose is to stare straight ahead, whisper directions into the client's ear after each question, and smile knowingly when the client says, "On the advice of my attorney, I decline to answer on the grounds that it may incriminate me pursuant to the Fifth Amendment of the United States Constitution" in response to every substantive question.

For reasons that were not apparent in 1950 and make no more sense today, Davis decided to depart from this script. After Halley got his and Russell's basic information on the record, Davis broke in with the following narrative:

MR. DAVIS: May I interrupt at this moment and make a statement for the record? Mr. Russell, I might tell you, is perfectly willing to come here and answer all of your questions. He doesn't claim, tend to claim any privilege—I don't know whether it is legally necessary—for the purpose of the record I am going to state he is not going to claim his privilege under 3486, Title 18, granting him any immunity.

SENATOR WILEY: What?

MR. HALLEY: You must specifically claim your immunity in each such case.

MR. DAVIS: Yes, that is right.

MR. HALLEY: And with regard to any privilege against self-incrimination, the law is that a witness before this committee is privileged to refuse to answer any questions which would tend to incriminate him under the Federal law.

MR. DAVIS: That is right.

MR. HALLEY: But that privilege does not extend to such incrimination under the State law.

MR. DAVIS: I am well aware of the law on the subject.[60]

If Davis had truly been "well aware of the law," one can only wonder why he was determined for Russell to testify *against* his own interests and to admit involvement in conduct that could have left him vulnerable to a state or federal prosecution for conspiracy to commit illegal gambling.

Russell, you see, was a "commission broker."[61] If you wanted to place a bet on a football game, baseball game, or an election, he was your man to see. "I would ask you how much do you want to place and you give me the amount," Russell said, adding that he would next ask what odds you would seek for the action, whether at 2-1 or whatever. Once Russell had that, he would look for someone else to take the other end of the bet, rather than assume that role himself, as a conventional bookie would. "If I can't place your—place your order, rather. . . . I would call you and tell you that I was unable to place the commission," he said. In that case, the bettor's money was refunded.[62]

However, since Russell worked with people like Leo "Bookie" Schaffer of Chicago, who would be arrested seven years later and charged with leading the largest illegal international[63] gambling ring discovered to that point by federal authorities,[64] presumably he did not fail often in finding a counterpart to his customer's action. Assuming Russell was successful, he would charge five percent of the amount wagered as his commission. In 1949, his business grossed him $32,000[65]—or $319,107.23 in 2015 dollars.[66]

Which, of course, gets us back to Davis's boneheaded decision to have Russell *explicitly waive* any Fifth Amendment privilege against self-incrimination. A year before the hearing, the U.S. Supreme Court reminded prosecutors and witnesses alike that "[I]t was established that *absolute immunity from federal criminal prosecution for offenses disclosed by the evidence must be given a person compelled to testify after claim of privilege against self-incrimination.*"[67] Thus, if Russell had simply *asserted* the privilege, the committee could have granted him immunity and forced him to testify, and the hearing would have proceeded as before—but he would not have exposed himself to potential prosecution on a federal level.

Although it is true that the Kefauver hearings predated most of the statutes banning interstate gambling in effect today, it is also true that—as Professor G. Robert Blakey noted in a 1984 paper—"Prior to 1950, gambling activity was, with some exceptions, generally prohibited at the federal and state levels."[68]

Based on Russell's testimony and the books from his enterprise, which he presented pursuant to the committee's subpoena,[69] any halfway competent federal prosecutor could have built a case for conspiracy to engage in interstate gambling (particularly given Russell's admitted business connections to Schaffer). Russell was potentially—again, assuming that Brown or Lynch or their successors had any interest in actually enforcing California's gambling laws, which was a fact not in evidence—in deeper trouble on a state level.

Ironically, seven years earlier, the California Legislature passed Government Code Section 9410, which held "A person sworn and examined before the Senate or Assembly, or any committee, can not [sic] be held to answer criminally or be subject to any penalty or forfeiture for any fact or act touching which he is required to testify." Furthermore, the California statute granted immunity for documents produced to the committee, in contrast to federal law at the time.

Granted, Government Code Section 9410 was intended to apply to state, rather than federal, investigations. But if Davis had not explicitly waived the privilege on behalf of his client, Russell would have had a decent argument against any state prosecution. Given the local disinterest in prosecuting gamblers or enforcing state or federal gambling laws, Russell likely dodged a bullet and Davis a malpractice claim. But the entire scrape could have been avoided.

BEWARE OF RAMBLING POLICE CHIEFS

The committee closed that day's testimony with San Francisco's then current chief of police, Michael Mitchell, as well as hearing from two men who would later hold that office, Frank Ahern and Thomas Cahill.

Put yourself in the position of the committee. Over the past several hours, you have been told by San Francisco's top prosecutor that gambling and narcotics are huge problems in the City, but that he has zero interest in prosecuting those who—by his own admission—are running an illegal lottery by playing "26." Next, you have had a businessperson show up with his idiot lawyer intentionally waiving his client's privilege against self-incrimination without even being *asked* by the committee to do so—and then heard the said businessperson spin a tale of the huge profits he has made in matching gamblers with those who want their action.

What do you do for Act III? Why, you invite the police chief to ramble at you, that is what!

> MR. HALLEY: I had thought that *rather than ask the witnesses specific questions on the subject of gambling activities and the Mafia,* that *we ask the chief and his staff if they would just care to tell us about it;* if not, we would ask specific questions, *but we would rather you went about it in your own way to give the committee what help you can.*
> MR. MITCHELL: That is O.K. with me.[70]

When given the choice between being allowed to ramble or to answer specific questions, it would have been surprising if Chief Mitchell had chosen the second option. And so the sultan of spin took center stage. "Regarding the gambling activity in San Francisco, I would say that the condition of the city is good," he said. "We know in the past there have been individuals that tried to violate the law, such as bookmaking, and probably running a crap game or something of that sort, *but in every instance where we have received any reports there has been an arrest made* and everything done in our power to wipe it out and clear the trouble up"[71] (emphasis added). As we have seen in chapters 5 through 8, this hardly describes the interaction between the SFPD and organized crime, other than perhaps inside the fervid imaginations of police boosters.

Given the testimony from Brown and Lynch about the prevalence of gambling in the City and Russell's immunity-free saga of how he grossed *10 times* the median household income simply by playing matchmaker to gamblers and bookmakers, Sen. Kefauver could not remain silent after this.

THE CHAIRMAN: While we are talking about gambling and what not, are there any big-time operators in San Francisco?

MR. MITCHELL: No, there is not. To my knowledge, there are no big-time operators in San Francisco.

THE CHAIRMAN: What about these betting commissioners?

MR. MITCHELL: I will say that there are two commission houses. One, Kyne's, formerly was an old bookmaker and he drifted into the commission business, and Corbett's* is the other commissioner, which has been going on for years. . . . They, as well as the others, have no authority to violate any law. My orders are specific on that, and the captain and the men on the beat know it. The only reports that have been given me were that they have been checked and found no violations of the law at the time they were being checked.[72]

And gong, gong, gong went the alarm bells—or should have. Although Penal Code Section 182, California's law on conspiracy, has been modified several times since it was initially enacted in 1872, the operative portion has remained constant, namely "(a) If two or more persons conspire: (1) To commit any crime." Given that it was illegal to gamble on sporting events and elections in California at the time, and the entire purpose of Corbett's business was to facilitate gambling on sporting and events and elections by matching bettors with bookmakers, the chief's position seemed, to put it charitably to him, odd.

Enter Senator Charles W. Tobey. The former Republican governor of New Hampshire, Tobey, had a controversial past in Congress—among other things, as late as September 1941, three months before Pearl Harbor, he was still addressing isolationist groups like the America First Committee about a supposed "conspiracy" to lure the United States into World War II.[73] Even so, he was not inclined to let Chief Mitchell off the hook when it came to Corbett's. The exchange is hilarious enough to make it worth reprinting in full.

SENATOR TOBEY: Is it your contention that they are not violating the law?

MR. MITCHELL: I take my reports from my men, and these reports are that at the time of their visit they found no violations whatever.

SENATOR TOBEY: Did they look at his records?

---

*That is, Russell's operation.

MR. MITCHELL: That I cannot say.

SENATOR TOBEY: Wasn't it superficial if they didn't look at his books?

MR. MITCHELL: I don't know; I can't say.

SENATOR TOBEY: He simply said that he was not doing any business and that is all?

MR. MITCHELL: They report to me that they found no violation of the law on their visits.

SENATOR TOBEY: What do they do there? Here is a man comes before the committee and shows his records; that he is violating the law. And then we ask the chief of police and you say he isn't. We have no trouble getting the evidence. We come here to get it, and you are here all the time.

MR. MITCHELL: I don't want to bring up any point, except as far as we know if he is working on commission he must be doing something that he is getting a commission on.

SENATOR TOBEY: There is a record in dollars and cents day after day there.

MR. MITCHELL: My men that went in there to report, they have never told me anything about searching the records.

SENATOR TOBEY: Didn't you tell them to go back and get the goods on him?[74]

Apparently, "betting commissioners" who did not spontaneously confess when the police paid a visit were safe from prosecution on Chief Mitchell's watch.

SENATOR TOBEY: Let us look at the picture. I will be very frank with you. You are the chief. This is your job. You are in charge, and yet we come down here strangers in a strange town and we have the evidence and we have the books before us; we have them admit to us that they are breaking the law, and there is the dollars-and-cents income. Yet your men are here all the time, and haven't done a thing except walk in and walk out again.[75]

After several more delusory questions, Tobey gave up, but threw a zinger the chief's way. "I haven't any more to ask about these *pro forma police officer's* activities"[76] (emphasis added).

If Tobey had recalled Brown to the stand, he might have elicited more interesting answers. As Ethan Rarick pointed out in "California Rising: The Life and Times of Pat Brown," in his 1943 campaign for district attorney, *Brown* arranged a 5-1 bet on *himself* with Corbett's competitor, Tom Kyne. "The result of course was to drive down the odds on himself, adding heft to the campaign's aura," wrote Rarick. "But Brown added an ingenious personal twist. He demanded his chit in the form of fifty $10 tickets, then handed them around to campaign volunteers and told each worker that a $60 payoff awaited if he won."[77] Translating those figures to 2015 dollars, each volunteer would clear $823.13.[78]

In any case, apparently inspired by Tobey, Kefauver then asked Mitchell why "26" was continued to be played across San Francisco. His response is epic.

MR. MITCHELL: The ":26" game has been stopped. I do allow it to be played between individuals, not by the man that owns—that is the proprietor of the cigar store or his clerk. They shoot the game of "26" between customers.
THE CHAIRMAN: Is the "26" game legal?
MR. MITCHELL: You pick out your number and try to make 26 on it. You shoot with 10 dice.
THE CHAIRMAN: I think they play "26" with the establishment for merchandise.
MR. MITCHELL: That is what I mean; yes.[79]

Thus, in less than a few minutes the chief took three positions, each of which was inconsistent with each other: (1) "26" has been shut down; (2) "26" can be played by and between customers, but the business owner or clerk cannot participate; and (3) "26" can be played by the customers and winners receive merchandise from the store. When Kefauver asked him whether this activity—which Brown had already confessed was likely a violation of California law—was ever "bothered" by San Francisco's allegedly finest, Chief Mitchell said it was not.[80]

On to James English, then the chief of inspectors for the SFPD and the closest thing the department had to a Mafia expert.

MR. ENGLISH: In January 1948, a new administration came into operation in San Francisco, and we had specific instructions at that time from the mayor of the city to exterminate or eliminate organized crime as such.

   We were aware of the fact that some organization existed. It wasn't at that time hardly in our field, although we adopted it into our division and conducted investigations which would tend to prevent this type of criminal operation.

   There were several things that made us aware of it and interested us in this particular field. One was a murder which occurred in 1947, which is prior to the time this administration took over, and through that investigation—-
THE CHAIRMAN: What was that murder?
MR. ENGLISH: That was the DeJohn murder.[81]

The "new administration" was that of Elmer Robinson, who had previously served as a municipal and superior court judge in San Francisco before his election. Later historians remember him as "presid[ing] during an era that has been described as 'the last of the city's old-time good times,' when vice quietly flourished."[82]

In any case, Inspector Ahern claimed that before he was killed, DeJohn started going "to the Poodle Dog restaurant out here on Polk Street. The Poodle Dog[83] restaurant was owned by *James Franzone, who is the leader of the mob here,* whom I never knew at that time."[84] Ahern did not explain why he believed Franzone was the leader of the local Mafia or why he considered him to be a San Franciscan, given Franzone's other addresses in Akron, Chicago, and Tampa.[85] Furthermore, as we saw in Chapter 8, although Franzone was an initial suspect in DeJohn's murder, he was never prosecuted for it.

Indeed, Ahern later admitted—in response to questioning from Halley—that Franzone stated he was associated with Hymie "Loud Mouth" Levin,[86] a collector for the Chicago Outfit[87] and Jack Perkins, who was indicted in 1935 by a San Francisco federal grand jury for harboring "Baby Face" Nelson.[88]

With regard to Calamia, Ahern said he was "fooling around with the purported owners, the mob that was hanging around down at the Sunland Sales Oil & Cheese Co., which was located at 25 Drumm Street here in San Francisco, and these particular characters had entered the case or connected via this particular concern."[89] According to Ahern, "from our investigation we learned they shipped the narcotics in a can of olive oil. They would have a round glass tube that would be the same length as the height of the can, so that it would not rattle, and they would put the morphine in it and ship it right in the olive oil."[90]

Sunland's records—once seized by Ahern's men—"brought in this Jack Dragna in Los Angeles and this Giralamo Adamo—that is Momo Adamo."[91] At the time, Dragna was the head of the Los Angeles *La Cosa Nostra* family, with Adamo as his underboss.[92] In addition, Ahern claimed that Nani was connected with Joseph Profaci in New York.[93]

All well and good, but for the failure to convict anyone for DeJohn's murder—or to bust anyone for the morphine in the olive oil cans.

WHAT DID IT ALL MEAN?

Brown went on to become California's attorney general and governor, as would his son, Edmund Gerald "Jerry" Brown—who still serves in the latter office. It does not appear that Russell was ever prosecuted for his admissions to the committee. Mitchell was replaced a year later by Michael Gaffey as police chief, apparently for reasons unrelated to anything he said before the Kefauver Committee. Other than Ahern, no other observer has declared Franzone the boss of the San Francisco Mafia in the late 1940s. And contrary to English's comments, far from being "exterminated" after the DeJohn killing, the Mafia in the City by the Bay continued its operations, more or less unmolested by law enforcement for years, aided and abetted by the committee's failure to call either Tony Lima or Mike Abati as witnesses, let alone James Lanza.

Once again, the San Francisco family had managed to keep to the shadows and dodge a bullet for the moment.

Chapter 10

The Apalachin Debacle

On the surface, by late 1957 the American Mafia seemed to be at the height of its power. As we see, with some limited exceptions it was the consensus view of federal law enforcement that either the Mafia *did not* exist or, if it did, there was precious little that could be done about it, given the state of federal law at the time. State and local law enforcement in most places, except in matters of the gravest provocation by organized crime (like bodies piling up in the streets during the Booze Wars in San Francisco in the 1930s, or the death of Nick DeJohn in the late 1940s when the grand jury got involved) could generally be distracted, appeased, bought off, or otherwise neutralized just as San Francisco's was.

Seventeen million Americans—the highest number since World War II and before Vietnam—were members of a union,[1] providing a fertile ground for labor racketeering for the Mafia. Control over unions and union leaders gave control over union pension funds, which the Mafia then loaned to the men who built what we now know as the Las Vegas Strip. The Tropicana Hotel opened that year[2] to huge acclaim, joining existing properties like the Thunderbird, the Desert Inn, the Sands, the Sahara, and the Riviera—and most, if not all, were Mafia affiliated, controlled, or influenced to one degree or another.[3]

If this were a work of fiction, critics would say a plot development where the discovery of a meeting in upstate New York suddenly imperiled Mafia operations across the country was an example of the book's author engaging in the worst type of *deus ex machina*. However, as we see in this work of history, that is *exactly* what occurred—and James Lanza was in the middle of it.

SEE NO EVIL

Even the man who would eventually do more than most to upset the Mafia's cheery state of affairs—G. Robert Blakey, the father of the Organized Crime Control Act of 1970—posed no threat to the Mafia at this point, given his status as a first-year law student at the University of Notre Dame in 1957.

The man who *could have*—J. Edgar Hoover of the FBI—was obsessed instead with chasing a nonexistent Communist Fifth Column,[4] leaving the Mafia as the near exclusive territory of Harry J. Anslinger and his Bureau of Narcotics. Historians attribute Hoover's refusal to acknowledge the existence of the Mafia up into the late 1950s to a variety of causes. In *J. Edgar Hoover: The Man and the Secrets*, Curt Gentry contends that it stemmed from a combination of Hoover's obsession with crime clearance statistics, his reluctance to expose his agents to the ability of *La Cosa Nostra* to corrupt and subvert them, his distaste for undercover operations, and his ongoing bureaucratic cat fight with Harry J. Anslinger, who led the Federal Bureau of Narcotics and Hoover's relationship with New York Mafia boss Frank Costello, whom Hoover once told "You stay out of my bailiwick and I'll stay out of yours."[5] As a result "Costello for the most part stayed clear of federal crimes, and especially those over J. Edgar Hoover claimed jurisdiction, and Hoover, for his own still-mysterious reasons, refused to admit that a national criminal organization existed."[6]

Other historians like Anthony Summers have contended that the Mafia had photographic proof of Hoover's homosexual activities, which it used to blackmail him.[7] Given that this was an era where being gay was punishable by a prison sentence in many places and was considered a legitimate reason by the federal government to yank security clearances and end a person's employment across the country, Hoover's reluctance to ask too many questions is comprehensible, if reprehensible.

Although Anslinger had been a foe of the Mafia since the early 1930s,[8] his agency lacked the FBI's heft or cachet and was focused on only a single line of Mafia business—drug trafficking. As Gentry[9] and others have noted, Anslinger was willing—as Hoover was not, at least publicly—to push the bounds of ethics in search of what he saw as a greater good. For example, in 1940 Anslinger—concerned about possible disruption to the United States' supply of morphine due to World War II—stockpiled 300 tons of the stuff in Treasury Department vaults in Washington, D.C., thereby causing the domestic price to jump by 300 percent.[10] His intelligence was not always the best either—around the same time he was publicly conflating the Mafia, the *Unione Siciliana* and the "Black Hand" into one organization.[11]

Although the *Unione* was often run by men with close ties to the Outfit, it was always a separate organization on paper. As for the Black Hand, we saw in Chapter 2 that the term was most accurately applied to a *style* of extortion rather than a specific overarching criminal organization and that Black Hand gangs often crossed ethnic lines.

Finally, he *did* target Costello's narcotics operations during World War II, with one investigation ending "with the arrest of 106 smugglers in Mexico, including several Germans, and the conviction of seventeen Mafia smugglers in the U.S."[12] Still, because of the Mafia's assistance (through Lucky Luciano and Joseph "Socks" Lanza in New York) on the Brooklyn and New York waterfront and to U.S. forces in Sicily and the Italian mainland, even Anslinger could not touch Costello.[13]

Notwithstanding these and other flaws, Anslinger has to be given his due. Because he (a) believed in the Mafia's existence and (b) as a direct consequence of (a) took steps to combat its involvement in the drug trade, he served as the federal government's primary warrior against the Mafia from the 1930s until the late 1950s. It was reportedly *his* files that provided the primary investigative support for the Kefauver Committee and its work, some of which we saw in Chapter 9.[14]

Indeed, the original organized crime file of Anslinger's Bureau of Narcotics, which leaked and was later published in 2007 as *Mafia: The Government's Secret File on Organized Crime* (with a foreword by Sam Giancana, nephew and namesake to the former Chicago Outfit boss), is a key research tool for Mafia historians and has been repeatedly cited in this book. Those files would soon become of interest to persons outside of Anslinger's empire, because Hoover's veil of denial about the existence of the Mafia was about to be shredded.

MOBSTERS NEED TO PROCESS

Given the nature of their business, it is not surprising most Mafia leaders prefer to settle business between each other in person. For this reason, the tradition of Mafia leaders from across the country meeting in person has a long provenance.

The first we know of took place in Cleveland on December 5, 1928, two years before the start of the Castellammarese War, described more fully in Chapter 5, and long before the founding of the commission.[15] Another conference followed in May 1929 after the St. Valentine's Day massacre in Chicago,[16] which allowed the attendees to relax in Nucky Johnson's Atlantic City while they attended to business. After that, the commission tried to meet every five years.[17]

The inconvenient distractions of World War II and the subsequent deportation of Lucky Luciano to Italy made it hard for the commission to this schedule, but they still managed a major summit in Havana in December 1946[18] before returning to the prewar schedule.

Because the San Francisco family was not directly represented on the commission during this period, it had to route its concerns and receive communications through the Chicago Outfit, which *was* directly represented.[19] This may explain why the San Francisco family was willing to go along with (and allegedly assist) in the murder of Nick DeJohn, as we saw in Chapter 8—there was little to be gained by providing succor to a fugitive from Outfit authority, especially when that fugitive seemed to be getting dangerous ideas about muscling in on local rackets. Moreover, as Joe Bonanno pointed out, during this period the commission had a working majority so long as the Five Mafia Families from New York City were present and united,[20] so although respected, the Outfit's views were never dispositive unless one or more New York families agreed with them.

In any case, 1956 marked the last "regular" commission meeting before the world would change beyond recognition for the Mafia and James Lanza personally.[21] Its location would become infamous just a year later: Apalachin, New York.[22]

ANSLINGER'S REVENGE AND A TRIP TO SICILY

As we saw in Chapter 9, federal narcotics penalties at the time were laughably light. Even after the government brought a 155 count indictment against 14 coconspirators involved in the heroin ring that touched Tampa and Kansas City (and swept in Sebastiano Nani), none of the major trafficking defendants were sentenced to more than six years in prison—and some did only a day.

Given that this did little to either deter narcotics conspiracies or encourage lower-level defendants to turn informants (what soldier would risk death as a snitch if the *worst* prison exposure they were facing was six years or less in federal custody?), Anslinger went to work on Congress and President Dwight Eisenhower.[23] His efforts paid off when the president signed the Narcotic Control Act of 1956, which imposed a base penalty of 2 to 10 years in prison for a first offense, 5 to 20 years for a second offense, and 10 to 40 years for a third.[24] The Act also raised the stakes for narcotics and marijuana smugglers, who were now looking at a minimum sentence of 5 years on a first offense.[25] Even more draconian, the Act provided that anyone convicted of trafficking heroin to juveniles could face a death sentence at the jury's discretion—and if the death penalty was not imposed, the defendant had to serve at least 10 years and could get a life sentence.[26]

With penalties like these in their arsenal, Anslinger's agents had increased leverage to encourage cooperation with the government—but the Mafia has over a century of practice honed to two continents in circumventing those police who could not be corrupted or otherwise eliminated.

THE MAFIA'S RESPONSE

About a year after Eisenhower signed the Act into law, Joe "Joe Bananas" Bonanno met with Lucky Luciano and a slew of the most dangerous *mafiosi* in two countries at the Grand Hotel et des Palmes in Palermo to find ways to keep the heroin pipeline from Europe to America open.[27] Despite Bonanno's reported misgivings,* the American Mafia "agreed to receive and sell regular shipments of heroin processed in Sicily and in Marseilles—the fabled 'French Connection,' operated with help from Corsican mobsters."[28] Until it was smashed in the 1970s, approximately 5,000 pounds per year of heroin flowed through the French Connection pipeline from Sicily and Corsica and into the veins and lungs of U.S. users every year.[29]

Assuming one has access to raw opium, making heroin is effectively child's play, although it can be time consuming.[30] First, the morphine is extracted from the opium through the use of boiling water and the addition of chemicals.[31] Second, the resulting morphine is further heated for six hours with the addition of other chemicals, filtered, and refiltered.[32] It takes about 10 kilograms of opium to make 1 kilo of morphine, but thanks to the other chemicals added in the transformation process from morphine to heroin, about 1 kilo of morphine will create 1 kilo of heroin[33]— or 2.2 pounds in the United States. Of course, the purity of that kilo (or 2.2 pounds) of heroin will be repeatedly diluted or "cut" by the addition of other substances or narcotics as it passes from smuggler to domestic trafficker to wholesaler to retailer to user so that the volume of heroin is maximized and supplies maintained until the next shipment.

This begs the question of why the Mafia chose to work with the French and the Corsicans at all rather than developing and controlling their own

---

*It is a point of debate of how hard Bonanno *actually* fought to prevent the Mafia from getting into wholesale trafficking of heroin, given his connections with and technical control over the Montreal Mafia family—without which the French Connection could not operate.

laboratories. According to some historians, this had to do with the Mafia's lack of qualified cookers at the time and the fact that the tradition ran from Marseilles to Montreal, Canada, and from there to New York City.[34] Given that this meant dealing with the Mafia boss of Montreal, Vincent "Vic the Egg" Cotroni, an Italian immigrant to Francophone Quebec,[35] it made more sense to let the Corsicans handle the shipment issues from Marseilles to New York City, since they spoke the language. Besides, when the Mafia *tried* (through Carmine Galante, a member of Bonanno's family, who applied for permanent residence in Canada) to take direct control of the Montreal rackets, it suffered the same fate as the previous U.S. invasions of Canada in 1775 and 1812—that is, an ignominious defeat and retreat.[36]

However, although the Royal Canadian Mounted Police ultimately forced Galante to be deported,[37] thanks to their connections with Cotroni through the Bonanno family, the Mafia maintained a presence in Montreal and elsewhere in Quebec.[38] Indeed, Cotroni was allegedly appointed a *caporegime* in the Bonanno family during this period.[39]

Finally, there was more than enough money for everyone. In the 1950s, "the morphine base would come in from Beirut, via Sicily, at around $1,000 a kilo, and the refineries in Marseilles would then turn it into 90 percent pure heroin, worth $7,000 a kilo. By the time it arrived in the United States it would be worth $30,000 a kilo [and] [o]n the streets . . . it would fetch $300,000 a kilo at 1950s prices."[40] With money like that at stake, it is easy to see how the leaders of the Mafia could convince themselves that heroin trafficking was a can't-miss proposition. Although the Narcotic Control Act of 1956 was a worrying development, there seemed no reason not to believe that the structure that had served them so well since the Mafia's early days in Sicily would protect the organization's top echelon. Sure, some soldiers would probably be caught moving heroin by Anslinger's men. Some might even be convicted. However, so long as they were insulated through their underboss and *caporegimes* from their soldiers and associates and all parties agreed that *omertà* was to be maintained at all costs, the bosses could believe they could reap the profits of heroin and drug trafficking without running the real risks. Still, *some* order needed to be maintained so that families did not fight over territories or engage in price wars with each other,[41] and the only way to hash out a binding nationwide agreement was for the bosses to meet face to face.

ORDER OUT OF CHAOS

Besides dividing up the flow of heroin that was about to swamp U.S. cities, the commission also had to end the violence in New York City after the failed assassination of Costello[42]—a failure that was particularly costly, as a slip of paper found on him by the New York City Police Department (NYPD) exposed the Mafia's interest in the Tropicana Casino in Las Vegas[43]—finds a way to divide up the economic plums of Cuba that satisfied the Tampa and New Orleans families as well as Frank DeSimone, the new boss of the Los Angeles family.[44] Given that DeSimone's cousin was James Lanza's sister-in-law,[45] the outcome would likely also have an impact on San Francisco family operations. Similarly, the commission had to finalize the division of garment district spoils between the Lucchese and Gambino families in New York.[46]

Although his was a minority view, Anslinger believed the commission was also trying to determine how to come up with the cash it would need to cement its control over Nevada's politicians.[47] Most other observers, including me, find this a bit of a stretch. At the time, Nevada's governor was Charles H. Russell who—although generally deemed painfully honest and dull by local politicos—still gave Benny Binion a gaming license despite Binion's decades of involvement with non-Mafia-organized crime in Texas and elsewhere, which included at least one murder.[48] Given that the primary goal of Nevada politicians—especially those in Southern Nevada, who had long played second fiddle to Northern Nevada in terms of both population and political power—was to maximize investment in the Silver State through any source necessary, it is not clear why it would have been necessary to buy *any* Nevada politicians, since they were generally in alignment with the Mafia's economic objectives, although for different reasons.

The agenda more or less set, it came time to pick a place. Sam Giancana of the Outfit offered Chicago—which, beyond being an appropriate neutral ground for the New Yorkers to settle their post-Costello drama, would have likely have been a secure location—but for whatever reason, Stefano Magaddino, the boss of the Buffalo family, insisted both the gathering taking place in Apalachin and at holding it at Joseph Barbara's home again, as they had done in 1956.[49]

According to Bonanno, even Barbara thought his house was too hot for the commission and asked Bonanno to help Magaddino understand that, but neither could sway the boss of Buffalo.[50] So the Barbara ranch it was—and the stage was set for the biggest debacle in the modern U.S. Mafia's history.

YOU ARE CORDIALLY INVITED

Besides scheduling the meeting in a location where they had already met before and that was known to be hot, or under some degree of police scrutiny, the organizers of the Apalachin meeting erred by violating one of the cardinal rules of the Mafia.

La Cosa Nostra has never been a small-d democratic organization. Although the commission offered a limited forum for the heads of the Five Families of New York City and the Outfit in Chicago (as well as a sprinkling of bosses from other areas) to discuss issues and mediate disputes, it was never intended to be a congress of the underworld. At the end of the day, the real purpose of the commission was to minimize conflict between violent killers who accepted only two laws: that which they imposed and that of superior force. Because of this, it is not surprising that—as Bonanno has pointed out previously—that the commission was structured so that agreement on a matter between New York's Five Families—which were then the strongest Mafia families in the United States when acting in concert—was sufficient to bind the rest of the American Mafia to a decision[51] at least in theory. By having only the most powerful families represented on the commission, the Mafia kept those with a right to be heard to a manageable size *and* improved their operational security. Although it can be challenging to bring 9 or 10 notorious killers, some or all of whom can be assumed to be under police surveillance at least to some degree, together in one place without alerting law enforcement, it is a far easier problem than inviting 60 or more Mafia bosses to the same meeting.

By inviting *every* Mafia boss in the United States to attend the Apalachin sitdown,[52] the organizers turned these wise precepts on their head. Instead of having the Five Families and a few key players from outside New York make the decisions (and control how those decisions would be explained to the rest of the American Mafia), the planners seemed to think they were creating the Mafia's version of France's *États-Généraux* of 1789—without remembering what happened to King Louis XVI and *his* underboss and *caporegimes* after His Majesty let the assembly genie out of the bottle. As more than one oligarch has learned, in a system closed to mass participation, a little democracy can have a tremendously corrosive effect on discipline.

On a more prosaic level, by inviting *every* leader of a family to Apalachin meant giving the event a far higher profile than it would have had otherwise, which was bound to—and indeed did create—trouble. Some leaders like Bonanno[53] were prescient enough to see this and sent their underbosses to represent them rather than appear themselves.[54] Ironically, this did not help Bonanno, who was misidentified as being at the meeting after his driver's license—which he had asked a friend to renew— ended up on the person of one of the Apalachin detainees.[55]

Happily, the same could not be said for Abati, who sent James Lanza— in the latter's capacity as underboss—to represent the San Francisco family's interests.[56] Until the end of his life, Lanza repeatedly denied being at the meeting, but the contemporaneous records tell a different tale. As early as March 1958—four months after the meeting—the FBI had verified that Lanza "was registered at a hotel in the vicinity of the Apalachin meeting on November 13, 1957, and shared rooms with three individuals who were known participants of this meeting."[57] Lanza stayed at the Casey Hotel in Scranton, Pa.,[58] which was about 70 miles away from Barbara's ranch outside of Apalachin. Unfortunately for him, the FBI learned Russell Bufalino, who would go on to run the northeastern Pennsylvania family, was the one who made the reservations.[59]

Given that Bufalino also put up Joe Cerrito—who went on to take over the San Jose family two years after Apalachin[60]—as well as Frank DeSimone, who was already running the Los Angeles family,[61] and DeSimone's underboss[62] Simone Scozzari in the same hotel, with all costs to be paid by Bufalino,[63] Lanza's later denials would ring as hollow as a *cannoli* shell. At least Lanza, who ended up sharing Room 316 with DeSimone,[64] got a chance to catch up on family business in both senses of the word.

Lanza had been clever in another way as well. As part of its efforts to deport Bufalino post-Apalachin, the Immigration and Naturalization service learned that Lanza had been registered at the Hotel New Yorker in New York City on November 11, 1957 (he shared Room 1641 with Joseph Cerrito) and checked out on November 15, 1957.[65] However, neither Lanza nor Cerrito occupied the room on November 13, 1957—the day both were registered at the Hotel Casey in Scranton.[66]

In fairness to Bufalino, at the time the 11-story Hotel Casey was one of the best hotels Scranton had to offer[67]—and but for an imbroglio at another hotel in Apalachin, it is likely no one would have ever known that his California guests were in town.

MOBSTERS CHECK IN, BUT THEY DON'T CHECK OUT

On a freezing November 13, 1957, New York State Police Sergeant Edgar Croswell visited the Parkway Motel in Apalachin after the owner discovered a guest had used a bad check to pay for their hotel room.[68] Although he and his partner interviewed the owner, Joseph Barbara's son came to the hotel to reserve "three 'double' rooms" for six men he could not name, but who would be there soon.[69] It was the possibility of *exactly* this sort of unfortunate coincidences happening that made a large city like Chicago (or for that matter, Atlantic City) a far better venue for the largest Mafia sitdown in history than Apalachin, New York. In a large city, reserving a block of rooms at a hotel would have been wholly unremarkable. But, in a small town like Apalachin, it was guaranteed to rouse

Croswell's suspicions, which led him to launch his own surveillance of Barbara's ranch, where he found several high-end vehicles with out-of-state plates.[70] As a result, "that night, before going to sleep at the Vestal barracks, Croswell telephoned his boss . . . to report his suspicion of a gangland summit in the making."[71]

Croswell returned to watch developments at Barbara's house the next day, until the family leaders there discovered what was going on.[72] Sadly, most made exactly the *wrong* decision, which was to flee on foot or in their cars. As historian Michael Newton points out, "It is a rule of thumb . . . that whenever someone runs away from the police, the runner instantly invites detention and interrogation."[73] In this particular case, Vito Genovese, the boss of the New York family, which bore his name, and 58 or more[†] other legitimate businessmen ended up in Croswell's bag.[74] At the time, Croswell admitted "We haven't a thing on them. But we made it clear we wanted them out of the area."[75]

How could he justify doing this without any probable cause? "We broke up the meeting because we were convinced it was being held for an unlawful purpose," Croswell said.[76] "They're all hoodlums, there's no doubt about it."[77] Besides Genovese, Croswell collared DeSimone, the boss of the Los Angeles family, as well as future New York bosses Paul Castellano and Carlo Gambino.[78] However, Cerrito and Lanza stayed out of his net.

As the FBI later discovered, although Lanza checked into Hotel Casey at 3:39 p.m. on November 13, 1957, for one night, "the guest registration pertaining to LANZA failed to note a checkout time."[79] In *The Valachi Papers*, Peter Maas stated he "can't be sure" if Lanza was at Apalachin[80] and, as stated previously, Lanza denied being there to the end of his life. However, based on the FBI's records (which Maas did not have access to), given that Bufalino had put up Lanza and DeSimone in the same room (and Cerrito in the same hotel) for the conference, it seems more reasonable to infer that Lanza and Cerrito either were present in Apalachin and evaded the police dragnet or were en route to Barbara's home and turned back once they heard of the raid.

FROM HERO TO INSPECTOR JAVERT

Although the United States cobbled together a conspiracy case—*U.S. v. Bufalino, et al.*—against Bufalino, DeSimone, and multiple others who were detained by Croswell and his colleagues, purportedly based on their

---

[†]Accounts of how many people were arrested vary and have been revised repeatedly since the meeting.

collective decision to lie about the gathering, the jury's guilty verdict was tossed in 1960 by the Second Circuit Court of Appeals. Writing for the court, Chief Judge J. Edward Lumbard pointed out that the government had utterly failed to meet its evidentiary burden:

Indeed, the pervasive innuendo throughout this case that this was a gathering of bad people for an evil purpose would seem to us to rebut any possible argument that only as a result of group action would any individual lie. Even an otherwise law abiding citizen who is stopped and interrogated by police, and who is given no reason for his detention and questioning, may feel it his right to give as little information as possible and even perhaps to respond evasively if he believes he might thereby be earlier rid of police inquiry. *U.S. v. Bufalino*, 285 F. 2d 408, 415 (1960)

His colleague, Judge Charles Edward Clark, went even further in his concurring opinion. To Clark, "Perhaps the most curious feature of this strange case is the fact that after all these years there is not a shred of legal evidence that the Apalachin gathering was illegal or even improper in either purpose or fact."[81] He went on to compare Croswell[82]—for his 13-year pursuit of Barbara without result—to Inspector Javert, the villain of Victor Hugo's *Les Misérables* who pursues Jean Valjean without mercy (or any sense of proportion) for decades.

Croswell's reaction to the court's ruling was deliciously uncomplicated if legally inappropriate—he publicly vowed to do what he did in 1957 again if he was given the chance.[83] Sadly or fortunately for everyone (depending on your point of view), by 1960 this was impossible, as Barbara had died of a heart attack the year before.[84]

Although Croswell failed in his efforts to shut down Barbara's crime family, which would continue to grow after its patriarch's death, his actions at Apalachin and their aftermath removed—once and for all—the ability of J. Edgar Hoover to deny the fact of the Mafia's existence. However, as we see in Chapter 11, Hoover's recognition of a problem did not mean that problem would or could be solved, much to the benefit of Lanza and his family.

Chapter 11

From Anonymity to "Top Hoodlum"

Although J. Edgar Hoover fully deserves the criticism he received for his willful blindness to *La Cosa Nostra* from the 1930s until the Apalachin debacle in 1957, the bureau's devil must be given his due—when he had to pivot, he did so quickly.

Less than two weeks after the bosses had fled Joseph Barbara's ranch, Hoover inaugurated the FBI's "Top Hoodlum" program, under which every field office had to prepare "a list of ten 'top hoodlums'—no more and no less—within the jurisdiction of [the] office."[1] Then again, it was far easier for Hoover to issue orders than for his minions to comply with them. James Lanza's file with the agency, released pursuant to a Freedom of Information Act (FOIA) request, indicates what appear to be several rounds of nudging from headquarters to the San Francisco Field Office before Special Agent in Charge W. Webb Burke finally named Lanza a "Top Hoodlum" on February 20, 1958.[2]

At the time, Lanza and his wife lived at 213 Anita Road, Apt. 7 in Burlingame, California,[3] about 20 miles south of San Francisco. He maintained his office at 559 Washington Street in San Francisco, just outside of North Beach.[4]

WE KNOW WHO YOU HAVE BEEN CALLING AND WHO SENDS YOU MAIL

Twenty-four hours after Burke added Lanza to the bureau's "Top Hoodlum" list, his agents had gained access to Lanza's telephone number

(Diamond 3-0618) and his long distance toll records. A teletype issued in the evening of February 21 to East Coast field offices and the director screamed "NEW YORK, PITTSBURG AND PHILADELPHIA REQUESTED TO IDENTIFY SUBSCRIBERS AND FURNISH BACKGROUND DATA."[5]

The fact that the bureau already had access to the numbers Lanza was calling (although it did not know who they belonged to) illustrates how much things have changed in the intervening decades. Currently, the installation* of pen registers—devices that track which number is called by a particular phone number without recording the conversation—is governed by 18 U.S.C. 3121 *et seq.*, which requires law enforcement agencies to secure a court order before installation of the pen register.[6]

Although the burden on law enforcement to obtain the order is about as minimal as it gets—all they need to do is demonstrate that the information is "likely to be obtained is relevant to an ongoing criminal investigation"[7]—the lifespan of the register is supposed to be limited to 60 days, with the possibility of a 60-day extension on court approval.[8] In contrast, in 1958 pen registers occupied a gray area. Although in 1937 the U.S. Supreme Court ruled in *Nardone v. United States*[9] that wiretap evidence was inadmissible in a criminal trial† (and, in a later proceeding involving the same players, determined two years later that leads originating from wiretap evidence were also tainted),[10] it remained unsettled whether pen registers, which simply recorded the number a person called, were admissible, let alone whether they required a court order or not.

Apparently untroubled by these seeming technicalities, Burke and his agents pressed on. They demanded (and got) headquarters' approval for a 30-day "mail cover"‡ on Lanza's home[11] and office,[12] but that was not enough. By mid-March, the San Francisco Office had asked headquarters for authorization to conduct a "survey relative to the installation of a misur in the premises at 559 Washington Street, San Francisco, California, in

---

*There are exceptions for Pen Registers installed under the Foreign Intelligence Surveillance Act ("FISA"), but these are beyond the scope of this book and not relevant to the bureau's investigation of Lanza in any case.

†Because it was not willing to overrule its 1928 decision in *Olmstead v. U.S.*, which had held that wiretapping did not violate the Fourth Amendment, the *Nardone* court based its ruling on the Communications Act of 1934 and the Act's prohibition of disclosure of radio messages.

‡A mail cover is the procedure by which the U.S. Postal Service makes a record of the outside of each item of mail received by the subject at a particular address and turns over that record to law enforcement.

which the Lanza Brothers Olive Oil company is located."[13] A "misur" is FBI-speak for "microphone surveillance." In other words, the San Francisco Office was asking for permission to see whether it would be feasible to break into Lanza's office and install a bug—notwithstanding the fact that any evidence that came from it would be inadmissible under the U.S. Supreme Court's ruling in *Nardone*.

The operative part of the San Francisco Office's application is worth repeating in full. "There is *no possibility* of obtaining the desired information by other means unless a live informant is present," wrote Burke (emphasis added). "Live informant coverage cannot reasonably be expected to be sufficient to provide all the information a misur can provide. Misurs are further superior since they can furnish verbatim coverage."[14] Translation: we cannot subvert anyone in Lanza's inner circle and even if we could, they would not be around during all of the time Lanza was in his office. Besides, would we really trust a man who would betray Lanza *not* to lie to us in turn?

One might hope that FBI headquarters would have addressed the legal issues caused by one of its offices proposing a burglary and an illegal wiretap, but if so, one would be sorely disappointed. Instead, the FBI's leadership was more concerned about whether the misur would be productive than if it would be legal. At the time, FBI Section Chief F.L. Price wrote "There is a good possibility that Lanza will eventually prove to be a valuable source of information concerning the Apalachin meeting since he will be most anxious to avoid the possibility of any publicity concerning his presence in the area at the time the meeting was held."[15] Still, Price was concerned that the San Francisco Office had failed to determine "*whether* Lanza does, in fact, *meet with hoodlum associates* at above-described premises"[16] (emphasis added). Price's concerns did not trouble Hoover, who approved the survey the next day.[17]

On March 26, 1958, Special Agent Curtis P. Irwin penned the first of many reports he and his colleagues in the San Francisco Office would write about Lanza in the coming decades. This one was notable because it was the first to point out Lanza's primary vulnerability—whether or not his U.S. citizenship was valid at all, as it was derivative of his late father Francesco Lanza's Petition for Naturalization, which itself was riddled with outright lies. "It is pointed out that in 1921, date of FRANCESCO LANZA obtaining his citizenship papers, JAMES would have been under 21 regardless whether he was born in 1902 or 1903," Irwin wrote.

However, it appears a little questionable that 3 of petitioner's children would be residing in New York and the only one who could obtain citizenship by derivation was reportedly residing in San Francisco with him at the time of his obtaining citizenship. *It is further noted that unless JAMES was actually residing with FRANCESCO in San Francisco in 1921, he is fraudulently claiming citizenship by derivation.*[18] (Emphasis added)

It is not clear from those portions of Lanza's file that have been released pursuant to FOIA whether Burke ever considered using this as leverage over Lanza or, whether he did consider it and ultimately decided not to do so, why Burke made that decision. It may have been a function of the FBI's organizational myopia about discovering what the Apalachin meeting was supposed to have been about that caused Burke to lose sight of what should have been his overall goal—that is, identifying and (presumably) prosecuting "Top Hoodlums" like Lanza.

In the meantime, Irwin did discover that Lanza often patronized the Tropical Café (which was owned by the then family boss Mike Abati) on 324 Drumm Street as well as the Poodle Dog Restaurant on 112 Polk Street and LaRocca's Corner at 957 Columbus Avenue,[19] the latter two that were made infamous in the aftermath of the murder of Nick DeJohn, as we saw in Chapter 8.

Intriguingly, Irwin also found out that Lanza had helped Sebastiano Nani, one of the three alleged killers of DeJohn, buy a house in San Mateo—and somehow got a portion of the broker's commission for himself in the bargain.[20] Still, although Irwin and his colleagues had not figured out that Lanza was the underboss and Abati the head of the family, in practical terms it did not matter. Irwin noted that Abati "has been ordered deported by INS and is presently on bond while the case is being appealed."[21] Since Abati had entered the United States as a stowaway in 1922,[22] it did not take an expert in immigration law to predict that the odds of him beating the case were minimal.

On the more humorous side, an informant within the San Francisco Police Department (SFPD)—whose identity the FBI continues to redact—told Irwin that although he thought Lanza was "influential within the Sicilian Element" (i.e., the Mafia) and believed Lanza was engaged in criminal activity, "it would be most difficult, in his opinion, to ascertain activity of Subject *as Subject is a very cautious operator*"[23] (emphasis added). More than half a century later, it is impossible to read those words and not imagine Lanza smiling at the compliment—or at least, smiling as much as a cautious operator would allow himself.

Alas, some of his colleagues were less cautious. Irwin connected the dots between Abati, the late Frank Scappatura, and their olive oil company in Oroville, California, which was owned by Henry Irving, at least on paper.[24] Worse, although Hoover and Federal Bureau of Narcotics (FBN) Chief Harry J. Anslinger's personal and interagency catfight made both the FBI and the FBN less effective against the Mafia than they each otherwise would have been, the feud did not always extend to street-level agents. Through an FBN colleague, Irwin learned Anthony DePinto, who was "considered a major operator in narcotics . . . on the West Coast between Seattle, Washington and San Francisco, in the late 1930s and early 1940s,"[25] had sent Lanza a postal money order for $64.50 (or $1,093.44 in 2015 dollars)[26] for no discernible reason.[27] Fortunately for Lanza, later that year "DePinto . . . was arrested by local[§] authorities for contributing to the delinquency of a minor, and four days later his parole was violated and he was returned to the Oregon State Prison,"[28] which ended the FBN's investigation of DePinto before it got closer to San Francisco.[29]

Similarly, when the FBN busted Pasquale Siragusa in 1939—another "major operator"[30] in narcotics working between Seattle and San Francisco—and locked him up in the federal prison on McNeil Island in 1940, Siragusa "executed the usual mail and visitor's lists."[31] However, one of Siragusa's lists only had four names on them—one from New York, one from Seattle, and one from Los Angeles (all of which the FBI continues to keep secret) and James Lanza's, with the 559 Washington Street address.

Meanwhile, agents from the California Department of Public Health, who were responsible for inspecting the Lanza's olive oil operation when they still packed and sold the stuff under their own label, told Irwin that Lanza "had not been active in the packaging or processing of olive oil since 1954 at least."[32] Still, their recollection of the last inspection of their plant in 1952 was revealing.

He believed JAMES was the one who was the more difficult to do business with. The older brother,[¶] as he recalled, was very pleasant when the State Agents made an inspection and assisted them. He believed it was the younger brother that would usually speak in Italian to people who might be around the plant and tell them to clear out when an inspector came in the plant.

[NAME REDACTED] stated he could understand Italian and knew what this brother said to the men who would be around. After this brother spoke to the men around the plant, they would always leave. [NAME REDACTED] stated that the men around were in his opinion always "tough looking Italians."[33]

This incident reveals in bas relief the price Hoover was paying for fighting so hard to keep the FBI a preserve of White Anglo-Saxon Protestants (WASPs), which made it harder to find agents who (a) spoke Italian

---

[§]In Roseburg, Oregon.
[¶]That is, Anthony Lanza.

and (b) could move within Italian communities with little or no notice. In contrast, Anslinger cast a far greater net in his search for talent, which made it easier for his agents to make cases.[34]

By March 1958, James's brother Anthony was advising the federal Food and Drug Administration (FDA) that James was handling the olive oil brokerage business, which—as the FDA agent recounted—"*was conducted primarily for the benefit of old friends and old customers*"[35] (emphasis added). Given that one of their two sources of supply for olive oil was the Oro Olive Oil Company that Abati was managing, government reports on the Lanzas have rarely been so apt. Meanwhile, on April 1, 1958, Burke advised FBI headquarters that it would be technically infeasible to install the bug in Lanza's office, due to the fact that the building's walls were made of solid brick and the underside of the floor of his office could be viewed from the basement.[36] The bureau's black bag squad was balked, for now.

A SLIPPERY TRIP

A month later, Burke and Irwin thought they got lucky. The Lanzas had shipped seven cases of olive oil to Brooklyn on May 17, 1958, by ship,[37] which was due to arrive in Brooklyn on June 2. For whatever reason, the San Francisco Office—though it was working with the FBN—refused to include the San Francisco Office of the U.S. Customs Service in the tip,[38] which was odd, given that the FBN and the Customs Service worked closely together, particularly in San Francisco, as they were both part of the Department of the Treasury.[39]

Through a "confidential source" using a portable X-ray machine,[40] the San Francisco Office reported that tins No. 1, No. 5, and No. 6 contained what appeared to be a foreign object—that is, something that was not olive oil.[41] Since the bureau had personally observed Lanza dropping off the tins with the steamship company, there seemed to be a decent chain of evidence tying him to the suspected contraband,[42] assuming they found any when they opened the barrels.

Alas, their hopes were dashed. On May 21, 1958, FBI headquarters advised the San Francisco Office that "STUDY OF RADIOGRAPHS OF OIL CANS REVEALED NO FOREIGN MATERIALS OR CONTAINERS."[43] Still, headquarters pointed out that "RADIOGRAPHS EXTREMELY DARK AND THUS IT IS POSSIBLE THAT OBJECTS COULD BE PRESENT WHICH ARE NOT DETECTABLE DUE TO OVER EXPOSURE."[44]

The FBN was not giving up. On May 22, 1958, the FBI special agent in charge of New York City advised FBI headquarters and the San

Francisco Office that "it is FBN's intention to have agents of Food and Drug Administration . . . examine instant shipment upon its arrival at Brooklyn, NY. If narcotics found in olive oil tins, [NAME REDACTED] will allow delivery and then make seizure."[45] Ultimately, when the FBN x-rayed the tins on June 2, 1958, they found "that there was no foreign matter or substance in the olive oil tins."[46]

It is difficult to say from the available record what happened. It is possible, as the scientists at the FBI's headquarters cautioned, that the initial X-ray scan by the "confidential informant" had created a false positive reading because it was taken improperly and that there never was anything in the barrels but olive oil. Alternatively, it is also possible that Lanza or the buyer got wind of what was going on and arranged for the contraband to disappear before it ended up on the dock at Brooklyn where the FBN was waiting. Whatever the cause, the result was the same—the bureau was no closer to making a charge stick on Lanza.

They kept at it though, tracking another shipment of olive oil from Lanza to Charles Cassaro of Cleveland, Ohio, who claimed to be selling olive oil by the gallon to local Italians and asserted he had never met Lanza in person.[47] The FBI found it more curious that Cassaro had been arrested seven times—four in connection with homicide investigations—between June 1927 and August 1932 and had never been charged.[48] In yet another strange coincidence, in every one of the murder investigations, Cassaro was booked alongside Frank Brancato,[49] who would go on to become the underboss of the Cleveland Mafia family.[50] Evidently, Lanza had built up an exclusive clientele for his business and his "old friends" were far more interesting than the average wholesale peddler of olive oil.

Meanwhile, Irwin got to see another lead—with regard to Lanza allegedly being involved with passing counterfeit money in the late 1930s— go up in smoke after the San Francisco Office of the Secret Service advised him they had destroyed the file.[51]

Still, the bureau was starting to get a better sense of who they were up against. Lanza was in his office, usually with a cigar in his mouth, from 8 a.m. to 4 p.m., Monday through Friday.[52] Other than his weekend and holiday visits to local racetracks and his weekly card game with his counterparts in the San Jose Mafia family, Lanza did not appear to have any hobbies other than making money.[53]

BRING IN THE BLACK BAG SQUAD

After a year of digging and gumshoeing by his agents seemed to bring his office no closer to infiltrating Lanza's rackets, Burke got impatient and reverted to his original plan, which was to send in the FBI's black-bag squad. On March 17, 1959, he advised headquarters that multiple persons on the bureau's radar were known to be visitors to Lanza's office at 559 Washington Street and that "all of them have been suspected of associating with members of the Sicilian groups in the San Francisco Area."[54] Furthermore, Irving—owner of the Oro Olive Oil Company and one of Lanza's primary suppliers—told the FBI that Irving considered Lanza "as the 'King-pin' of the Sicilian element in the San Francisco area."[55]

Irving's decision to bad-mouth Lanza was particularly *infame*, given that Irving—as the FBI report delicately puts it—"has been the accountant for several Sicilians whose names have come to the attention of law enforcement offices."[56] His client list included the Tropical Bar and Café as well as the Sunland Cheese and Olive Oil Company, which Nick DeJohn was thought to have attempted to muscle in on before he ended up on the wrong end of a garrote.[57]

Finally, thanks to some ill-advised renovations at 559 Washington Street by the Lanzas, the technical objections to installing the misur had evaporated, although—as Burke bluntly put it—"it appears that trespass will be involved."[58] FBI Section Chief L.N Conroy was less concerned with the trespass than the fact the misur installation could "be completed with maximum security and no risk of detection."[59] Based on Burke's representation that it could be, Conroy recommended the bureau give its approval to the scheme.[60] Of course, there was no discussion—from Burke, Conroy, or Alex Rosen at FBI headquarters—about the legalities (or lack thereof) of what they were doing, much less any nagging concerns about the Fourth Amendment's protection of Lanza's privacy and how they were about to ride roughshod over it. At no time did Conroy or Rosen say: "Hey, what about the Supreme Court's decision in *Nardone*? Won't all the evidence we gather be tainted and inadmissible? And if so, why the hell is Burke proposing we commit felony burglary?"

Instead, on April 1, 1959, Hoover approved the installation of the misur at 559 Washington Street for 30 days.[61] After it went live at 10 a.m. on April 24, 1959,[62] it would be in place for most of the next six years.

Chapter 12

Legitimate Businesses

Thanks to their illegal installation of the bug at James Lanza's office at 559 Washington Street, FBI Special Agent in Charge Webb Burke and his agents now had their supposed Holy Grail—verbatim coverage of everything Lanza said while in the office. Sadly—from the perspective of law enforcement, at any rate—it did them little good.

On May 22, 1959, Burke asked for a six-month extension of the misur, but Hoover was unpersuaded. Instead, Burke got a 30-day extension from June 1, 1959, and a scolding that "renewal beyond that period will be contingent upon continued justification on the basis of material developed from this source."[1]

A few weeks later, Special Agent Herbert K. Mudd took over the Lanza case from Special Agent Curtis Irwin. Mudd would live to regret this achievement, as it ultimately led to his forced early retirement from the FBI and public disgrace several years later after FBI files were leaked to *Look* magazine, but in 1959 (from the tenor of his reports, anyway) he appears to have been just as dedicated as Irwin was in the pursuit of Lanza.

THE WAGES OF OLIVE OIL AND REAL ESTATE

Today, Mudd would likely have paid greater attention to the real property owned by Lanza, either with his brother Anthony or in the name of his sister Rose in an effort to determine whether it had been purchased with the proceeds of criminal activity, because if it had been, the property would have been potentially vulnerable to a criminal asset forfeiture claim by the government. In the late 1950s, that was not as practical an option because the Racketeer Influenced and Corrupt Organizations (RICO) Act did not exist,[2] which was a pity for Mudd, as those holdings Lanza had that the FBI knew about were fairly sizable.

Besides the 559 Washington Street headquarters, the Lanza family (through Rose) owned units at 2178 to 2182 Bush Street, as well as additional properties at 2184 to 2188 Bush Street and at 1900 to 1906 Fillmore Street, all of which seem to have been mixed-use commercial and residential properties.[3] Thanks to Lanza's other investments, as of 1956 the bureau estimated his and his wife Josephine's gross income from legitimate sources was $10,000 a year (or $87,255.88 in 2015 dollars).[4]

Given the current (as of this writing) overheated state of the San Francisco real estate market, Lanza's on-the-books income, adjusted for inflation, may not sound princely by today's standards, but it does not tell the whole story. Remember, in 1956 it was still possible to buy a four-level house in the Outer Mission in San Francisco for $10,950[5] or rent a two-bedroom apartment in the Castro for $35 a month.[6] In contrast, by the end of 2015, the *median* home price in San Francisco had broken the $1.2 million[7] mark and the median rent in the Castro for an apartment was around $3,320 a month.[8]

Moreover, in 1956 the median annual income for men across the United States was $3,600, with the median income for women being $1,100,[9] which meant that their combined family income (since Josephine worked) was about 112 percent above the national median. As a result, much to the likely annoyance of the SFPD, Lanza was probably one of the only suspected mobsters in the City who was immune to a vagrancy charge, which the cops used on a massive scale during the Booze Wars of the 1920s and 1930s (as we saw in Chapter 5) and to a lesser extent after Nick DeJohn was killed (as we saw in Chapter 8).

Still, law enforcement had other means of letting Lanza know he was on their radar, including but not limited to grand jury subpoenas. As we saw with the Apalachin debacle in Chapter 11, Lanza would end up getting wrapped up in the drama taking place in someone else's city.

GOING TO THE GRAND JURY

On January 13, 1959, the U.S. Department of Justice impaneled a special grand jury in Los Angeles to gather information on "100 top hoodlums."[10] The main difference between a "special" and a standard grand jury is that the former exists primarily to investigate and gather information about crimes (although it can also issue indictments), where the latter's purpose is simply to indict* persons the prosecution requests it to. Since the federal government—thanks to Hoover's ostrich-like approach to organized crime until Apalachin—was largely operating in the dark when it came to the Mafia, it had to start from square one. Still, it is not entirely clear what Lloyd F. Dunn, who had previously been an Assistant U.S. Attorney in Los Angeles before getting promoted to a special assistant attorney general, hoped to accomplish by summoning suspected mob leaders to account for themselves, other than the potential of indicting them for perjury depending on what they said, or jailing them for contempt if they refused to speak.[11]

Sure enough, among the first batch of witnesses subpoenaed were Joe "Joe Bananas" Bonanno, who retained his slot as boss of his own family as well as his seat on the commission despite having traded the cold of New York for the warmth of Arizona, Frank DeSimone—boss of the Los Angeles family (and Lanza's cousin-in-law) as well as Simone Scozzari, DeSimone's underboss.[12]

Lanza's turn came on March 17, 1959, when he was ordered to appear with Joe Cerrito. At the time, the *Los Angeles Times* referred to both as "San Francisco businessmen,"[13] proving the *Times*' ignorance of northern California geography matched their cluelessness about Mafia operations north of Ventura Boulevard.[†]

Initially, Lanza invoked his Fifth Amendment right not to testify on the ground his answers might incriminate him criminally. That led U.S. District Judge Leon R. Yankwich to grant Lanza immunity, which required him to testify (since whatever he said at that point could not be used against him).[14] This was the first judicial grant of immunity before the special grand jury, but at the time, Dunn seemed to be pleased—he described Lanza as a "co-operative witness" when Lanza returned to testify on May 19, 1959.[15]

His brother Anthony and sister Rose had a far less pleasant visit to Los Angeles to testify. Thanks to their train being two-and-a-half hours late, U.S. District Judge Benjamin Harrison issued bench warrants for both Anthony and Rose, with $1,000 bail (or $8,155.88 in 2015 dollars)[16] for each.[17] As the *Los Angeles Times* reported, just as the jury was

---

*As Sol Wachter, the former chief judge of the New York Court of Appeals famously pointed out, the prosecutor's control over a general grand jury is usually sufficient to get it to "indict a ham sandwich" if that were the whim of the government.
†While businessmen both Cerrito and Lanza certainly were, Cerrito's main center of operations was in San Jose, which is nearly 50 miles south of San Francisco.

filing out of the courtroom, a secretary burst in to announce breathlessly "They're here, they're here."[18]

Anthony remained annoyed about this when he sat down or a chat with Special Agents Mudd and Frank Warner on June 9, 1959. After repeatedly denying that James was at Apalachin (though, since he was not there, it was not clear how he would know this), Anthony "became highly incensed that his family, who have for forty years operated a clean and honest business, should be embarrassed by all of the publicity appearing in the local newspapers and their individual appearances before the special Federal Grand Jury in Los Angeles."[19]

Despite all this, FBI headquarters remained skeptical about the value of the Lanza misur, granting only a 30-day extension on June 1, 1959, rather than the 6-month extension the San Francisco Office sought.[20]

Eighteen days later, the misur picked up an excited conversation in Italian and English between Anthony and an unidentified male, which seemed to indicate they would draw and aim weapons at FBI agents under the right circumstances.[21] As the bureau's phlegmatic report "In view of the . . . statements made, it is suggested that the subject JAMES LANZA and his brother ANTHONY LANZA be considered armed and dangerous."[22]

The incident is curious for a number of reasons. Although both Anthony and James could be hotheaded at times, no one has ever suggested that Anthony was involved in any of the family's illegal operations. Similarly, neither had been known to carry weapons. Then again, the San Francisco Office was locked in an ongoing battle with FBI headquarters to keep the misur in place and so they may have felt any tidbits that made that more likely were worth passing along to headquarters, even if it was just Anthony blowing off steam.

On June 25, 1959, the misur picked up Lanza talking about his grand jury appearance. "They asked him if I was there[‡] . . . if [NAME REDACTED] was there . . . how should I know what someone did twenty years ago? Truthfully, I never knew anything about it . . . we just have to stick together."[23]

One wonders whether his next sentence was a result of his instinctive caution or, whether he thought the government was listening, his desire to issue a *sotto voce* challenge to the FBI. "I don't know anything about heroin being in olive oil or anything like that."[24]

---

‡That is, at the Apalachin meeting.

END OF THE TRAIL?

On August 28, 1959, the patience of FBI headquarters with the less-than-fruitful misur having been exhausted, FBI officials ordered the San Francisco Office to disconnect the misur.[25] The San Francisco Office complied on September 1, 1959.[26] Two months later, Mudd placed the Lanza investigation into "inactive" status.[27] On February 18, 1960, the San Francisco Office advised headquarters that it was closing its investigation of Lanza due to lack of sufficient evidence to prove his association with the Mafia or his engagement in criminal activity.[28]

Still, Hoover—for whatever reason—had not forgotten about the Lanzas. On June 2, 1960, he "suggested"[29] to the San Francisco Office that they consider reinstalling a misur at the Lanza's new offices on 560 Merchant Street (which were on the other side of the 559 Washington Street building). During this period, Hoover's "suggestions" tended to be followed by his agents with alacrity. After San Francisco went through the motions of formally requesting authorization for the misur, headquarters approved its installation on July 12, 1960[30] and the black bag squad was back in business. On the night of August 2, 1960, bureau burglars entered the building and placed misurs "in the wall of the space to be occupied by LANZA."[31]

By December 1960, the FBI was referring to local lawyer (and future mayor of San Francisco) Joseph Alioto as a "close associate" of Lanza[32] after the misur picked up James apparently telling Anthony that he had just come from Alioto's office where he had helped Alioto secure a $200,000 settlement in a case,[33] although he apparently had to give back $100,000 to Alioto for whatever unexplained reason.[34]

IT IS NOT ALL OLIVE OIL AND GRAND JURIES

This iteration of the misur picked up Lanza in a different role—as the *padrone* of those who sought his counsel or assistance. On April 4, 1961, he met with a man who was upset his wife had filed for divorce and who feared his soon-to-be-ex-spouse would grab all their money.[35] After advising the man that California was a community property state and that his soon-to-be-ex-wife would get half of his assets, Lanza called the attorney for the man's ex-wife. "My name is LANZA. I don't know if you know me? I've known of you, we know your brother real well too. [NAME REDACTED] is here, he's a good friend of mine. He's kind of upset about what's going on."[36]

Having shown a glimpse of the steel inside his velvet glove, Lanza returned to the velvet approach. "He asked if I knew you. I told him you were a good attorney. Yeah, I told him he shouldn't do that,§ just have one attorney and then do as he is told to do by the attorney."[37] Given that the other attorney was ethically bound to hang up the phone and not discuss the case with Lanza, who—as a non-lawyer—could not represent the man, it is striking that the conversation went on for more than a few seconds. Whoever the lawyer was, he clearly knew *who* Lanza was.

Other interactions were less pleasant. On April 19, 1961, the FBI spoke with one of Lanza's neighbors near his new home at 19 Wildwood Drive in San Mateo, California, who reported him as the neighborhood grouch. According to Mudd's report, Lanza

has bitterly complained to the parents of the [neighborhood] children when a ball or other object may land on his lawn . . . LANZA indicated that because of the fact he had a very beautiful home and that it cost him $55,000.00, he did not want to have it damaged in any way by children playing on the lawn or in any way close to the front of the house where possibly a window could be broke.[38]

This was an uncharacteristically foolish move on Lanza's part. Then and now, the house at 19 Wildwood Drive lies at the bottom of a hill in a cul-de-sac and the homes are so close they appear to almost touch each other. Given these environmental constraints, it would be difficult, if not impossible, for the FBI to surveil Lanza's house (where his famous poker games took place every Friday with his San Jose colleagues) without cooperation from his neighbors, as the car would be noticed.

It is difficult to conceive of a more effective way to get his neighbors to snitch on him or to persuade them to offer hospitality to the bureau than for Lanza to harangue them about their children acting like children. That is why bosses from Al Capone, whose generosity to Chicago residents was legendary,[39] to John Gotti[40] have historically gone out of their way to be pleasant to their neighbors.

To Lanza's credit, as we see, he mellowed in later years on this subject. However, given that Lanza was on Hoover's personal radar, the present was the time he needed every solid friend he could muster. Instead, as we see in Chapter 13, some old friends were about to become exceptionally problematic.

---

§Presumably, that the husband should not get his own lawyer.

Chapter 13

The Swinging 1960s

Although the 1960s would turn out to be the most challenging decade for the Lanza family, it did not start out that way. It was not all James Lanza's fault, as some of those challenges were a direct result of forces unleashed by people above his pay grade.

NEVER TRUST AN EX-BOOTLEGGER

As a start, despite the fact that the then Vice President Richard Nixon was reportedly working with both the CIA and the Mafia to eliminate Fidel Castro ahead of the 1960 presidential election,[1] the Chicago Outfit decided—on the advice of Sam "Mooney" Giancana—to back Nixon's challenger John F. Kennedy instead.[2] Evidently, Joseph Kennedy Sr., father of John and his brother (and future attorney general) Robert Kennedy, supposedly promised Giancana that if Kennedy was elected "'his boys would back off the Outfit, especially in their Las Vegas business.' Mooney bragged about the assurances he got from [Joe] Kennedy."[3] Although Joe Kennedy had more credibility with the Outfit than, say, Nixon's* father would have had because of Joe Kennedy's past work as a bootlegger during Prohibition, all he had to offer were words. Giancana forgot that talk is cheap and talk from a politician's father especially so.

---

*Lanza's reaction, as a registered Republican, to these developments is sadly not extant.

After Kennedy was elected, he promptly appointed his brother Robert attorney general, thereby giving the United States its first top law enforcement officer (at least on paper) who was actually serious about going after the Mafia in the modern history of the organization. As a result, on September 13, 1961, Kennedy signed a slew of bills[4]—including the Interstate Travel in Aid of Racketeering ("ITAR") Act, which made travel or the use of "any facility in interstate or foreign commerce, including the mail" to commit or facilitate a crime a separate felony.[5] Thanks to ITAR, if FBI Agent Herbert K. Mudd could only catch Lanza talking to someone on the phone about a crime or Lanza using a ship or a train to send contraband inside olive oil tins out of state or internationally, Lanza was now in danger of spending the next few decades behind bars.

EVERYTHING WOULD BE FINE IF IT WERE NOT FOR THESE MEDDLING AGENTS

On the brighter side, on May 30, 1961, Governor Pat Brown signed a bill repealing California's vagrancy statute,[6] thereby depriving the SFPD of its primary tool to harass legitimate businessmen like Mike Abati (and before him, scores of mobsters during the Booze Wars of the 1920s and 1930s, as we saw in Chapter 5). Even better—at least from Lanza's perspective—on June 17, 1961, the Immigration and Naturalization Service ordered Mike Abati—whose appeals had finally been exhausted— to either leave for Italy by August 1 or be removed there.[7] This cleared the way for Lanza to assume his role as boss of the family, the role he had been groomed for since his father's day.

It was a busy month for Lanza, as he somehow got stuck with coordinating Abati's taxes with attorney Joseph Alioto and Abati's accountant (and FBI snitch) Henry Irving, on top of Lanza's other business.[8] He also had a private sit-down scheduled with Joe "Joe Bananas" Bonanno on June 16, 1961,[9] while Bonanno was in town for his son-in-law Gregory Genovese's graduation from dental school.[10]

Beyond Mudd's general interest in all things related to Lanza, at the time Bonanno was ducking a subpoena from a federal grand jury in Phoenix, which was enough to put both men on the agent's radar. Alas, even though Mudd and his colleagues from the bureau and the U.S. Marshal's service placed the Jack Tar Hotel on Van Ness Avenue under surveillance that night, they only saw Genovese, not Lanza or Bonanno.[11]

Once again, the government was bested—the following Monday, Lanza told Anthony (and the misur) "Joe Bonanno came this past week from Phoenix . . . they wanted to show this . . . racket so they had a subpoena for the Federal grand jury for Joe Bonanno."[12] One can almost imagine the likely chuckle in Lanza's voice when he closed with "Joe didn't show himself for the subpoena."[13] Over the coming years, the FBI seemed to conclude Genovese was the conduit by which Lanza and Bonanno passed messages to each other, although it would prove to be another channel they largely failed to penetrate.

It did not always please him though. Later that year, the misur picked up Lanza complaining to Bonanno's attorney that despite having put Bonanno together with Alioto on a case that resulted in a $100,000 settlement and having shown them around San Francisco and taken them to dinner, he had not received a piece of the spoils.[14] Shortly thereafter, Lanza had to listen to his colleague Vito Bruno complain that Genovese had filled two of his teeth rather than just pulling them, which Bruno attributed to Genovese's attempt to make money.[15]

By the end of the year, Lanza came up with a new idea. In November 1961, San Francisco's crab fishing boats stayed moored at Fisherman's Wharf because the boat owners demanded 25 cents per pound for their catch and the crab wholesalers were only willing to pay 18 cents.[16] On December 19, the misur picked up Lanza telling a friend that if the crab fishermen were properly organized, they could, as the FBI report summarized, "get rid of all of the men that caused them any trouble."[17]

Since the crab fishermen already had their own association, Lanza's comment is fascinating. Was he thinking about muscling in on the Crab Boat Owners Association to control it like Joseph "Socks" Lanza ran the Fulton Fish Market in New York City, as we saw in Chapter 6? Or was he proposing creating a new union to supplant the Crab Boat Owners Association? Sadly, the subject never came up again in those portions of Lanza's FBI file that have been released pursuant to the Freedom of Information Act, but in light of the Lanza family's long connections to Fisherman's Wharf through their association with the Aliotos in running the Exposition Fish Grotto for several years, it is a question worth pondering, even if it cannot be answered at present.

BONANNOS, BAD CHECKS, AND A BANANA WAR

In January 1962—on top of his other business with the Bonannos—Lanza and Genovese were tasked with an effort to spare the family some embarrassment. Joe Bonanno's son Bill wrote a bad check while he was in San Francisco, and Genovese and Lanza attempted to cover it by depositing money into Bonanno's account at the Crocker-Angelo bank at 16th and Mission.[18] Bill would continue to have trouble managing money until he was ultimately busted for using a stolen credit card in 1968 and was sent to prison for nearly three years.[19]

Long before then, the Bonannos were causing Lanza bigger headaches. In the fall of 1964, Joe Bonanno decided that the moment was ripe to recreate Salvatore Maranzano's role as "boss of all bosses" on the Mafia's commission. To do this, he planned to whack New York bosses Carlo Gambino and Tommy Lucchese and Lanza's cousin-in-law Frank DeSimone, the boss of the Los Angeles family.[20] Alas for Joe Bonanno, the plan was quickly discovered by his adversaries and the commission demanded he report to them to explain himself.[21] Instead, "Joe Bananas" went on the run.[22]

It is difficult to tell from Lanza's October 16, 1964, conversation with Steve Zoccoli, then a *caporegime* in the San Jose family (and later its *consigliere*), what about this turn of events annoyed him the most—the fact that Bonanno was foolish enough to launch a war against the commission or that he was incompetent enough to lose it. "There is no discipline," said Lanza, in earshot of the FBI's misur. "However, mistakes have to be paid for."[23]

He then turned to the inability of Bill Bonanno to secure his father's compliance with the commission's summons. "He said that he had called his father . . . but, tell me, Sir, what can I say to this man?" said Lanza to Zoccoli. "Aren't we the Commission? What would the Commission be for if it did not understand these things? The Commission knows all these things—it is human—the Commission may be right or wrong, but [it] is human."[24] On hearing that, any remaining doubts within the FBI with regard to Lanza's involvement with the Mafia must have burned off faster than San Francisco fog at high noon. Sadly for the bureau, the misur was about to be converted from a source of intelligence into an unexploded bomb for both Lanza and Joe Alioto.

L.B.J. PULLS THE PLUG AND *LOOK* MAGAZINE GOES DOWN THE DRAIN

In July 1965, President Lyndon Baines Johnson ordered all federal agencies to disconnect all existing wiretaps and misurs except those being used in national security investigations.[25] Since the Lanza investigation did not fall within that exception—and the Omnibus Crime Control Act, which would later provide a legal framework for the FBI to obtain court-ordered wiretaps—was still three years away, the bureau shut down the misur on Lanza, although they continued to observe him for their own edification and to keep J. Edgar Hoover happy.

Four years later, freelance reporters Richard Carlson and Lance Brisson, who were working on a story about the Mafia for *Look* magazine, persuaded Mudd to leak them part of the FBI's file on Lanza. At the time,

Mudd claimed he had not known the focus of the piece would be Joseph Alioto, who had gone from being a lawyer who did some work with Lanza to mayor of San Francisco.

The opening sentence of Carlson and Brisson's article "San Francisco's Mayor Alioto and the Mafia," in the September 23, 1969, issue of *Look*, was sufficient to cause terminal *agita* from North Beach to Lanza's home in San Mateo: "Mayor Joseph L. Alioto . . . is enmeshed in a web of alliances with at least six leaders of La Cosa Nostra."[26] Lanza was named as the boss of the San Francisco family whom James "Jimmy the Weasel" Fratianno had gone to before trying to secure a loan from Alioto's new bank for Fratianno's trucking firm.[27]

Also making appearances in the article as "The Mafia Men in the Mayor's Life" were Salvatore and Angelo Marino of the San Jose family, the deceased gambler Emilio Giorgetti (whom Alioto had represented during the Kefauver Committee hearings, as we saw in Chapter 9), Frank Bompensiero of the Los Angeles family, and Frank LaPorte of the Chicago Outfit.[28]

Predictably, Alioto promptly filed a libel suit against *Look* magazine's founder and publisher as well as his publishing company, Cowles Communications. After four inconclusive trials and two appeals to the Ninth Circuit Court of Appeals—and one unsuccessful request for U.S. Supreme Court review—the case finally ended in 1981, when the court found in Alioto's favor and awarded him $350,000 in damages, plus costs. The victory proved beyond Pyrrhic for Alioto who—although voters re-elected him as mayor in 1971—neither went on to higher office nor received a penny from the judgment against *Look*, as it ended up being assigned to his law firm's creditors.

As for Lanza, thanks to *Look*, he was now notorious on a national level and would have to get used to being referred to as the boss of San Francisco's Mafia family until the end of his days. Although it was written before the *Look* article, those in the know could quickly see how the "Anthony Molinari" character in Mario Puzo's *The Godfather* (first published in 1969) was inspired by Lanza. Molinari "had the impassive face of the professional gambler and it was known he had something to do with dope smuggling over the Mexican border and from the ships plying the oriental oceans."[29]

To a boss who was so cautious that he refused to make, or initiate, new soldiers for years to replace those who had died because he feared attracting FBI attention, this newfound fame must have been galling, particularly as it came as a result of other people's mistakes. Still, Lanza pressed on.

Epilogue: The Lion in Winter

As the 1960s turned into the 1970s, James Lanza saw the San Francisco he came of age in begin to change beyond recognition. His old building at 559 Washington Street had long since been sold and demolished to create space for the Transamerica Pyramid, which—when completed in 1972—would be the tallest building in the City by the Bay.

Joe Alioto—whom he had known for years until they had to deny each other like Peter in the garden during the *Look* magazine litigation—had gone back to practicing law after his second term as mayor. He was replaced by George Moscone, another Italian American, but one of a very different generation than Alioto and Lanza.

Although Lanza's name continued to appear on public reports the state of California issued on organized crime, the FBI bothered him less and less. Evidently, the bad odor that surrounded Mudd's leak to *Look* and J. Edgar Hoover's death in 1972 caused the bureau to lose interest in him. *Look* itself was dead by then too, a casualty of changing tastes and Alioto's lawsuit.

Although Jimmy "The Weasel" Fratianno become a government witness in the late 1970s, the wisdom of Lanza's standard practice of keeping him at arm's length (except for that meeting leaked by Mudd to *Look*) became evident. Although Fratianno's testimony sent, by his own account, "30 guys away, six of them bosses,"[1] Lanza was not among them.

Lanza had mellowed in some ways since the late 1950s and 1960s. As her aunt was his neighbor for many years, Madeleine* and some members of her family remember James Lanza well in the 1970s. "The first thing people said when she bought the house was 'Do you know you've bought the house next to a mobster?'" Madeleine said. "All the neighbors knew who he was." When Madeleine was a child "we were always instructed *not* to let our balls go in his yard when we were playing kickball and to aim away from there," she says today with a laugh. "He had an impeccable yard and his garden was spotless."

Evidently the message Lanza left with the neighbors a decade before was still well remembered. "My aunt used to say [Lanza] looked tough, but was always very friendly and polite," Madeleine said. "He had lots of male visitors and they all spoke Italian, with never a word of English." Ironically, Madeleine's dad was a retired member of law enforcement at the time.

"One year for Halloween, my female cousin dressed up like an actual mobster, with a plastic machine gun, hat and suspenders," said Madeleine. "My aunt and uncle told us to avoid Lanza's house that year, but there was no way we were going to do that—he gave out *full* candy bars! My dad, on the other hand, thought if anything Lanza would be amused."

Although Madeleine does not remember how Lanza reacted that night, during this period he tended to take interactions with his neighbors in stride. "One day, my grandfather accidentally hit (Lanza's) perfect hedge and mailbox with his car and was really worried," said Madeleine. "But Lanza came out and said 'No problem, no problem' and wouldn't even let him pay for the damage."

During those years, Madeleine and her family remember Lanza's biggest passion as spending time at the Bay Meadows Racetrack. "He always had a driver," she said. Lanza "drove a nice car, a Cadillac, but he never liked to park it at Bay Meadows." Besides watching the horses run, "Lanza would go down [there] with a roll of quarters to do his business," Madeleine said. "Back then, the government couldn't tap pay phones or so everyone thought." In addition, "Whenever he went out, to the market or downtown, he was never alone," Madeleine said. "He always had a man that looked like a bodyguard with him who he always introduced as a 'nephew,' even when it was a different guy."

Meanwhile, Lanza's wife Josephine worked at Roos Brothers, one of San Mateo's downtown department stores. "She always dressed classy,"

---

*Per Madeleine's request, her last name has not been used. The stories listed here are both her own recollections and those of her family members, who preferred not to be interviewed directly or be named in this book.

Madeleine said. "Not over the top, but always elegant. And she drove a Cadillac too."

Despite all the class and bonhomie and no matter how nice Lanza was to neighborhood children and their parents, the reality of Lanza's world was never far away. "One day, out of the blue, the police came and searched the two Cadillacs," Madeleine said. "They pulled them out of the garage so the police could search them—maybe they were afraid if the cops searched them in the garage they'd end up searching the house."

According to those members of her family who went inside, the Lanza's home "was immaculate," Madeleine said. "In the days before Costco, he had bulk packages of chips and mints in his garage. Whether he took those home from the Bay Meadows racetrack or got them from someplace else, I never knew. There was probably bulk alcohol too, but as kids we never noticed things like that."

Behind the garage was Lanza's rec room, where his legendary poker games took place with his cronies from the San Jose family and others. With the perspective of history, one wonders why the FBI (which had zero compunction about illegally wiretapping Lanza's office, as we saw in Chapter 11) apparently never tried to conduct electronic surveillance on his rec room.

Other than random police harassment, which by then he must have become resigned, the next few decades were good times for Lanza. Besides getting to hand out full-size candy bars to children and wave away damages to his hedge like the proud *signore* of the manor he had become, he got to watch his son Frank succeed beyond his father's wildest dreams as the founder and president of L-3 Communications, which would become one of the nation's leading defense contractors,[2] and to see his grandchildren and great-grandchildren grow up.

When the reaper finally came for Lanza on February 14, 2006, he left this world as he would have wished—quietly and without fanfare. By this time, the *San Francisco Chronicle* had forgotten about him, so the only coverage of his death was an obituary (probably prepared by his family or the funeral home) that was riddled with inaccuracies. This is a pity—if not for Lanza, than for history. After all, despite the best efforts of the FBI, the Federal Bureau of Narcotics and the association of trained killers known as *La Cosa Nostra*, he had survived for more than a century to die free, wealthy, and in his own bed of natural causes. It was an achievement none of Lanza's predecessors, from Jerry Ferri on down, other than his father had managed—and James outlived Francesco by four decades.

In the end, he more than earned his reputation as the most successful mobster almost no one had heard of.

Notes

NOTES ON TERMS

1. Robert J. Schoenberg, *Mr. Capone: The Real—And Complete—Story of Al Capone* (William Morrow & Co., 1992), 79, 144.

CHRONOLOGY

1. County of San Francisco; Certification of Vital Record. Standard Certificate of Death, Francesco Lanza, Residence 1020 Francisco Street (Copy in author's possession).

2. Russo, *The Outfit*, 455. *See* also Jack Anderson, "LBJ Slows Wiretapping," Washington Merry-Go-Round, *Ocala Star-Banner* (December 28, 1965).

CHAPTER 1: DISARMING THE BODYGUARD: SAN FRANCISCO MAFIA MYTHS AND REALITIES

1. "Summary of the third regular session of the Teheran Meeting" (November 30, 1943). Typed memorandum. Facsimile. W. Averell Harriman Papers, Manuscript Division, Library of Congress (208); http://www.loc.gov/exhibits /churchill/wc-unity.html (accessed October 18, 2014).

2. Herbert Asbury, *The Barbary Coast: An Informal History of the San Francisco Underworld*, Alfred A. Knopf (1933), rep. by Thunder's Mouth Press, New York (2002), 49.

3. Ibid., 50.

4. Ibid., 55.

5. Ibid., 64.

6. Ibid., 65.

7. Porter Garnett, ed., *Papers of the Committee of Vigilance of 1851* (Berkeley: University of California, 1910), 291. https://books.google.com/books?id =AJIJAQAAIAAJ&printsec=frontcover&dq=editions:7sPIM0bCyp8C&hl=en &sa=X&ei=8JNzVYTuI9CsogTTx4KQCQ&ved=0CCQQ6AEwAQ#v =onepage&q&f=false (accessed June 6, 2015).

8. Asbury, *The Barbary Coast*, 70–74.

9. Ibid., 75.

10. Garnett, *Papers of the Committee.*

11. Michelle Jolly, "Sex, Vigilantism, and San Francisco in 1856," *Common -Place.org,* 3, No. 4 (July 2003). http://www.common-place.org/vol-03/no-04 /san-francisco/ (accessed April 17, 2016).

12. Ibid.

13. Ibid.

14. "Letter from London," *San Francisco Chronicle* (August 18, 1874), 2.

15. "No Regrets," *San Francisco Morning Call* (March 17, 1891), 1.

16. "Vendetta Murders: Statements Concerning the Operations of New Orleans Desperadoes," *San Francisco Morning Call* (October 21, 1890), 1.

17. "The New Orleans Lynching," *San Francisco Morning Call* (March 17, 1891), 4.

18. Ibid.

19. "Terribly Slashed," *San Francisco Morning Call* (February 5, 1892), 3.

20. Ibid.

21. Ibid.

22. "Rivaled The Frog Not the Nightingale: Di Franchi Thought He Could Sing," *San Francisco Call* (December 7, 1898), 5.

23. Ibid.

24. "Mankiller May Be Hiding in or Close to City, Police Think," *San Francisco Call* (April 11, 1905), 3.

25. "Assassination of Petrosino: Local Italian Newspaper Says Murder of Detective in Sicily Proves Gang is Organized," *San Francisco Call* (March 15, 1909), 6.

26. Nan Boyd, *Wide Open Town: A History of Queer San Francisco to 1965* (University of California Press, 2005), 143.

27. Ian Haney López, *Dog Whistle Politics: How Coded Racial Appeals Have Reinvented Racism and Wrecked the Middle Class* (New York: Oxford University Press, 2014).

28. Bernard Averbuch, *"Crab Is King"—The Colorful Story of Fisherman's Wharf in San Francisco* (Mabuhay Publishing Co., 1973), 16.

29. Ormando Willis Gray, *San Francisco Atlas Map* (Philadelphia, PA: O.W. Gray & Son, 1878).

30. Averbuch, *Crab Is King*, 17.

31. Ibid., 18.

32. Asbury, *The Barbary Coast*, 75–76.

33. Ibid.

CHAPTER 2: SICILIAN REALITIES AND AMERICAN DREAMS

1. Province of Palermo, Castelbuono, "Castelbuono Castle." http://etnaportal .it/castelbuono/castello_di_castelbuono (accessed March 21, 2016).

2. Eva Wallander, "Production of Manna in Sicily." http://www.oleaceae.info /fraxinus/manna.html (accessed April 4, 2015).

3. Veronica DiGrigoli, "Manna from Heaven? Or from Sicily?" http:// siciliangodmother.com/2012/09/14/manna-from-heaven-or-from-sicily/ (accessed March 21, 2016).

4. Wallander, "Production of Manna." Others dispute the legend that the manna of Sicily is that which is referenced in Exodus, *see* generally N. Gray Bartlett and Albert E. Ebbert, eds., *The Pharmacist and Chemical Record*, Vol. III (Chicago: Chicago College of Pharmacy, 1870), 8.

5. In the interest of brevity, "Francesco" will be used to refer to Francesco Lanza/Proetto in this chapter unless otherwise noted.

6. Ministero Di Agricoltura, Industria E Commercio Direzione Generale Della Statistica, *Censimento Della Popolazione Del Regno D'italia* (February 10, 1901), 247.

7. Istituto Nazionale di Statistica, *Popolazione residente censita al 2001 (popolazione legale) e al 1991, differenze e densità abitativa, per comune— Censimento 2001.* http://dawinci.istat.it/plDownload/TavPopLegaleComuniIta .xls (accessed March 29, 2015).

8. Province of Palermo, Castelbuono, "Castelbuono Castle." http://etnaportal .it/castelbuono/castello_di_castelbuono (accessed March 21, 2016).

9. Joshua Whatmough, *The Foundations of Modern Italy* (New York: Haskell House Publishers, 1937), 359.

10. Selwyn Raab, *Five Families: The Rise, Decline, and Resurgence of America's Most Powerful Mafia Empires* (St. Martin's Press, 2006), 14.

11. Ibid.

12. Salvatore Lupo, *History of the Mafia.* Translated by Anthony Shugaar (Columbia University Press, 2009), 198.

13. Ibid., 15.

14. Cesare Mori, *The Last Struggle with the Mafia* (Putnam, 1933), 30.

15. Lupo, *History of the Mafia*, 27.

16. Raab, *Five Families*, 15.

17. George Macaulay Trevelyan, *Garibaldi and the Making of Italy* (London: Longmans, Green & Co., 1911), 50.

18. Raab, *Five Families,* 15.

19. Giuliano Procacci, *History of the Italian People* (Harper & Row, 1971), 277.

20. Ibid., 270.

21. Ibid.

22. Ibid., 271.

23. At the time of the liberation of Rome by Risorgimento forces, approximately 78 percent of Italians were illiterate and most of the country was existing at a barely subsistence level economically. Procacci, *History of the Italian People*, 275.

24. Lupo, *History of the Mafia*, 31.

25. Lucy Riall, *Sicily and the Unification of Italy: Liberal Policy and Local Power 1859–1866* (Oxford University Press, 1998), 157.

26. Lupo, *History of the Mafia*, 31–32.

27. Ibid., 39.

28. Ibid.

29. John Dickie, *Blood Brotherhoods: Italy and the Rise of Three Mafias* (Perseus Books Group, 2014), 56.

30. Arcangelo Dimico, Alessia Isopi, and Ola Olsson, "Origins of the Sicilian Mafia: The Market for Lemons." Scandinavian Working Papers in Economics No. 532 (Department of Economics, School of Economics and Commercial Law, Göteborg University, 2012), 6.

31. Ibid.

32. Ibid.

33. Ibid., 7.

34. "Inflation Calculator 2016," *DaveManuel.com.* http://www.davemanuel .com/inflation-calculator.php (accessed January 11, 2016).

35. Dimico et al., "Origins of the Sicilian Mafia," 7.

36. Ibid., 12.

37. Paul M. Johnson, *A Glossary of Political Economy Terms* (Department of Political Science, Auburn University). http://www.auburn.edu/~johnspm /gloss/rent-seeking_behavior (accessed April 4, 2015).

38. Lupo, *History of the Mafia,x.*

39. Paolo Buonanno et al., "Poor Institutions, Rich Mines: Resource Curse and the Origins of the Sicilian Mafia." Quaderni Working Paper (2012).

40. Ibid., 3.

41. Ibid., 10.

42. Ibid.

43. Ibid.

44. Ibid.

45. Ibid., 11–12.

46. Lupo, *History of the Mafia, x.*

47. Provincia Di Palermo, Commune Di Castelbuono, *Estratto Riassunto Dal Registro Degli Atti Di Nascita* (Caterina Albanese Lanza) (translated copy in author's possession).

48. Immigration and Naturalization Service File, James J. Lanza, 33; Released pursuant to FOIA Request (copy in author's possession).

49. Ibid., 12–13.

50. Ibid., 18.

51. Ibid., 30.

52. Proetto, Mariono Vince, Passenger Record, S.S. Sicilia, Arrival February 10, 1905. https://www.libertyellisfoundation.org/passenger-details/czoxMjoi MTAyOTkyMDYwMjMzIjs=/czo5OiJwYXNzZW5nZXIiOw== (accessed April 12, 2015).

53. Luigi Barzini, *The Italians*, Hamish Hamilton (1964), 264.

54. Palizzolo Gravina, *Il blasone in Sicilia: ossia, Raccolta araldica.* Italian ed., Kindle LOC 577 (March 19, 2012). Kindle ed.

55. George Macaulay Trevelyan, *Garibaldi and the Making of Italy.* Kindle ed., Kindle LOC 502–504 (December 12, 2012).

56. Marcello Sorgi. *Il grande dandy: Vita spericolata di Raimondo Lanza di Trabia, ultimo principe siciliano* (2011). Italian ed., Kindle ed.

57. Ibid.

58. New York State Census, "Index and Images," *FamilySearch* (1905). https://familysearch.org/pal:/MM9.3.1/TH-1-159385-57600-5?cc=1463113 (accessed May 10, 2015). New York, Manhattan, A.D. 12, E.D. 11, image 28 of 48; county offices, New York.

59. Immigration and Naturalization Service File, 43.

60. Immigration and Naturalization Service File, 45.

61. Ibid.

62. Thomas Monroe Pitkin and Francesco Cordasco, *The Black Hand: A Chapter in Ethnic Crime* (Totowa, NJ: Littlefield, Adams & Co., 1977), 15.

63. Ibid., 34, 44, 122.

64. Ibid., 58. Indeed, Pitkin notes that the Black Hand symbol was used for extortion purposes in Louisiana in 1855. Pitkin and Cordasco, *The Black Hand*, 46.

65. Pitkin and Cordasco, *The Black Hand*, 45.

66. Ibid., 80.

67. Ibid., 80–81.

68. Francesco is *believed* to have entered the United States on or about July 11, 1904, but the INS was unable to verify this. Immigration and Naturalization Service File, 39.

69. The *Fasci Siciliani* called for land and other reforms. Lupo, *History of the Mafia*, 148. There is no direct link between them and Mussolini's later Fascist movement other than the similarity in their names, both of which stem from *Fasces*, which are a "bundle of rods and among them an ax with projecting blade borne before ancient Roman magistrates as a badge of authority." *See* http://www.merriam-webster.com/dictionary/fasces (accessed April 12, 2015).

CHAPTER 3: TO THE MEAN STREETS OF NEW YORK

1. Special Agent Curtis Irwin, "James Joseph Lanza" (September 15, 1958), FBI Report Form 263, 40.

2. Kenneth T. Jackson, "1904–2004; If the Subway Had Never Been," *New York Times* (March 28, 2004). http://www.nytimes.com/2004/03/28/nyregion/1904-2004-if-the-subway-had-never-been.html (accessed March 21, 2016); *see* also "1904: New York City Subway Opens," *History.com.* http://www.history.com/this-day-in-history/new-york-city-subway-opens (accessed March 21, 2016)

3. Victor Zarnowitz, *Business Cycles: Theory, History, Indicators, and Forecasting* (University of Chicago Press, 2007) (Google e-Book), 228–229.

4. Edgar L. Murlin, *The New York Red Book* (Albany, NY: J.B. Lyon Publishers, 1905), 26–27. https://books.google.com/books?id=fgg3AQAAMAAJ &printsec=frontcover&source=gbs_ge_summary_r&cad=0#v=onepage&q&f =false (accessed March 21, 2016).

5. Great Britain, Parliament, House of Commons, "Accounts and Papers 1906," Vol. 126 Session (February 13, 1906–December 21, 1906), 9.

6. Marilyn Chase, *The Barbary Plague: The Black Death in Victorian San Francisco* (Random House, 2004).

7. U.S. Bureau of the Census, *Estimates of Population 1904, 1905, 1906: Including the Census Returns of States Making an Intercensal Enumeration U.S. Govt* (Printing Office, 1907) (Google e-Book), 18.

8. Herbert Asbury, *The Gangs of New York* (Thunder's Mouth Press, 1990) (prev. pub. 1927–1928), 19–20.

9. Frank J. Cavaioli, "Patterns of Italian Immigration to the United States," *Catholic Social Science Review*, 13 (2008): 214.

10. Ibid.

11. Joan Rapczynski, *The Italian Immigrant Experience in America (1870–1920)* (Yale-New Haven Teachers Institute, 1999). http://www.yale.edu/ynhti /curriculum/units/1999/3/99.03.06.x.html (accessed June 10, 2015).

12. Asbury, *The Gangs of New York*, 336.

13. Ibid., 20.

14. Ibid., 21.

15. Terry Golway, *Machine Made: Tammany Hall and the Creation of Modern American Politics* (New York: W.W. Norton & Co., 2014), 154.

16. Tim Newark, *Lucky Luciano: The Real and the Fake Gangster* (New York: St. Martin's Press, 2010), 16.

17. Asbury, *The Gangs of New York*, 34–35.

18. Tyler Anbinder, *Five Points: The Nineteenth Century New York City Neighborhood* (Free Press, 2010), 271.

19. "Johnny Torrio's First Mob," *Infamous New York* (March 21, 2014). http://infamousnewyork.com/2014/03/21/johnny-torrio-and-his-first-mob-the -james-street-gang/ (accessed March 21, 2016).

20. Asbury, *The Gangs of New York*, 260.

21. Ibid., 261.

22. Ibid.

23. Ibid.

24. Ibid., 266.

25. Federico Varese, *Mafias on the Move: How Organized Crime Conquers New Territories* (Princeton University Press, 2013), 114; see also Asbury, *The Gangs of New York*, 315.

26. Howard Abadinsky, *Organized Crime*. 10th ed. (Belmont, CA: Wadsworth/ Cengage, 2007), 314.

27. Newark, *Lucky Luciano*, 19.

28. David Critchley, *The Origin of Organized Crime in America: The New York City Mafia 1891–1931* (New York: Routledge, 2009), 72.

29. Ibid.

30. Ibid., 77.

31. Ibid.

32. Ibid., 74.

33. Sen. William Dillingham, *Reports of the Immigration Commission: Immigrants in Industries* (Parts 21 and 22) (Government Printing Office, June 15, 1910), 393.

34. Ibid.

35. Ibid., Part 24, 493.

36. Kenneth T. Jackson and David S. Dunbar, eds., *Empire City: New York through the Centuries* (Columbia University Press, 2005), 432.

37. H. R. 4075, *Sixty-Seventh Congress, Session I, Ch. 8* (1921). http://library .uwb.edu/guides/usimmigration/42%20stat%205.pdf (accessed July 3, 2015).

38. U.S. Census, "Chapter VII–Country of Birth of the Foreign Born Population" (1910), 781.

39. U.S. Census, "Table 32 Foreign Born Population, Distributed According to Country of Birth By States and Territories" (1890), 608.

40. U.S. Department of State, "The Immigration Act of 1924." https://history .state.gov/milestones/1921-1936/immigration-act (accessed March 21, 2016).

41. Irwin, "James Joseph Lanza" (September 15, 1958), 40.

42. New York State Census, "Index and Images," 52.

43. Ibid.

44. "The Street Necrology of the Lower East Side," *Forgotten New York* (April 16, 2000). http://forgotten-ny.com/2000/04/lower-east-side-necrology/ (accessed May 28, 2015).

45. City of New York, *The City Record* (October 16, 1905), 8730.

46. New York State Census, "Index and Images," 52.

47. William Mailly, "The New York Rent Strike," *The Independent* 64 (January–June 1908): 149.

48. Rebecca Krucoff, *New York Neighborhoods: The Lower East Side* (New York Public Library, 2012), 34, 42. http://www.nypl.org/sites/default/files /lowereastsideguide-final_0.pdf (accessed May 28, 2015).

49. Greg Young and Tom Meyers, "Who Were the Short Tails? The Crazy Violent Habits of the Real Lower East Side Gang," *The Bowery Boys: New York City History* (February 14, 2014). http://www.boweryboyshistory.com/2014/02 /who-were-short-tails-gang-crazy-violent.html (accessed May 28, 2015).

50. Ibid.

51. Melissa Kimaldi, "The Power of New York's 'Burned-Over' Districts" (September 25, 2012). http://www.nycreligion.info/power-yorks-burned-dis tricts/ (accessed June 30, 2015).

52. Bella Spewack, *Streets: A Memoir of the Lower East Side* (New York: The Feminist Press at the City University of New York, 1995), 81.

53. Ibid.

54. "General City News—An Alleged Murder in Goerck Street," *New York Times* (July 6, 1862).

55. Ibid.

56. William Lawrence, "New York Election Frauds: Supplemental Report," 40th Congress, 3rd Session, Report No. 41 (March 1, 1869), 630.

57. "Held Up by Boy Highwaymen," *The Evening World* (March 27, 1891), 1.

58. "Alleged 'Fence' Raided," *The Evening World* (January 30, 1894), 1.

59. U.S. Census, "Index and Images," *FamilySearch* (1920). httpsllfamily search,org/paIlMM9, 1 VMJ PR-XNT (accessed November 09, 2014). Francisco Lanza, Brooklyn Assembly District 2, Kings, New York, United States; citing sheet 6B, family 127, NARA microfilm publication T625 (Washington, DC: National Archives and Records Administration); FHL microfilm 1821147.

60. *Copartnership and Corporation Directory Boroughs of Manhattan and Bronx* (R.L. Polk & Co., 1915), 572.

61. Ibid., 474.

62. "Real Estate Records: New Buildings," *Brooklyn Daily Eagle* (June 19, 1915), 18.

63. Bureau of Labor Statistics, "CPI Inflation Calculator." http://data.bls.gov /cgi-bin/cpicalc.pl?cost1=15%2C000&year1=1915&year2=2015 (accessed July 9, 2015).

64. "Real Estate Records," 18.

65. *Copartnership and Corporation*, 603.

66. Special Agent Curtis Irwin, "James Joseph Lanza" (November 18, 1958), FBI Report Form 263, 60.

67. Ibid.

68. "Judgments Satisfied," *Brooklyn Daily Eagle* (August 15, 1918), 17.

69. *Documents of the Assembly of the State of New York, One Hundred and Fortieth Session* (J.B. Lyon Company Printers, 1917), 200.

70. U.S. Census, Index and Images. *FamilySearch* (1920). Francisco Lanza, Brooklyn Assembly District 2, Kings, New York, United States; citing sheet 6B, family 127, NARA microfilm publication T625 (Washington, DC: National Archives and Records Administration, n.d.); FHL microfilm 1,821,147.

71. Ibid.

72. "$500,000 Fire Sweeps Luna Park; Coney Threatened By 5-Alarm Blaze," *Brooklyn Daily Eagle* (August 13, 1944). http://bklyn.newspapers.com/image /53859700/ (accessed May 30, 2015).

73. U.S. Census, "New York—Race and Hispanic Origin for Selected Large Cities and Other Places: Earliest Census to 1990." http://www.census.gov /population/www/documentation/twps0076/NYtab.pdf (accessed May 30, 2015).

74. *Brooklyn Chamber of Commerce Bulletin*, III, No. 45 (July 22, 1922), 7 (Google e-Book).

75. Hamilton v. Kentucky Distilleries & Warehouse Co., 251 U.S. 146 (1919).

76. Michael A. Lerner, *Dry Manhattan: Prohibition in New York City* (Harvard University Press, 2008), 42.

77. Ibid.

78. Hamilton v. Kentucky Distilleries & Warehouse Co., 251 U.S. 146 (1919).

79. Ibid.

80. Hamilton v. Kentucky Distilleries & Warehouse Co., 251 U.S. 146, 157 (1919).

81. Hamilton v. Kentucky Distilleries & Warehouse Co., 251 U.S. 146, 156–157 (1919).

82. Hamilton v. Kentucky Distilleries & Warehouse Co., 251 U.S. 146, 161 (1919).

83. Richard F. Hamm, *Shaping the 18th Amendment: Temperance Reform, Legal Culture and the Polity* (University of North Carolina Press, 1995), 247.

84. "Wartime Prohibition Law Is Upheld; Court Is Silent on Enforcement Act; Liquor Men Here to Sue for Their Loss," *New York Times* (December 16, 1919), 1.

85. "My Name? Poke Easy," *Brooklyn Daily Eagle* (January 8, 1919), 3.

86. "Government Hears of Scheme to Open 'Kitchen Stills,'" *Brooklyn Daily Eagle* (February 2, 1919), 18.

87. Ibid.

88. "Brooklyn Life Editorials," *Brooklyn Life* (May 1, 1920), 9.

89. Deposition of James J. Lanza, *Joseph Alioto v. Gardner Cowles and Cowles Communications* (December 15, 1969), 54, ln. 4.

90. Ibid., 63, ln. 21–26.

91. Edward Behr, *Prohibition: Thirteen Years That Changed America* (Arcade Publishing, 2000), 85.

92. Ibid.

93. Ibid.

94. Ibid., 86.

95. Ibid.

96. Federal Judicial Center, *Olmstead v. United States: The Constitutional Challenges of Prohibition Enforcement.* http://www.fjc.gov/history/home.nsf/page/tu_olmstead_doc_5.html (accessed July 28, 2015).

97. Bureau of Labor Statistics, "CPI Inflation Calculator." http://data.bls.gov/cgi-bin/cpicalc.pl?cost1=1000&year1=1920&year2=2015 (accessed July 28, 2015).

98. Mark Thornton, *The Economics of Prohibition* (University of Utah Press, 1991), 102.

99. Federal Judicial Center, *Olmstead v. United States.*

100. U.S. Bureau of the Census, *Population of the 100 Largest Urban Places: 1920.* https://www.census.gov/population/www/documentation/twps0027/tab15.txt (accessed July 28, 2015).

CHAPTER 4: GO WEST, YOUNG MAN, 'CAUSE IT'S PROHIBITION

1. U.S. Census, "Table 10: Composition and Characteristics of the Population, for Cities of 10,000 or More" (1920), 118.

2. Ibid.

3. California Department of Finance, "20th Century Industries." http://www.dof.ca.gov/HTML/FS_DATA/HistoryCAEconomy/20th_century_1900.htm (accessed August 12, 2015).

4. U.S. Census, "Table 6: Country of Birth of the Foreign Born White" (1920), 109.

5. Ibid.

6. Ibid., 679.

7. Jerry Flamm, *Hometown San Francisco* (Scottwall Associates, 1994), 28–29.

8. Ibid., 30.

9. Ibid.

10. Ibid., 29.

11. Ibid.

12. Ibid.

13. Marianne Costantinou, "Last Call at the Gold Spike/Italian Family's Saloon a Place Where Memories Were Made," *San Francisco Chronicle* (February 21, 2006). http://www.sfgate.com/restaurants/article/Last-call-at-the-Gold -Spike-Italian-family-s-2540953.php (accessed August 13, 2015).

14. Ibid.

15. Flamm, *Hometown San Francisco*, 32–33.

16. "San Francisco Snapshots," *San Francisco Business* (July 15, 1921), 2.

17. Ibid.

18. Ibid.

19. Special Agent Curtis P. Irwin, "James Joseph Lanza" (March 26, 1958), FBI Report 263, 2–3.

20. Ibid., 2.

21. Ibid., 3.

22. Ibid.

23. Ibid.

24. *Crocker-Langley San Francisco City Directory 1921* (H.S. Crocker & Co., 1921), 189, 1075.

25. U.S. Census, "Database with Images," *FamilySearch*. https://familysearch .org/ark:/61903/1:1:MJPR-XNT (accessed August 8, 2015). Francisco Lanza, Brooklyn Assembly District 2, Kings, New York, United States; citing sheet 6B, family 127, NARA microfilm publication T625 (Washington, DC: National Archives and Records Administration, n.d.); FHL microfilm 1,821,147.

26. Special Agent Curtis P. Irwin, "James Joseph Lanza" (March 26, 1958), FBI Report 263, 3.

27. U.S Naturalization Law of March 26, 1790 (1 Stat. 103). http://rs6.loc .gov/cgi-bin/ampage?collId=llsl&fileName=001/llsl001.db&recNum=226 (accessed August 8, 2015).

28. INA §101(f)(6); *see* also 8 C.F.R. 316.10(b)(2)(v).

29. U.S. Citizenship and Immigration Services, *USCIS Policy Manual,* Vol. 12, Part F, Ch. 5 (July 21, 2015). http://www.uscis.gov/policymanual/Print /PolicyManual-Volume12-PartF-Chapter5.html (accessed August 10, 2015).

30. Irwin, "James Joseph Lanza" (March 26, 1958), 4.

31. *Crocker-Langley San Francisco City Directory 1923* (H.S. Crocker & Co., 1923), 1018.

32. Ibid.

33. Howard Seftel, "Government Regulation and the Rise of the California Fruit Industry: The Entrepreneurial Attack on Fruit Pests, 1880–1920," *The Business History Review* 59, No. 3 (Autumn 1985): 373.

34. Ibid., 384–388.

35. Ibid., 401.

36. R. L. Nougbaet, "Report of the Viticultural Service," Second Report of the California Department of Agriculture (1921), 627.

37. Ibid.

38. Ibid.

39. Merritt Barnes, "'Fountainhead of Corruption': Peter McDonough, Boss of San Francisco's Underworld," *California History* (1979), 58, No. 2: 145.

40. Ibid.

41. Ibid.

42. Flamm, *Hometown San Francisco*, 38.

43. Ibid.

44. Barnes, "Fountainhead of Corruption," 145; *see also* Shane Bauer, "Inside the Wild, Shadowy, and Highly Lucrative Bail Industry," *Mother Jones* (May/June 2014). http://www.motherjones.com/politics/2014/06/bail-bond-prison-industry (accessed September 17, 2015).

45. Barnes, "Fountainhead of Corruption," 146.

46. Ibid.

47. Ibid.

48. Ibid., 146–147.

49. Ibid., 147.

50. Ibid.

51. Ibid., 145.

52. Ibid.

53. Ibid., 148.

54. Cohen v. Commissioner of Internal Revenue, 266 F.2d 5 (9th Cir. 1959).

55. Edward J. Clarke, *Deviant Behavior: A Text Study in the Sociology of Deviance* (Worth Publishers, 2008), 554.

56. Barnes, "Fountainhead of Corruption," 148.

57. Bureau of Labor Statistics, "CPI Inflation Calculator." http://data.bls.gov/cgi-bin/cpicalc.pl?cost1=10&year1=1927&year2=2015 (accessed September 19, 2015).

58. Barnes, "Fountainhead of Corruption," 148.

59. Ibid., 149.

60. Ibid.

61. *Crocker-Langley San Francisco City Directory 1924* (H.S. Crocker & Co., 1924), 850.

62. *Crocker-Langley San Francisco City Directory 1925* (H.S. Crocker & Co., 1925), 1109.

63. Irwin, "James Joseph Lanza" (November 18, 1958), 5.

64. Ibid., 6.

65. *Crocker-Langley San Francisco City Directory 1926* (R.L. Polk & Co., 1926), 1237.

66. *Crocker-Langley San Francisco City Directory 1927* (R.L. Polk & Co., 1927), 1283.

67. Irwin, "James Joseph Lanza" (November 18, 1958), 6.

68. Ibid., 6.

69. *Crocker-Langley San Francisco City Directory 1928* (R.L. Polk & Co., 1928), 922.

70. *Crocker-Langley San Francisco City Directory 1929* (R.L. Polk & Co., 1929), 917.

71. *Crocker-Langley San Francisco City Directory 1930* (R.L. Polk & Co., 1930), 810.

72. *Crocker-Langley San Francisco City Directory 1931* (R.L. Polk & Co., 1931), 819.

73. *Crocker-Langley San Francisco City Directory 1932* (R.L. Polk & Co., 1932), 690.

74. *Crocker-Langley San Francisco City Directory 1933* (R.L. Polk & Co., 1933), 667.

75. *Crocker-Langley San Francisco City Directory 1934* (R.L. Polk & Co., 1934), 635.

CHAPTER 5: FERRI MEETS HIS MAKER

1. "Beer Baron Held Slain for Revenge," *San Francisco Chronicle* (November 25, 1928), 54.

2. Ibid.

3. Nan Alamilla Boyd, *Wide Open Town* (University of California Press, 2003), 44.

4. "Corporal J.J. Muldoon Victim of Dastardly Crime," *Douglas 2-0 Police Journal* (San Francisco Police Department, January 1929), 11.

5. Daniel Steven Crafts, "Historical Essay: Mayor 'Sunny Jim' Rolph." http://foundsf.org/index.php?title=Mayor_%22Sunny_Jim%22_Rolph (accessed June 1, 2014).

6. Herbert Asbury, *The Barbary Coast* (New York: A.A. Knopf, 1933), 309.

7. Crafts, "Historical Essay."

8. Ibid.

9. Samuel Dickson, *San Francisco Is Your Home* (Stanford, CA: Stanford University Press, 1947), 209.

10. Ibid.

11. "Gunmen Kill Racketeer in S.F. Feud of Gangsters," *Oakland Tribune* (October 24, 1928), 1.

12. Ibid.

13. "Gunmen Foe Is Quizzed in S.F. Killing," *Oakland Tribune* (November 25, 1928), 73.

14. Ibid.

15. "Police Name Partner as Ferri Slayer," *San Francisco Chronicle* (December 2, 1928), 68.

16. Ibid.

17. "Avengers Kill 2 S.F. Gunmen, Carry Feud to Sacramento," *San Francisco Chronicle* (December 20, 1928), 1.

18. Ibid.

19. "Police Hunt S.F. Bootlegging," *San Francisco Chronicle* (December 15, 1928), 3.

20. Ibid.

21. "'Joe.' Named by Victim, Is Clue in Rum Killing," *Oakland Tribune* (December 15, 1928), 3.

22. "Bootleg Chiefs Quizzed after Murder in S.F.," *Oakland Tribune* (December 14, 1928), 49.

23. "Still Blast at S.F. Hotel Stirs Prohi Inquiry," *Oakland Tribune* (May 26, 1926), 2.

24. Ibid.

25. Ibid.

26. "Women Who Slew Husband Sent Home to Children," *Oakland Tribune* (December 2, 1928), 18.

27. "Police Hunt S.F. Bootlegging," *San Francisco Chronicle* (December 15, 1928), 3

28. "Underworld Death Traffic Held Proved," *Woodland Daily Democrat* (Woodland, CA, July 6, 1932), 5.

29. "Gang Slays S.F. Man on North Beach Death Ride," *San Francisco Chronicle* (July 31, 1929), 1.

30. "Underworld Death Traffic," 5.

31. Ibid.

32. "Gang Slays," 1.

33. Ibid.

34. U.S. Bureau of the Census, "Population of the 100 Largest Urban Places" (June 15, 1998). https://www.census.gov/population/www/documentation/twps 0027/tab16.txt (accessed October 1, 2015).

35. Selwyn Raab, *Five Families: The Rise, Decline and Resurgence of America's Most Powerful Mafia Empires* (St. Martin's Press, 2005), 26.

36. Ibid.

37. Ibid., 28.

38. Ibid.

39. Robert J. Schoenberg, *Mr. Capone: The Real and Complete Story of Al Capone* (Harper Collins, 1993), 37.

40. Raab, *Five Families*, 26.

41. Ibid., 27.

42. Ibid., 26.

43. Joseph Bonanno, *A Man of Honor: The Autobiography of Joseph Bonanno* (St. Martin's Press, 1983), 122.

44. Raab, *Five Families*, 28.

45. James R. Holmes, "Everything You Know about Clausewitz Is Wrong," *The Diplomat* (November 12, 2014). http://thediplomat.com/2014/11/everything -you-know-about-clausewitz-is-wrong/ (accessed October 3, 2015).

46. Michael Pollak, "Coney Island's Big Hit," *New York Times* (June 29, 2012). http://www.nytimes.com/2012/07/01/nyregion/answer-to-a-question-about -a-mobsters-death-in-coney-island.html?_r=0 (accessed October 3, 2015).

47. Raab, *Five Families*, 28.

48. Ibid., 29.

49. Ibid.

50. Ibid., 30.

51. Ibid., 31.

52. Ibid., 32.

53. Humbert S. Nelli, *The Business of Crime: Italians and Syndicate Crime in the United States* (University of Chicago Press, 1976), 207.

54. Ibid.

55. Ibid.

56. "Bail Given Man in Deportation Case," *San Francisco Chronicle* (May 17, 1930), 15.

57. Bureau of Labor Statistics, "CPI Inflation Calculator." http://data.bls .gov/cgi-bin/cpicalc.pl?cost1=5000&year1=1930&year2=2015 (accessed October 1, 2015).

58. "Suspect Nabbed in Murder 12 Years Ago," *Oakland Tribune* (May 14, 1930), 3.

59. "Bail Given Man."

60. "Suspect Nabbed," 3.

61. "Deportation Case Arguments Offered," *San Francisco Chronicle* (May 20, 1930), 23

62. "Five Jailed in Murder of Mafia King," *Oakland Tribune* (October 14, 1930), 1.

63. Bureau of Labor Statistics, "CPI Inflation Calculator." http://data.bls.gov /cgi-bin/cpicalc.pl?cost1=1500&year1=1930&year2=2015 (accessed October 5, 2015).

64. "Five Jailed," 1.

65. Ibid.

66. Ibid.

67. Ibid.

68. "Wife Menaced by S.F. King of Blackhand, Says Victim," *Oakland Tribune* (October 15, 1930), 3.

69. Merritt Barnes, "Corruption Central: Peter P. McDonough," *FoundSF*. http://foundsf.org/index.php?title=CORRUPTION_CENTRAL:_PETER_P. _McDONOUGH (accessed October 7, 2015).

70. "Wife Menaced," 3.

71. Ibid.

72. Ibid.

73. "Rossi Named Mayor as Rolph Successor," *San Bernardino County Sun* (December 23, 1930), 1.

74. "Rossi New Mayor of San Francisco," *The News-Review* (Roseburg, OR, December 23, 1930), 1.

75. "Select Rossi as Successor to Mayor Rolph," *The Oregon Statesman* (Salem, OR December 21, 1930), 1.

76. "Esposito Freed after Quick Trial," *San Francisco Chronicle* (April 3, 1931), 4.

77. "Two More Men Jailed as Bad Bill Passers," *Oakland Tribune* (October 18, 1931), 12.

78. "Killing Ends Victim's Long Police Record," *San Francisco Chronicle* (May 20, 1932), 4.

79. Ibid.

80. Ibid.

81. Ibid.

82. Ibid.

83. Ibid.

84. "Folsom Prison Gun Plot Traced to 'Yacht Bandits,'" *Oakland Tribune* (August 15, 1931), 8.

85. "Bandits Owned Young Arsenal," *Spokane Daily Chronicle* (June 19, 1929), 51.

86. Bureau of Labor Statistics, "CPI Inflation Calculator." http://data.bls.gov/cgi-bin/cpicalc.pl?cost1=10000&year1=1929&year2=2015 (accessed October 8, 2015)

87. "Bandits Owned," 51.

88. "Folsom Prison Gun Plot," 8.

89. David Bird, "Peter Joseph Licavoli Sr., 81, Ex-Crime Leader in Detroit," *New York Times* (January 12, 1984). http://www.nytimes.com/1984/01/12/obituaries/peter-joseph-licavoli-sr-81-ex-crime-leader-in-detroit.html (accessed October 8, 2015).

90. "Head of Gun Plot Denied Habeas Writ," *Oakland Tribune* (August 16, 1931), 3.

91. Ibid.

92. Ibid.

93. "Colson Makes Probation Plea," *Oakland Tribune* (March 28, 1933), 3.

94. Ibid.

95. "Gangster Shot in Bootleg Row at S.F. Resort," *Oakland Tribune* (May 16, 1932), 9.

96. "S.F. Gangster Executed in Busy Street," *San Francisco Chronicle* (May 19, 1932), 1.

97. Ibid.

98. Ibid.

99. "California, San Francisco County Records, 1824–1997," Database with Images, *FamilySearch* (Luigi Malvese, 1932). https://familysearch.org/ark:/61903/1:1:QKD4-PM81 (accessed October 17, 2015).

100. Luigi Malvese, "City and County of San Francisco Coroner's Office, Necropsy Department, No. 875" (May 19, 1932), 1–2.

101. "S.F. Gangster," 1.

102. Ibid., 1, 14.

103. "Jury Verdict Says Police Know Killer," *Oakland Tribune* (May 27, 1932), 1.

104. "Mobster Love Best, Weeps Gang 'Widow,'" *San Francisco Chronicle* (May 20, 1932).

105. Ibid.

106. "San Francisco Wants No Capones or Gang Methods," *San Francisco Chronicle* (May 20, 1932), 1.

107. Ibid.

108. "Killing Starts Police War on Gangsters," *San Francisco Chronicle* (May 20, 1932), 1.

109. "S.F. Suspect Hunted for Gang Killing," *San Francisco Chronicle* (May 22, 1932), 1

110. Ibid.

111. Bureau of Labor Statistics, "CPI Inflation Calculator." http://data.bls.gov/cgi-bin/cpicalc.pl?cost1=1000&year1=1932&year2=2015 (accessed October 17, 2015)

112. "S.F. Suspect," 1.

113. Ibid., 3.

114. Ibid.

115. Ibid.

116. Ibid., 1.

117. Ibid., 3.

118. Ibid.

119. "Police Death Squad Chief Loses Post," *San Francisco Chronicle* (May 25, 1932), 6.

120. "Killer Known, Jury Finds in Gang Slaying," *San Francisco Chronicle* (May 27, 1932), 9.

121. Ibid.

122. "Man Who Slew S.F. Gangster Is Located," *The Bakersfield Californian* (May 30, 1932), 7.

123. "Man Arrested in Racketeer Killing," *Oakland Tribune* (February 10, 1933), 19.

124. Sebastian Fichera, *Italy on the Pacific: San Francisco's Italian Americans* (St. Martin's Press, 2011), 122.

125. Paul Drexler, "I Left My Crime Family in San Francisco," *San Francisco Examiner* (December 20, 2015). http://www.sfexaminer.com/i-left-my-crime-family-in-san-francisco/ (accessed December 22, 2015).

126. Fichera, *Italy on the Pacific*, 122.

CHAPTER 6: THE END OF PROHIBITION AND THE BIG STRIKE

1. *Crocker-Langley San Francisco City Directory 1935* (R.L. Polk & Co., 1935), 665.

2. Carl Nolte, "Tough Times, Tough People," *San Francisco Chronicle* (May 2, 1999). http://www.sfgate.com/bayarea/article/TOUGH-TIMES-TOUGH-PEOPLE-The-Great-Depression-2933187.php (accessed November 7, 2015).

3. Kevin Starr, *Endangered Dreams: The Great Depression in California* (Oxford University Press, 1996), 80.

4. Kate Bronfenbrenner, "California Farmworkers' Strikes of 1933" (Cornell University Industrial Labor Relations School, 1990). http://digitalcommons .ilr.cornell.edu/cgi/viewcontent.cgi?article=1561&context=articles (accessed November 7, 2015).

5. Ibid.

6. Starr, *Endangered Dreams*, 81–82.

7. *San Francisco in the 1930s: The WPA's Guide to the City by the Bay* (University of California Press, 2011), 35.

8. Ibid.

9. Nolte, "Tough Times."

10. Ibid.

11. Nathan Ward, *Dark Harbor: The War for the New York Waterfront* (Farrar, Straus and Giroux, 2010), 12.

12. Ibid., xix.

13. "'Tough Tony' Anastasio, 57, Pier Boss, Dies," *Chicago Tribune* (March 1, 1963), 41.

14. Ward, *Dark Harbor*, xix.

15. James B. Jacobs, Colleen Friel, and Robert Radick, *Gotham Unbound: How New York City Was Liberated from the Grip of Organized Crime* (New York University Press, 1999), 41.

16. Ibid.

17. Bureau of Labor Statistics, "CPI Inflation Calculator." http://data.bls.gov /cgi-bin/cpicalc.pl?cost1=25000&year1=1931&year2=2015 (accessed November 8, 2015).

18. Jacobs et al., *Gotham Unbound*, 41.

19. Ibid.

20. Ibid., 47.

21. "Fall of Lucky Gives Gangland Stunning Blow," *Brooklyn Daily Eagle* (June 8, 1936), 6.

22. Tim Newark, *Mafia Allies* (Zenith Press, 2007), 98.

23. Ibid., 105.

24. Mike Quin, *The Big Strike* (Olema Publishing Co., 1949), 30.

25. Ibid., 31.

26. Ibid., 39.

27. "Christmas for the Shipowners," *Waterfront Worker* 1, No. 1 (December 1932): 1.

28. Bureau of Labor Statistics, "History of Wages in the United States from Colonial Times to 1928," *Revision of Bulletin No. 499 with Supplement* (1929–1933): 570.

29. Jerry Flamm, *A Good Life in Hard Times: San Francisco in the '20s & '30s* (Chronicle Books, 1978), 51.

30. Quin, *The Big Strike*, 31.

31. Ibid.

32. Ibid., 40.

33. Ibid.

34. Ibid., 40–41.

35. Ibid., 41.

36. Ibid.

37. Ibid.

38. Ibid.

39. Ibid.

40. Ibid., 45.

41. Starr, *Endangered Dreams*, 98.

42. Quin, *The Big Strike*, 59.

43. Ibid., 60.

44. Ibid., 48.

45. Ibid.

46. Ibid., 48–49.

47. Ibid.

48. Ibid., 51.

49. "Text of Atherton's Report on Police Graft Probe," *San Francisco Examiner* (March 17, 1937), 9.

50. Quin, *The Big Strike*, 75.

51. Ibid., 99.

52. Ibid., 137.

53. Ibid., 141.

54. Ibid., 151.

55. Ibid.

56. Ibid., 196–197.

57. Ibid., 197.

58. Ibid., 198.

59. "Riot at Pier of Karlsruhe Short-Lived, One Is Jailed," *Oakland Tribune* (March 2, 1935), 1.

60. Quin, *The Big Strike*, 199.

61. Simone Carlota Cezanne De Santiago Ramos, "Showing the Flag: War Cruiser Karlsruhe and Germandom Abroad" (PhD diss., University of North Texas, August 2013), 137.

62. Ibid., 138.

63. Virtual Museum of the City of San Francisco, "'Red' Suspects Demand Jury." http://www.sfmuseum.org/hist4/maritime16.html (accessed November 28, 2015) (Original article *The Daily News*, July 18, 1934).

64. American Federation of Labor, "Report of Proceedings of the Forty-First Annual Convention Held at Denver, Colorado" (The Law Reporter Printing Co., 1921), 352.

65. "Webb Says Brady Not Disqualified in Mooney Trial," *Modesto News-Herald* (Modesto, CA, March 28, 1933), 3.

66. "Mooney Acquitted on Superior Judge's Directed Verdict," *Santa Cruz Sentinel* (May 25, 1933), 1–2.

67. Ibid., 2.

68. Kevin Starr, *The Dream Endures: California Enters the 1940s* (Oxford University Press, 1997), 141.

69. "Text of Atherton's Report," 1.

70. Ibid., 2.

71. Ibid.

72. Ibid., 4.

73. Bureau of Labor Statistics, "CPI Inflation Calculator." http://data.bls.gov /cgi-bin/cpicalc.pl?cost1=27%2C000.00&year1=1936&year2=2015 (accessed November 28, 2015).

74. "Text of Atherton's Report," 2.

75. Ibid., 6.

76. Bureau of Labor Statistics, "CPI Inflation Calculator." http://data.bls.gov /cgi-bin/cpicalc.pl?cost1=15000&year1=1936&year2=2015 (accessed December 1, 2015).

77. "Text of Atherton's Report," 3.

78. Ibid., 6.

79. Ibid.

80. Ibid.

81. Ibid.

82. Ibid.

83. Ibid.

84. Ibid., 4.

85. Ibid.

86. Ibid., 8.

87. Bureau of Labor Statistics, "CPI Inflation Calculator." http://data.bls.gov /cgi-bin/cpicalc.pl?cost1=1000000&year1=1936&year2=2015 (accessed December 1, 2015).

88. "Former G Man Names Police in S.F. Vice Pay Off," *The Fresno Bee* (March 16, 1937), 1.

89. "Text of Atherton's Report," 18.

90. Ibid.

91. Starr, *The Dream Endures*, 141.

92. Merritt Barnes, "Fountainhead of Corruption," *California History 58*, No. 2 (Summer 1979): 152.

93. Ibid.

94. County of San Francisco; Certification of Vital Record. Standard Certificate of Death, Francesco Lanza, Residence 1020 Francisco Street (Copy in author's possession).

95. Mayo Clinic, "Aplastic Anemia." http://www.mayoclinic.org/diseases-conditions/aplastic-anemia/basics/definition/con-20019296 (accessed December 5, 2015).

CHAPTER 7: *MARONE*, WE CAN'T USE THE WHARF NO MORE?

1. U.S. Treasury Department, Bureau of Narcotics, *Mafia: The Government's Secret File on Organized Crime* (Harper Collins, 2007), 35.

2. Ibid.

3. "Newsy Paragraphs," *Indiana Weekly Messenger* (November 8, 1928), 5.

4. "Produce Dealer Is Shot to Death by Masquerader," *The Warren Tribune* (Warren, PA, October 31, 1928), 2.

5. Marcelo Bucheli, *Bananas and Business: The United Fruit Company in Colombia, 1899–2000* (New York University Press, 2005), 47–49.

6. "Tony Lima Acquitted of Murder at Ebensburg," *Lebanon Daily News* (Lebanon, PA, December 14, 1928), 15.

7. "Port of San Francisco, United States, to Pearl Harbor," *Ports.com*. http://ports.com/sea-route/port-of-san-francisco,united-states/pearl-harbor,united-states/ (accessed August 16, 2015).

8. U.S. Navy Naval History and Heritage Command, "Japanese Forces at Pearl Harbor." http://www.history.navy.mil/our-collections/photography/wars-and-events/world-war-ii/pearl-harbor-raid/japanese-forces-in-the-pearl-harbor-attack.html (accessed August 16, 2015).

9. "On This Day: Germany and Italy Declare War on the U.S.," *British Broadcasting Corporation*. http://news.bbc.co.uk/onthisday/hi/dates/stories/december/11/newsid_3532000/3532401.stm (accessed August 23, 2015).

10. Rose D. Scherini, "Executive Order 9066 and Italian Americans: The San Francisco Story," *California History* 70, No. 4 (Winter 1991/1992): 367.

11. Ibid.

12. Ibid.

13. National Park Service, "World War II in the San Francisco Bay Area." http://www.nps.gov/nr/travel/wwiibayarea/intro.htm (accessed August 17, 2015).

14. National Park Service, "One Camp, Ten Thousand Lives; One Camp, Ten Thousand Stories." http://www.nps.gov/manz/index.htm (accessed August 17, 2015).

15. U.S. Department of Justice, "Report to the Congress of the United States: A Review of the Restrictions on Persons of Italian Ancestry during World War II" (2001), 2.

16. Ibid.

17. Sen. Jack B. Tenney, "Report Joint Fact-Finding Committee on Un-American Activities in California," *California Legislature*, 15th Session (1943), 283.

18. Winston S. Churchill, *Memoirs of the Second World War (Abridged)* (Houghton Mifflin Co., 1991), 66.

19. Ibid., 74–85.

20. "U.S. Sends Formal Apology to Mussolini; General to be Tried for Speech," *Reading Times* (Reading, PA, January 30, 1931), 1.

21. "Butler's Trial Called Off by Navy Department," *Reading Times* (Reading, PA, February 9, 1931), 1.

22. Noam Chomsky, *Deterring Democracy* (Harper-Collins, 1992), 40.

23. Ibid.

24. "On This Day: Germany."

25. Patricia Yollin, "A SECRET HISTORY/The Harassment of Italians during World War II Has Particular Relevance Today and Serves as a Warning of

What Could Happen," *San Francisco Chronicle* (October 21, 2001). http://www
.sfgate.com/magazine/article/A-SECRET-HISTORY-The-harassment-of-Italians
-2866287.php (accessed September 2, 2015).

26. Stanley Schneider, "Peace and Paranoia." In *Even Paranoids Have Ene-mies*, edited by Joseph H. Berke, Stella Pierides, Andrea Sabbadini, and Stanley Schneider, 208 (Routledge, 1998).

27. Tenney, "Report Joint Fact-Finding Committee," 284.

28. University of California Berkeley Library, "The Loyalty Oath Contro-versy, University of California, 1949–1951." http://www.lib.berkeley.edu/uchistory /archives_exhibits/loyaltyoath/timelinesummary.html (accessed August 23, 2015).

29. Alfred W. McCoy, *Policing America's Empire: The United States, the Phil-ippines, and the Rise of the Surveillance* (State University of Wisconsin Press, 2009), 340.

30. Sen. Jack B. Tenney, *Zion's Trojan Horse* (Standard Publications, 1954), 246–247.

31. Tenney, "Report Joint Fact-Finding Committee," 284.

32. Ibid., 284–285.

33. Ibid., 285.

34. Ibid.

35. Ibid.

36. Ibid.

37. Ibid., 286–287.

38. Ibid., 287.

39. Ibid., 299.

40. Ibid.

41. Ibid.

42. Ibid., 286.

43. Ibid.

44. Ibid.

45. Ibid.

46. Ibid., 287.

47. Ibid., 311.

48. Ibid.

49. "L'Italia Pays Tribute to Action of U.S.," *San Francisco Chronicle* (Febru-ary 4, 1917), 36.

50. Tenney, "Report Joint Fact Finding Committee," 313.

51. Ibid.

52. Ibid., 296.

53. Ibid.

54. Ibid., 294.

55. "12 Arrested in Anti-Nazi Frisco Riots," *El Paso Herald-Post* (October 3, 1938), 7.

56. Ibid.

57. Ibid.

58. Tenney, "Report Joint Fact-Finding Committee," 294.

59. Ibid.

60. Robert J. Cressman, *The Official Chronology of the U.S. Navy during World War II* (Naval Institute Press, 2000), 46.

61. U.S. Department of State: Office of the Historian, "A Guide to the United States' History of Recognition, Diplomatic, and Consular Relations, by Country, since 1776: Italy." https://history.state.gov/countries/italy (accessed August 29, 2015).

62. Ibid.

63. John Patrick Diggins, *Mussolini and Fascism: The View from America* (Princeton University Press, 1972), 84.

64. "Nazi Flag Display Arouses Unionists in San Francisco," *The Milwaukee Journal* (May 26, 1937): 3.

65. "Nazi Flags Used: San Francisco Bridge Opening: Mayor's Apology for Earlier Incident," *The Sydney Morning Herald* (May 29, 1937), 17.

66. Tenney, "Report Joint Fact Finding Committee," 291.

67. Ibid., 253.

68. Salvatore John LaGumina, *The Humble and the Heroic: Wartime Italian Americans* (Cambria Press, 2006), 56.

69. Ibid.

70. Howard Zinn, *LaGuardia in Congress* (Cornell University Press, 1958), 111.

71. Ibid.

72. David B. Green, "This Day in Jewish History: U.S. Apologizes for Insulting Hitler," *Haaretz* (March 5, 2014). http://www.haaretz.com/news/features/this-day-in-jewish-history/.premium-1.578174 (accessed August 29, 2015).

73. Ibid.

74. Tenney, "Report Joint Fact Finding Committee," 298.

75. Ibid.

76. Ibid.

77. Ibid.

78. Ibid., 257.

79. Ibid.

80. Glen Jeansonne, *Women of the Far Right: The Mothers Movement and World War II* (University of Chicago Press, 1996), 45–56.

81. Tenney, "Report Joint Fact Finding Committee," 320.

82. Ibid., 321.

83. Ibid.

84. Rose D. Scherini, "When Italian-Americans were 'Enemy Aliens.'" In *Una Storia Segreta: The Secret History if Italian American Evacuation and Internment during World War II* (Heyday Books, 2001), 22.

85. Ibid.

86. Tenney, "Report Joint Fact-Finding Committee," 286.

87. Ibid., 285.

88. Lawrence DiStasi, *Una Storia Segreta: The Secret History if Italian American Evacuation and Internment during World War II* (Heyday Books, 2001), 64.

89. Ibid., 64–65.

90. Scherini, "Executive Order 9066," 369.

91. Ibid.

92. Ibid.

93. Letter from Capt. R.F. McCullough, U.S.N., and Lt. Cmdr. R.E. Law-rance U.S.N.R. to FBI Special Agent In Charge N.J.L. Pieper, February 10, 1942, CONFIDENTIAL (Declassified by and in possession of National Archives), 2–3.

94. U.S. Department of Justice, "Report to the Congress," 31; *see also* "Mem-orandum from the Commandant, United States Coast Guard, to District Coast Guard Officers and Captains of the Port" (May 12, 1942).

95. Ibid.

96. Bernard Averbuch, *Crab Is King: The Colorful Story of Fisherman's Wharf in San Francisco* (Mabuhay Publishing Co., 1973), 68.

97. DiStasi, *Una Storia Segreta*, 68.

98. Tenney, "Report Joint Fact Finding Committee," 318.

99. "West Coast Ouster Hits Draft Head, 45 Others," *The News-Review* (Roseburg, OR, October 12, 1942), 1.

100. "Lapham Wins Mayor Race in Bay City," *The Bakersfield Californian* (November 3, 1943), 1.

101. San Francisco Recreation and Parks, "Angelo J. Rossi Playground." http:// sfrecpark.org/destination/angelo-j-rossi-playground/ (accessed March 21, 2016).

102. Scherini, "Executive Order 9066," 371.

103. Janny Hu, "Sabella & La Torre Still a Family Affair," *San Francisco Chronicle* (October 1, 2013). http://www.sfgate.com/restaurants/article/Sabella -amp-La-Torre-still-a-family-affair-4850005.php (accessed August 31, 2015); *see also* "Sabella and La Torre History." http://www.sabellalatorre.com/ordereze /Content/3/Summary.aspx (accessed August 31, 2015).

104. Federal Bureau of Investigation, "James Joseph Lanza Anti-Racketeering" (June 5, 1958), File No. 92–123, 1.

105. Judith Russell and Renee Fantin, *Studies in Food Rationing* (Office of Temporary Controls, Office of Price Administration, Gen. Publication No. 13, May 29, 1947), 185.

106. Ibid., 183.

107. Ibid., 186.

108. Ibid., 183.

109. Ibid., 196.

110. Ibid., 197.

111. Ibid., 240.

112. "Eberts Super Market Department Store" (advertisement), *Santa Cruz Sentinel* (March 7, 1944), 8.

113. Bureau of Labor Statistics, "CPI Inflation Calculator." http://data.bls .gov/cgi-bin/cpicalc.pl?cost1=2.64&year1=1944&year2=2015 (accessed Sep-tember 7, 2015).

114. Olga Senise Barrio and Hoy Carman, "Olive Oil: A 'Rediscovered' Cali-fornia Crop," *UPDATE: Agricultural and Resource Economics* 8, No. 5 (May/ June 2005): 2.

115. "Black Market Told," *Press-Courier* (Oxnard, CA, April 17, 1946), 7.

116. Robert Weintraub, *The Victory Season: The End of World War II and the Birth of Baseball's* (Golden Age Back Bay Books, 2014), 162.

117. "Chronology of 1944 San Francisco War Events," *The Virtual Museum of City of San Francisco.* http://www.sfmuseum.org/war/44.html (accessed September 13, 2015).

118. James Ciment and Thaddeus Russell, eds., *The Home Front Encyclopedia: United States, Britain and Canada in World Wars I and II* (ABC-CLIO, 2007), 783.

119. U.S. Department of Agriculture, "The Fats and Oils Situation," FOS 113 (November 1946), 7.

120. Special Agent Curtis P. Irwin, "James Joseph Lanza," Federal Bureau of Investigation, FD-263 (March 26, 1958), 5.

121. Special Agent Charles P. Irwin, "James Lanza," Federal Bureau of Investigation, FD-263 (November 18, 1958), 5.

122. Special Agent [Name Redacted], "James Joseph Lanza," Federal Bureau of Investigation, FD-263 (April 14, 1958), 11.

123. Irwin, "James Joseph Lanza," (April 14, 1958), 11.

124. SA Curtis P. Irwin, "James Joseph Lanza," Federal Bureau of Investigation, FD-263 (September 15, 1958), 8.

125. Drew Pearson, "Washington Merry-Go-Round: Gunmen Rule West Coast Underground," *Ocala Star-Banner* (February 9, 1962), 2.

126. Michael Newton, *The Mafia at Apalachin* (McFarland and Company, 2012), 182.

127. Special Agent Frank A. Warner, "James Joseph Lanza," Federal Bureau of Investigation, FD-204 (September 9, 1960), 1.

128. Newton, *The Mafia at Apalachin, 1957*, 87.

129. Ibid., 102.

130. Special Agent [Name Redacted], "James Joseph Lanza," 11.

131. Irwin, "James Joseph Lanza," (March 26, 1958), 9.

CHAPTER 8: DEJOHN TAKES THE BIG SLEEP

1. John H. Mollenkopf, *The Contested City* (Princeton University Press, 1983), 151.

2. Ibid.

3. "Fillmore Timeline 1860–2001," *PBS.org.* http://www.pbs.org/kqed/fillmore/learning/time.html (accessed December 12, 2015).

4. Mollenkopf, *The Contested City*, 151.

5. Merritt Barnes, "Corruption Central: Peter P. McDonough." http://foundsf.org/index.php?title=CORRUPTION_CENTRAL:_PETER_P._McDONOUGH (accessed December 12, 2015).

6. Emil Bartos "Ace Assassin for Capone Is Shot to Death," *Belvidere Daily Republican* (February 15, 1936), 1.

7. Ibid.

8. "Hoodlum's End in S.F. Laid to Gang Vengeance," *The Times* (San Mateo, CA, May 10, 1947), 2.

9. Ibid.

10. "Triggermen Kill Ex Alky Suspect in Barber Chair," *Belvidere Daily Republican* (Belvidere, IL, December 6, 1943), 2.

11. "Chicago Hunts Victim's Friend," *The Decatur Herald* (Decatur, IL, March 13, 1944), 10.

12. "Search for Friend of Jas. DeAngelo," *Dixon Evening Telegraph* (Dixon, IL, March 14, 1944), 1.

13. "Body in Sewer Is Identified," *The Decatur Herald* (Decatur, IL, April 9, 1945), 5.

14. Ibid.

15. Frederic Sondern Jr., *Brotherhood of Evil: The Mafia* (Farrar, Straus and Cudhy, 1959), 239.

16. "Hoodlum's End," 2.

17. Ibid.

18. "Rival of Capone Gang Strangled in Car Here!" *San Francisco Chronicle* (May 10, 1947), 1.

19. Ibid., 3.

20. Ibid., 1.

21. "Search for DeJohn Killer," *San Francisco Chronicle* (May 13, 1947), 1.

22. "DeJohn Murder," *San Francisco Chronicle* (May 15, 1947), 1.

23. "The DeJohn Murder Case," *San Francisco Chronicle* (May 17, 1947), 1.

24. "De John Friend and Ex-Con Being Held In The Slaying," *San Francisco Chronicle* (May 22, 1947), 1.

25. Ibid.

26. Ibid.

27. "DeJohn Case Break 'Near,'" *San Francisco Chronicle* (May 23, 1947), 1.

28. Ibid., 9.

29. Ibid.

30. "Police Hint at De John Murder Charges Today" *San Francisco Chronicle* (May 24, 1947), 1.

31. Ibid.

32. Special Agent Curtis P. Irwin, "James Joseph Lanza," Federal Bureau of Investigation FD-263 (March 26, 1958), 18.

33. Ibid.

34. "DeJohn Case Oil Firm Investigated," *San Francisco Chronicle* (June 3, 1947), 22.

35. "DeJohn Murder: Calamia Charged But Police Say Case Not Solved," *San Francisco Chronicle* (May 25, 1947), 1.

36. Ibid.

37. Ibid.

38. "The DeJohn Murder Case: Capece Is Released; Police Accused of Third Degree," *San Francisco Chronicle* (May 26, 1947).

39. "DeJohn Death Link," *San Francisco Chronicle* (May 27, 1947), 3.

40. Ibid.

41. Daniel Waugh, *Gangs of St. Louis: Men of Respect* (Arcadia Publishing, 2010), 209.

42. Ibid.

43. "DeJohn Death Link," 3.

44. Ibid.

45. Ibid.

46. "Heat on Gangsters: Dullea Orders Crackdown in DeJohn Case," *San Francisco Chronicle* (May 28, 1947), 1.

47. Ibid.

48. Herb Caen, "Herb Caen: It's News to Me," *San Francisco Chronicle* (May 28, 1947), 15.

49. Ibid.

50. Ibid.

51. Ovid Demaris, *The Last Mafioso: The Treacherous World of Jimmy ("the Weasel") Fratianno* (Ishi Press, 1981), 76.

52. "DeJohn Slaying: Scene of the Garroting Is Believed Found," *San Francisco Chronicle* (May 29, 1947), 1.

53. Ibid.

54. "Break in the DeJohn Case: Police Hold Former N.Y. Gangster in Local Hospital," *San Francisco Chronicle* (May 31, 1947), 1.

55. Ibid.

56. Ibid.

57. "DeJohn Murder: Calamia Freed; Police Offer No Case at Hearing," *San Francisco Chronicle* (June 1, 1947), 1.

58. "DeJohn Case Oil Firm," 22.

59. Bureau of Labor Statistics, "CPI Inflation Calculator." http://data.bls.gov/cgi-bin/cpicalc.pl?cost1=500000&year1=1948&year2=2015 (accessed December 21, 2015).

60. "DeJohn Inquest: Coroner Calls 19 Witnesses; Further Investigation Urged," *San Francisco Chronicle* (June 5, 1947), 24.

61. Ibid.

62. Ibid.

63. Ibid.

64. "DeJohn Case Contempt Hearing," *San Francisco Chronicle* (June 19, 1947), 13.

65. "Four Arrested in Nick DeJohn Killing," *San Francisco Chronicle* (November 21, 1948), 1.

66. Ibid.

67. "Pawned Jewelry New Clue in the DeJohn Gang Murder," *San Francisco Chronicle* (November 22, 1948), 1.

68. Ibid.

69. Bureau of Labor Statistics, "CPI Inflation Calculator." http://data.bls.gov/cgi-bin/cpicalc.pl?cost1=8000&year1=1947&year2=2015 (acesseed December 22, 2015)

70. "FBI Aids in DeJohn Case," *San Francisco Chronicle* (November 23, 1948), 15.

71. "The DeJohn Murder: Mrs. Lima Somehow Has the Idea Tony Won't Be Back for Holidays," *San Francisco Chronicle* (December 8, 1948), 29.

72. Ibid.

73. "DeJohn Case Fugitive Jailed; Fear of Gang Action Hinted," *San Francisco Chronicle* (December 24, 1948), 1.

74. "Calamia 'Put the Finger' on Other DeJohn Defendants, Police Say," *San Francisco Chronicle* (February 18, 1949), 1.

75. Ibid., 3.

76. Ibid.

77. "DeJohn Prosecution Rests Case; Ahern Sticks to Story of 'Squeal,' " *San Francisco Chronicle* (February 19, 1949), 7.

78. Ibid.

79. "DeJohn Murder: Defense Fails to Shake Testimony on Hearing Plot," *San Francisco Chronicle* (February 5, 1949), 1.

80. Ibid.

81. Ibid.

82. "DeJohn Murder Trial: Mrs. Venza Questioned on Bad Check," *San Francisco Chronicle* (February 9, 1949), 12.

83. "The DeJohn Trial: State Witnesses Stick to Switched Stories in Impeachment Attempt," *San Francisco Chronicle* (February 17, 1949), 14.

84. "Defense Is Opened in DeJohn Case," *San Francisco Chronicle* (February 24, 1949), 3.

85. "Still No DeJohn Verdict: Jury Is Locked Up For Night," *San Francisco Chronicle* (March 8, 1949), 1.

86. "The DeJohn Jury Is Dismissed While Still Seeking a Verdict," *San Francisco Chronicle* (March 9, 1949), 1.

87. "Lima, DeJohn Suspect, Freed," *The Times* (San Mateo, CA, April 20, 1949), 8.

88. Stan Gores, "DiBella Lived at Hotel, Headed Grande Cheese Firm," *Fond Du Lac Commonwealth Reporter* (Wis., March 12, 1966), 8.

89. Special Agent Curtis P. Irwin, "James Joseph Lanza" (November 18, 1958), FBI Report Form 263, 60.

90. Gores, "DiBella Lived at Hotel," 8.

91. Drew Pearson, "Mobsters' Migration Southward Points to Big Crime Conclave," Washington Merry-Go-Round, *The Herald-Mail* (Hagerstown, MD, February 2, 1962), 13.

92. "Figure in DeJohn Case Dies in S.F.," *The Times* (San Mateo, CA, November 28, 1952), 8.

93. "Suspect in DeJohn Killing Dies of Tumor," *The Fresno Bee* (November 30, 1952), 13.

94. "U.S. Deports Dreaded Mafia Leader Nani," *Independent Star-News* (Pasadena, CA, February 9, 1958), 1.

95. Ibid.

96. "Tony Lima, DeJohn Case Suspect, Back in Trouble," *San Francisco Chronicle* (November 18, 1952), 3.

97. "State Opens Case against Trio in Grape Theft Trial," *The Fresno Bee* (March 2, 1953), 9.

98. U.S. Treasury Department, Bureau of Narcotics, *Mafia: The Government's Secret File on Organized Crime* (HarperCollins, 2007), 35.

CHAPTER 9: THE KEFAUVER SHOW

1. U.S. Senate, "Special Committee on Organized Crime in Interstate Commerce (The Kefauver Committee)." http://www.senate.gov/artandhistory/history/common/investigations/Kefauver.htm (accessed April 20, 2014).

2. Ibid.

3. Ibid.

4. U.S. Bureau of the Census, *Statistical Abstract of the United States, 1961*, 8. http://www2.census.gov/prod2/statcomp/documents/1951-02.pdf (accessed April 20, 2014).

5. U.S. Senate, "Hearings before the Special Committee to Investigate Organized Crime in Interstate Commerce," Eighty First Congress, Second Session, Pursuant to S. Res. 202, Pt. 4 (September 28, 1950, Kansas City), 81.

6. Bureau of Labor Statistics, "CPI Inflation Calculator." http://data.bls.gov/cgi-bin/cpicalc.pl?cost1=3000&year1=1940&year2=2015 (accessed December 26, 2015).

7. U.S. Senate, "Hearings before the Special Committee" (September 28, 1950).

8. Ibid., 82–83.

9. Ibid.

10. Ibid., 83.

11. Ibid., 89.

12. Judith Moore, "When Everything Was Lost," *San Diego Reader* (March 18, 1999). http://www.sandiegoreader.com/news/1999/mar/18/cover-when-everything-was-lost/ (accessed April 11, 2014).

13. U.S. Senate, "Hearings before the Special Committee to Investigate Organized Crime in Interstate Commerce," Eighty First Congress, Second Session, Pursuant to S. Res. 202, Pt. 10 (November 21, 1950, San Francisco), 418–419.

14. Remember, *Roe v. Wade* is still over two decades away.

15. U.S. Senate, "Hearings before the Special Committee" (November 21, 1950), 422.

16. Ibid., 422–423.

17. Bay Area Census, "San Francisco City and County," http://www.bayareacensus.ca.gov/counties/SanFranciscoCounty50.htm (accessed March 21, 2016).

18. Dan Schrieber, "San Francisco at 1 Million: City's Population Is Booming Once Again," *San Francisco Examiner* (December 29, 2013). http://www.sfexaminer.com/sanfrancisco/san-francisco-at-1-million-citys-population-is-booming-once-again/Content?oid=2659836 (accessed April 12, 2014).

19. Ernest Beyl, "The Evolution of San Francisco Newspapers from 1846 until Today, Part 3," *Marina Times* (October 2013). http://www.marinatimes .com/2013/09/the-evolution-of-san-francisco-newspapers-from-1846-until -today-part-3/ (accessed April 12, 2014).

20. "Uniform Crime Reports for the United States and Its Possessions," *Federal Bureau of Investigation* (1950), XXI, No. 1, 22

21. Joshua Melvin, "Police Hiring Boom Hits Bay Area Departments," *San Jose Mercury News* (February 20, 2013). http://www.mercurynews.com/top -stories/ci_22623070/police-hiring-boom-hits-bay-area-departments (accessed April 16, 2014).

22. U.S. Senate, "Hearings before the Special Committee" (November 21, 1950), 423.

23. Ibid.

24. State of California, "Final Report of the State of California's Special Crime Study Commission on Organized Crime" (May 11, 1953), 47–49. According to the report, the commission reported the allegations to the San Francisco Police Department, which summarily dismissed them. Noting that the Merchants Club continued to operate unmolested for several years after the commission brought the issue to the attention of the SFPD, the report noted "The above report emphasizing as it does that the investigation officers of the S. F. D. as late as 1952 do not recognize Lewis, Waxman, and Gillespie and are in ignorance of their business verges on the ludicrous. However, the matter ceases to be funny when there is so clear a demonstration of the fact that known gamblers are being permitted in San Francisco either with the connivance of the police or more probably through the interference of their political masters."

25. The club was originally located at 365 Market Street when it opened in 1931 and moved to its present location at 1025 Columbus Avenue in 1951. At present, it is open only for special shows and corporate events—and there are no contemporary reports of dice boards. It remains family owned. http://www .bimbos365club.com/history (accessed April 12, 2014).

26. State of California, "Final Report of the State," 57.

27. Ibid., 58.

28. Bay Area Census, "San Francisco City and County" http://www.bay areacensus.ca.gov/counties/SanFranciscoCounty50.htm (accessed March 21, 2016).

29. Bureau of Labor Statistics, "CPI Inflation Calculator." http://data.bls.gov /cgi-bin/cpicalc.pl?cost1=20000&year1=1949&year2=2015 (accessed December 26, 2015).

30. U.S. Senate, "Hearings before the Special Committee" (November 21, 1950, 423.

31. Ibid., 424.

32. Ibid.

33. Ibid.

34. Ibid.

35. Ibid.

36. Ibid.

37. LaRocca's Corner Tavern still exists and is in operation at 957 Columbus Avenue, although its founder, Leo LaRocca, sadly passed away in 2006. *See* Marianne Costantinou, "Leo La Rocca—His North Beach Saloon Was Popular with All Types," *San Francisco Chronicle* (February 8, 2006). http://www.sfgate.com /default/article/Leo-La-Rocca-his-North-Beach-saloon-was-2541697.php (accessed April 20, 2014).

38. U.S. Senate, "Hearings before the Special Committee" (November 21, 1950), 424.

39. Ibid., 426.

40. Ibid.

41. Ibid., 427.

42. Ibid.

43. Ibid.

44. Ibid.

45. Ibid., 434.

46. In contrast to (most) "26" games in San Francisco, which were run by the shopkeeper or bartender, the Chicago variant was conducted by a "26 girl," whose job it was to schmooze the customers as well as run the game. Of course, some suspicious folk, like the Chicago Police Department saw this as a front for sex work. Bob Hughes, "The '26' Game And Its Girls Finally Run Out Of Luck," *Chicago Tribune* (March 16, 1986). http://articles.chicagotribune.com/1986-03 -16/features/8601190603_1_dice-taverns-girls (accessed April 16, 2014).

47. Hughes, "The '26' Game And Its Girls."

48. U.S. Senate, "Hearings before the Special Committee" (November 21, 1950), 435.

49. Calif. Pen. Code 319.

50. As passed in 1911 (and in effect in 1950) Penal Code. 330a only banned "card dice" and "dice with more than six faces" (in addition to "slot or card machine(s), contrivance(s), appliance(s) or mechanical device(s)") as gambling paraphernalia. Thus, mere possession of dice to play "26" was not a crime unless the dice had more than six faces.

51. *In re Portnoy*, 21 Cal.2d 237, 131 P.2d 1 (1942).

52. U.S. Senate, "Hearings before the Special Committee" (November 21, 1950), 439.

53. Ibid., 436.

54. That is, California's antigambling laws. *See* Penal Code 330–337z. There is no equivalent statute that explicitly imposes a similar requirement with regard to illegal lotteries, but it seems reasonable that a court would find that ignoring them would fall under dereliction of duty.

55. U.S. Senate, "Hearings before the Special Committee" (November 21, 1950), 437.

56. Ibid.

57. Ibid.

58. Ibid., 439.

59. Ibid.

60. Ibid., 448.

61. Ibid.

62. Ibid.

63. Schaffer operated on both sides of the Canadian–U.S. border and allegedly had operatives in some of Canada's major cities, including Montreal and Winnipeg. *See* "Events and Discoveries," *Sports Illustrated* (November 12, 1956). http://www.si.com/vault/1956/11/12/668266/events--discoveries (Accessed April 17, 2016).

64. Mike McCormick, *Terra Haute: Queen City of the Wabash* (Great Britain: Arcadia Publishing, 2005), 135.

65. U.S. Senate, "Hearings before the Special Committee" (November 21, 1950), 449.

66. Bureau of Labor Statistics, "CPI Inflation Calculator." http://data.bls.gov/cgi-bin/cpicalc.pl?cost1=32000&year1=1949&year2=2015 (accessed December 26, 2015).

67. *Smith v. United States* 337 U.S. 137, 147 69 S.Ct. 1000 (1949) (emphasis added).

68. G. Robert Blakey, "Legal Regulation of Gambling Since 1950," *The Annals of the American Academy of Political and Social Science* 474 (1984):12–13. Blakey is generally considered to be the father of the Racketeer Influenced and Corrupt Organizations ("RICO") Act, which was signed into law by President Nixon in 1970.

69. Under the then current federal law, Russell could not claim that the documents were privileged. However, he *might* have been able to do so under state law if he had asserted the privilege.

70. U.S. Senate, "Hearings before the Special Committee" (November 21, 1950), 489 (emphasis added).

71. Ibid.

72. Ibid., 490 (emphasis added).

73. Charles W. Tobey, "Wake Up America! The Hour Is Late THERE IS A CONSPIRACY TO GET US INTO WAR," Delivered before an America First Committee Rally at Carnegie Hall, New York (September 17, 1941). http://www.ibiblio.org/pha/policy/1941/1941-09-17a.html (accessed April 19, 2014).

74. U.S. Senate, "Hearings before the Special Committee" (November 21, 1950), 490.

75. Ibid., 491.

76. Ibid., 491 (emphasis added). To lawyers, the term "pro forma" signifies something done to satisfy form rather than substance—think Captain Renault in "Casablanca" ordering a roundup of "the usual suspects."

77. Ethan Rarick, *California Rising: The Life and Times of Pat Brown* (Berkeley: University of California Press, 2005), 36.

78. Bureau of Labor Statistics, "CPI Inflation Calculator." http://data.bls.gov/cgi-bin/cpicalc.pl?cost1=60.00&year1=1943&year2=2015 (accessed January 18, 2016).

79. U.S. Senate, "Hearings before the Special Committee" (November 21, 1950), 491–492 (emphasis added).

80. Ibid., 492 (emphasis added).

81. Ibid., 494.

82. "Biography," Elmer E. Robinson Papers (San Francisco, CA: SFH 6 San Francisco History Center, San Francisco Public Library). http://sfpl.org/pdf/libraries/main/sfhistory/mayoral-papers/robinson.pdf (accessed April 19, 2014).

83. Although not much is known about the Poodle Dog operation at 1115 Polk Street, it appears to have no connection to the original Poodle Dog and its successors. Lewis Baer, "The [Original, Old, Ritz, Bergez-Franks] Poodle Dog," *San Francisco Bay Area Post Card Club*, XXI, No. 4 (May 2006). http://www.postcard.org/sfbapcc2006-05-s.pdf (accessed April 19, 2014).

84. U.S. Senate, "Hearings before the Special Committee" (November 21, 1950), 495 (emphasis added).

85. Ibid.

86. Ibid., 497.

87. "Hymie 'Loud Mouth' Levin, Collector for Al Capone and the Chicago Outfit," *Chicago Tribune* (June 17, 1934); The Janet A. Ginsburg Chicago Tribune Collection. http://tomcat.lib.msu.edu/branches/dmc/tribune/detail.jsp?id=13678 (accessed April 19, 2014).

88. "U.S. Names 17 as Nelson Aids," *The Milwaukee Sentinel* (January 16, 1935). http://news.google.com/newspapers?nid=1368&dat=19350116&id=8lsaAAAAIBAJ&sjid=JA0EAAAAIBAJ&pg=6967,2508485 (accessed March 21, 2016).

89. U.S. Senate, "Hearings before the Special Committee" (November 21, 1950), 499–500.

90. Ibid., 502.

91. Ibid., 500.

92. Judith Moore, "When Everything Was Lost."

93. Profaci was then the boss of the Profaci family, with legitimate interests in olive oil and tomato paste and illegitimate interests in waterfront rackets and heroin importation and close allies with Joe Bonanno and the Bonanno family. After Profaci's death in 1962, the family was renamed the Colombo family. Anthony Bruno, "The Colombo Family: The Olive Oil King," *CrimeLibrary*. http://www.crimelibrary.com/gangsters_outlaws/family_epics/colombo/3.html (accessed April 19, 2014).

CHAPTER 10: THE APALACHIN DEBACLE

1. Lee Troy, "Trade Union Membership, 1897–1962" (National Bureau of Economic Research, 1965), 1.

2. Ed Reid and Ovid Demaris, *The Green Felt Jungle* (Pocket Cardinal, 1963), 87.

3. Ibid., 43.

4. Gil Reavill, *Mafia Summit* (St. Martin's Press, 2013), 136.

5. Curt Gentry, *J. Edgar Hoover: The Man and the Secrets* (W.W. Norton and Co., 1991), 328–329.

6. Ibid., 329–330.

7. Anthony Summers, *Official and Confidential: The Secret Life of J. Edgar Hoover* (Open Road Integrated Media, 2013), 290.

8. John C. McWilliams, *The Protectors: Harry J. Anslinger and the Federal Bureau of Narcotics, 1930–1962* (University of Delaware Press, 1990), 15.

9. Gentry, *J. Edgar Hoover*, 328–330.

10. McWilliams, *The Protectors*, 96.

11. Ibid., 129.

12. Douglas Valentine, *The Strength of the Wolf: The Secret History of America's War on Drugs*. Kindle ed. (Verso, 2006), LOC 1018.

13. Ibid.

14. McWilliams, *The Protectors*, 141.

15. Robert J. Schoenberg, *Mr. Capone: The Real—and Complete—Story of Al Capone* (HarperCollins, 1992), 232.

16. Ibid., 233.

17. Michael Newton, *The Mafia at Apalachin, 1957*. Kindle ed. (McFarland, 2012), LOC 841.

18. The Mob Museum, "Timeline." http://themobmuseum.org/timeline_events /havana-conference/ (accessed December 29, 2015).

19. Jerry Capeci, *The Complete Idiot's Guide to the Mafia*. 2nd ed. (Penguin Books, 2004), 35.

20. Joseph Bonanno, *A Man of Honor: The Autobiography of Joseph Bonanno* (St. Martin's Press, 1983), 177.

21. Capeci, *The Complete Idiot's Guide*, 36.

22. Newton, *The Mafia at Apalachin, 1957*, LOC 841.

23. Ibid., LOC 804.

24. Pub. L. 728, 84th Cong., 70 Stat. 567, 568 (July 18, 1956).

25. Pub. L. 728, 84th Cong., 70 Stat. 568, 570–571 (July 18, 1956).

26. Ibid.

27. Newton, *The Mafia at Apalachin, 1957*, LOC 796–807.

28. Ibid., LOC 807.

29. Ibid., LOC 883.

30. Martin Booth, *Opium: A History* (St. Martin's Press, 1996), 77.

31. Ibid.

32. Ibid., 77–78.

33. Ibid., 78.

34. Nigel Cawthorne, *Mafia: The History of the Mob*. Kindle ed. (Arcturus Publishing, 2012), LOC 2664.

35. Pierre de Champlain, "Le parrain discret: vie et carrière de Vincenzo Cotroni," *Huffington Post Canada* (September 9, 2014). http://quebec.huffing tonpost.ca/pierre-de-champlain/le-parrain-discret-vie-et-carriere-de-vincenzo -cotroni_b_5711181.html (accessed January 2, 2016).

36. Ibid.

37. Jean-Pierre Charbonneau, "On the Track of a Former Gestapo Agent," *Ottawa Journal* (July 5, 1976): 29.

38. de Champlain, "Le parrain discret."

39. Ibid.

40. Cawthorne, *Mafia: The History*, LOC 2669.

41. Newton, *The Mafia at Apalachin, 1957*, LOC 883.

42. Ibid., LOC 871.

43. Reid and Demaris, *The Green Felt*, 83.

44. Newton, *The Mafia at Apalachin, 1957*, LOC 874–877.

45. Special Agent Curtis P. Irwin, "James Joseph Lanza," Federal Bureau of Investigation, FD-263 (November 18, 1958), 5.

46. Newton, *The Mafia at Apalachin, 1957*, LOC 883–885.

47. McWilliams, *The Protectors*, 145.

48. Reid and Demaris, *The Green Felt*, 155.

49. Bonanno, *A Man of Honor*, 212.

50. Ibid.

51. Ibid., 177.

52. Newton, *The Mafia at Apalachin, 1957*, LOC 888.

53. Bonanno, *A Man of Honor*, 216.

54. Newton, *The Mafia at Apalachin, 1957*, LOC 930–934.

55. Bonanno, *A Man of Honor*, 216.

56. Newton, *The Mafia at Apalachin, 1957*, LOC 1046–1050.

57. F. L. Price, "James Joseph Lanza," Federal Bureau of Investigation, Standard Form 54 (March 20, 1958), 1.

58. Curtis P. Irwin, "James Joseph Lanza," FBI Form FD-263 (March 26, 1958), 1.

59. Ibid.

60. Capeci, *The Complete Idiot's Guide*, 92.

61. Ibid., 95.

62. Ibid.

63. Irwin, "James Joseph Lanza" (March 26, 1958), 13.

64. Ibid.

65. Curtis P. Irwin, "James Joseph Lanza," FD-263 (July 24, 1958), 16.

66. Ibid.

67. Cheryl A. Kashuba, "Hotel Casey Symbolized City's Affluence, Culture," *The Scranton Times-Tribune* (November 8, 2009). http://thetimes-tribune.com /news/hotel-casey-symbolized-city-s-affluence-culture-1.400770 (accessed January 10, 2016).

68. Newton, *The Mafia at Apalachin, 1957*, LOC 1062–1064, 1070–1073.

69. Ibid., LOC 1073.

70. Ibid., LOC 1082.

71. Ibid., LOC 1085.

72. Ibid., LOC 1091–1095.

73. Ibid., LOC 1101–1104.

74. "Mobster, Pals Scatter after Meeting Ends," *Kingston Daily Freeman* (November 15, 1957), 15.

75. Ibid.

76. Ibid.

77. Ibid.

78. Newton, *The Mafia at Apalachin, 1957*, LOC 1125–1126.

79. Curtis P. Irwin, "James Joseph Lanza," FD-263 (May 26, 1958), 14.

80. Peter Maas, *The Valachi Papers* (HarperCollins, 1968), 235.

81. *United States v. Bufalino*, 285 F. 2d 408, 419 (2nd Cir. 1960).

82. Ibid.

83. "Croswell Defends Role as Apalachin Raider," *Kingston Daily Freeman* (Kingston, NY, November 30, 1960), 34.

84. Capeci, *The Complete Idiot's Guide*, 8.

CHAPTER 11: FROM ANONYMITY TO "TOP HOODLUM"

1. Michael Newton, *The Mafia at Apalachin, 1957*. Kindle ed. (McFarland, 2012), LOC 1214.

2. SAC San Francisco to Director, "James Joseph Lanza," FD-36, Air-Tel (February 20, 1958).

3. Ibid.

4. Ibid.

5. SAC San Francisco to Director and SACS NEW YORK, PITTSBURG AND PHILADELPHIA, Teletype (February 21, 1958).

6. 18 U.S.C. 3122.

7. 18 U.S.C. 3122 (b).

8. 18 U.S.C. 3124 (c) (1)-(2).

9. Nardone v. United States, 302 US 379 (1937).

10. Victor S. Elgort, "Legal Constraints upon the Use of the Pen Register as a Law Enforcement Tool," *Cornell Law Review* 60, No. 6 (August 1975): 1031.

11. SAC San Francisco to Director, "James Joseph Lanza," FD-227 (February 25, 1958).

12. Ibid.

13. F. L. Price to Rosen, "James Joseph Lanza," Memorandum (March 20, 1958).

14. SAC San Francisco to Director, "James Joseph Lanza," FD-142 (March 17, 1958), 3.

15. Price to Rosen, "James Joseph Lanza," (March 20, 1958).

16. Ibid.

17. Director, FBI to SAC San Francisco, "James Joseph Lanza," (March 21, 1958).

18. Special Agent Curtis P. Irwin, "James Joseph Lanza," FD-263 (March 26, 1958), 4.

19. Ibid., 15.

20. Ibid., 16.

21. Ibid., 17.

22. "'Racketeer' Ordered Out of Country," *San Francisco Chronicle* (June 18, 1961), 3.

23. Irwin, "James Joseph Lanza" (March 26, 1958), 16.

24. Ibid., 17.

25. Ibid., 21.

26. Bureau of Labor Statistics, "CPI Inflation Calculator." http://data.bls.gov /cgi-bin/cpicalc.pl?cost1=64.50&year1=1940&year2=2015 (accessed January 14, 2016).

27. Irwin, "James Joseph Lanza" (March 26, 1958), 21.

28. Ibid.

29. Ibid.

30. Ibid.

31. Ibid.

32. Ibid.

33. Ibid., 34–35.

34. John C. McWilliams, *The Protectors: Harry J. Anslinger and the Federal Bureau of Narcotics, 1930–1962* (University of Delaware Press, 1990), 159.

35. Irwin, "James Joseph Lanza" (March 26, 1958), 37.

36. SAC San Francisco to Director, "James Joseph Lanza," Std Form 64 (April 1, 1958).

37. SAC San Francisco to Director and SAC New York, Teletype (May 20, 1958).

38. Ibid.

39. McWilliams, *The Protectors*, 155.

40. SAC San Francisco to Director FBI, "James Joseph Lanza," Memorandum (May 17, 1958), 1.

41. Ibid.

42. Ibid.

43. Director FBI to SAC San Francisco, Teletype, Urgent (May 21, 1958).

44. Director FBI to SAC San Francisco, id., May 21, 1958.

45. SAC New York to Director FBI, "James Joseph Lanza" (May 20, 1958).

46. SAC New York to Director FBI, "James Joseph Lanza" (June 2, 1958).

47. Irwin, "James Joseph Lanza" (June 10, 1958), 23.

48. Ibid.

49. Ibid.

50. John Johnson, Joel Selvin, and Dick Cami, *Peppermint Twist: The Mob, the Music, and the Most Famous Dance Club of the '60s* (St. Martin's Press, 2012), 173.

51. Irwin, "James Joseph Lanza" (June 10, 1958), 25.

52. Ibid., 32.

53. Ibid.

54. SAC San Francisco to Director, "James Joseph Lanza" (March 17, 1959), 2.

55. Ibid.

56. Irwin, "James Joseph Lanza," FD-263 (July 24, 1958), 5.

57. Ibid., 6.

58. SAC San Francisco to Director (March 17, 1959), 2.

59. L. N. Conroy to Rosen, "James Joseph Lanza" (April 1, 1959), 1.

60. Ibid., 2.

61. Director FBI to SAC San Francisco, "James Joseph Lanza" (April 1, 1959).

62. SAC San Francisco to Director, "James Joseph Lanza" Airtel (April 24, 1959).

CHAPTER 12: LEGITIMATE BUSINESSES

1. Director FBI to SAC San Francisco, "James Joseph Lanza" (June 1, 1959).

2. 18 U.S.C. 1963 (a) (3).

3. Special Agent Curtis P. Irwin, "James Joseph Lanza" (May 26, 1958), 29.

4. Bureau of Labor Statistics, "CPI Inflation Calculator." http://data.bls.gov /cgi-bin/cpicalc.pl?cost1=10%2C000&year1=1956&year2=2015 (accessed January 16, 2016).

5. "Sunny Outer Mission" Advertisement, *San Francisco Chronicle* (November 25, 1956), 41.

6. "Castro Nr. 14th," Advertisement, *San Francisco Chronicle* (October 29, 1956), 36.

7. Paragon Real Estate Group, "San Francisco Real Estate Market Reports." http://www.paragon-re.com/Market_Updates/ (accessed January 16, 2016).

8. "Median 1-Bedroom Rent, Fall 2015," *Zumper.com*. https://www.zumper .com/apartments-for-rent/san-francisco-ca (accessed January 16, 2016).

9. U.S. Department of Commerce, Bureau of the Census, "Current Population Reports: Consumer Income" (June 30, 1957), Series P-60, Vol. 25.

10. "U.S. Grand Jury Begins Crime Study," *Los Angeles Times* (January 14, 1959), 1.

11. Ibid.

12. "Moving on Top Hoodlums," *Kansas City Times* (January 15, 1959), 2.

13. "Atty DeSimone Quizzed by Federal Grand Jury," *Los Angeles Times* (March 18, 1959), 4.

14. SAC San Francisco to Director FBI, Airtel, FD-36 (May 12, 1959), 2.

15. Ibid.

16. Bureau of Labor Statistics, "CPI Inflation Calculator." http://data.bls.gov /cgi-bin/cpicalc.pl?cost1=1000&year1=1959&year2=2015 (accessed January 16, 2016).

17. "Late Train Has Crime Inquiry in Turmoil," *Los Angeles Times* (February 27, 1959), 4.

18. Ibid.

19. SA Herbert K. Mudd to File, "James Joseph Lanza," FD-204 (June 16, 1959), 6.

20. Director FBI to SAC San Francisco, Airtel (June 1, 1959).

21. SAC San Francisco to Director FBI, Airtel (June 19, 1959).

22. Ibid.

23. SA Herbert K. Mudd, "James Joseph Lanza," FD-263 (July 31, 1959), 11.

24. Ibid.

25. Rosen to L. N. Conroy, "James Joseph Lanza" (August 28, 1959).

26. SAC San Francisco to Director FBI, "James Joseph Lanza," Airtel (September 1, 1959).

27. SA Herbert K. Mudd, "James Joseph Lanza," FD-263 (November 14, 1959), 1.

28. SAC San Francisco to Director FBI, "James Joseph Lanza" (February 18, 1960), 2–3.

29. Director FBI to SAC San Francisco, "Top Hoodlum Program" (June 2, 1960).

30. Director FBI to SAC San Francisco, "James Joseph Lanza," Airtel (July 12, 1960).

31. SAC San Francisco to Director FBI, "James Joseph Lanza," Airtel (August 3, 1960).

32. SAC San Francisco to Director FBI "James Joseph Lanza," Airtel (December 21, 1960), 2.

33. Ibid.

34. Ibid., 4.

35. SAC San Francisco to Director FBI, "Justification for Continuation of Technical or Microphone Surveillance" (April 4, 1961), 2b.

36. Ibid.

37. Ibid., 2c.

38. SA Herbert K. Mudd, "James Joseph Lanza," FD-204 (May 10, 1961), 2.

39. Robert J. Schoenberg, *Mr. Capone: The Real–And Complete–Story of Al Capone* (HarperCollins, 1993), 170–179.

40. John H. Davis, *Mafia Dynasty* (HarperCollins, 1994), 366.

CHAPTER 13: THE SWINGING 1960s

1. Lamar Waldron, *Watergate: The Hidden History: Nixon, the Mafia, and the CIA* (Counterpoint Press, 2012), 88–91.

2. Gus Russo, *The Outfit* (Bloomsbury, 2001), 371–372.

3. Ibid.

4. Cecil Stoughton, *ST-202-7-61. President John F. Kennedy Signs Interstate Anti-Crime Bills* (Boston, MA: John Fitzgerald Kennedy Library).

5. Pub. L. 87-228, 62 Stat. 793 (87th Cong., 1961).

6. "Police Here Drop Vagrancy Arrests," *San Francisco Chronicle* (June 2, 1961), 37.

7. "'Racketeer' Ordered Out of Country," *San Francisco Chronicle* (June 18, 1961), 3.

8. SAC San Francisco to Director FBI, "Justification for Continuation of Technical or Microphone Surveillance" (July 3, 1961), 2a.

9. Ibid., 2b.

10. Ibid.

11. Ibid., 2d.

12. Ibid., 2d.

13. Ibid.

14. SAC San Francisco to Director FBI "James Joseph Lanza" (November 8, 1961), 2.

15. SAC San Francisco to Director FBI, "James Joseph Lanza" (November 29, 1961), 1.

16. Mike Thomas, "Hard Times by the Bay," *San Francisco Chronicle* (November 18, 1961), 5.

17. SAC San Francisco to Director FBI, "James Joseph Lanza" (December 20, 1961), 2.

18. SAC San Francisco to Director FBI, "James Joseph Lanza" (January 24, 1962), 3.

19. Jerry Capeci, *The Complete Idiot's Guide to the Mafia*. 2nd ed. (Penguin Group, 2004), 177–178.

20. Carl Sifakis, *The Mafia Encyclopedia*. 3rd ed. (Facts on File, 2005), 28.

21. Ibid., 49.

22. Ibid.

23. SAC San Francisco to Director FBI, "James Joseph Lanza" (November 10, 1964), 2.

24. Ibid., 3–4.

25. Jack Anderson, "LBJ Slows Wiretapping," Washington Merry-Go-Round, *Ocala Star-Banner* (Ocala, FL, December 28, 1965), 4. *See* also Russo, *The Outfit*, 455.

26. Richard Carlson and Lance Brisson, "San Francisco's Mayor Alioto and the Mafia," *Look Magazine* (September 23, 1969), 17.

27. Ibid., 18.

28. Ibid., 18–19.

29. Mario Puzo, *The Godfather* (G.P. Putnam's Sons, 1969), 282.

EPILOGUE: THE LION IN WINTER

1. Ray Loynd and Jean Merl, "Jimmy the 'Weasel' Fratianno; Mob Figure, Informant," *Los Angeles Times* (July 1, 1993). http://articles.latimes.com/1993 -07-01/news/mn-8855_1_mob-figure (accessed January 17, 2016).

2. Leslie Wayne, "Chief at Big Military Contractor Dies," *New York Times* (June 8, 2006). http://www.nytimes.com/2006/06/08/business/08arms.html (accessed January 17, 2016).

Selected Bibliography

Abadinsky, Howard. *Organized Crime.* 10th ed. Wadsworth/Cengage, 2007.

Anbinder, Tyler. *Five Points: The Nineteenth Century New York City Neighborhood.* Free Press, 2010.

Asbury, Herbert. *The Gangs of New York.* Alfred A. Knopf (1927), rep. by Thunder's Mouth Press, 1990.

Asbury, Herbert. *The Barbary Coast: An Informal History of the San Francisco Underworld.* Alfred A. Knopf (1933), rep. by Thunder's Mouth Press, 2002.

Averbuch, Bernard. *Crab Is King—The Colorful Story of Fisherman's Wharf in San Francisco.* Mabuhay Publishing Co., 1973.

Behr, Edward. *Prohibition: Thirteen Years That Changed America.* Arcade Publishing, 2000.

Bonanno, Joseph. *A Man of Honor: The Autobiography of Joseph Bonanno.* St. Martin's Press, 1983.

Booth, Martin. *Opium: A History.* St. Martin's Press, 1996.

Boyd, Nan. *Wide Open Town: A History of Queer San Francisco to 1965.* University of California Press, 2005.

Bucheli, Marcelo. *Bananas and Business: The United Fruit Company in Colombia, 1899–2000.* New York University Press, 2005.

Capeci, Jerry. *The Complete Idiot's Guide to the Mafia.* 2nd ed. Penguin Books, 2004.

Cawthorne, Nigel. *Mafia: The History of the Mob.* Kindle ed. Arcturus Publishing, 2012.

Chase, Marilyn. *The Barbary Plague: The Black Death in Victorian San Francisco.* Random House, 2004.

Chomsky, Noam. *Deterring Democracy.* Harper-Collins, 1992.

Churchill, Winston S. *Memoirs of the Second World War* (Abridged). Houghton Mifflin Co., 1991.

Ciment, James, and Thaddeus Russell, eds. *The Home Front Encyclopedia: United States, Britain and Canada in World Wars I and II.* ABC-CLIO, 2007.

Clarke, Edward J. *Deviant Behavior: A Text Study in the Sociology of Deviance.* Worth Publishers, 2008.

Cressman, Robert J. *The Official Chronology of the U.S. Navy during World War II.* Naval Institute Press, 2000.

Critchley, David. *The Origin of Organized Crime in America: The New York City Mafia 1891–1931.* Routledge, 2009.

Davis, John H. *Mafia Dynasty.* HarperCollins, 1994.

Dickie, John. *Blood Brotherhoods: Italy and the Rise of Three Mafias.* Perseus Books Group, 2014.

Dickson, Samuel. *San Francisco Is Your Home.* Stanford University Press, 1947.

Diggins, John Patrick. *Mussolini and Fascism: The View from America.* Princeton University Press, 1972.

DiStasi, Lawrence. *Una Storia Segreta: The Secret History of Italian American Evacuation and Internment during World War II.* Heyday Books, 2001.

Fichera, Sebastian. *Italy on the Pacific: San Francisco's Italian Americans.* St. Martin's Press, 2011.

Flamm, Jerry. *A Good Life in Hard Times: San Francisco in the '20s & '30s.* Chronicle Books, 1978.

Flamm, Jerry. *Hometown San Francisco.* Scottwall Associates, 1994.

Gentry, Curt. *J. Edgar Hoover: The Man and the Secrets.* W.W. Norton and Co., 1991.

Golway, Terry. *Machine Made: Tammany Hall and the Creation of Modern American Politics.* New York: W.W. Norton & Co., 2014.

Hamm, Richard F. *Shaping the 18th Amendment: Temperance Reform, Legal Culture and the Polity.* University of North Carolina Press, 1995.

Jackson, Kenneth T., and David S. Dunbar, eds. *Empire City: New York through the Centuries.* Columbia University Press, 2005.

Jacobs, James B., Colleen Friel, and Robert Radick. *Gotham Unbound: How New York City Was Liberated from the Grip of Organized Crime.* New York University Press, 1999.

Jeansonne, Glen. *Women of the Far Right: The Mothers Movement and World War II.* University of Chicago Press, 1996.

Johnson, John, Joel Selvin, and Dick Cami. *Peppermint Twist: The Mob, the Music, and the Most Famous Dance Club of the '60s.* St. Martin's Press, 2012.

LaGumina, Salvatore John. *The Humble and the Heroic: Wartime Italian Americans.* Cambria Press, 2006.

Lerner, Michael A. *Dry Manhattan: Prohibition in New York City.* Harvard University Press, 2008.

López, Ian Haney. *Dog Whistle Politics: How Coded Racial Appeals Have Reinvented Racism and Wrecked the Middle Class.* Oxford University Press, 2014.

Lupo, Salvatore. *History of the Mafia.* Translated by Anthony Shugaars. Columbia University Press, 2009.

Maas, Peter. *The Valachi Papers.* HarperCollins, 1968.

McCoy, Alfred W. *Policing America's Empire: The United States, the Philippines, and the Rise of the Surveillance State.* University of Wisconsin Press, 2009.

McWilliams, John C. *The Protectors: Harry J. Anslinger and the Federal Bureau of Narcotics, 1930–1962.* University of Delaware Press, 1990.

Mollenkopf, John H. *The Contested City.* Princeton University Press, 1983.

Mori, Cesare. *The Last Struggle with the Mafia.* Putnam, 1933.

Murlin, Edgar L. *The New York Red Book.* J.B. Lyon Publishers, 1905.

Nelli, Humbert S. *The Business of Crime: Italians and Syndicate Crime in the United States.* University of Chicago Press, 1976.

Newark, Tim. *Mafia Allies.* Zenith Press, 2007.

Newark, Tim. *Lucky Luciano: The Real and the Fake Gangster.* St. Martin's Press, 2010.

Newton, Michael. *The Mafia at Apalachin, 1957.* Kindle ed. McFarland and Co., 2012.

Pitkin, Thomas Monroe, and Francesco Cordasco. *The Black Hand: A Chapter in Ethnic Crime.* Littlefield, Adams & Co., 1977.

Procacci, Giuliano. *History of the Italian People.* Harper&Row, 1971.

Puzo, Mario. *The Godfather.* G.P. Putnam's Sons, 1969.

Quin, Mike. *The Big Strike.* Olema Publishing Co., 1949.

Raab, Selwyn. *Five Families: The Rise, Decline, and Resurgence of America's Most Powerful Mafia Empires.* St. Martin's Press, 2006.

Rarick, Ethan. *California Rising: The Life and Times of Pat Brown.* University of California Press, 2005.

Reavill, Gil. *Mafia Summit.* St. Martin's Press, 2013.

Reid, Ed, and Ovid Demaris. *The Green Felt Jungle.* Pocket Cardinal, 1963.

Riall, Lucy. *Sicily and the Unification of Italy: Liberal Policy and Local Power 1859–1866.* Oxford University Press, 1998.

Russo, Gus. *The Outfit.* Bloomsbury, 2001.

Schoenberg, Robert J. *Mr. Capone: The Real and Complete Story of Al Capone.* Harper Collins, 1993.

Sifakis, Carl. *The Mafia Encyclopedia.* 3rd ed. Facts on File, 2005.

Spewack, Bella. *Streets: A Memoir of the Lower East Side.* The Feminist Press at the City University of New York, 1995.

Starr, Kevin. *Endangered Dreams: The Great Depression in California.* Oxford University Press, 1996.

Starr, Kevin. *The Dream Endures: California Enters the 1940s.* Oxford University Press, 1997.

Summers, Anthony. *Official and Confidential: The Secret Life of J. Edgar Hoover.* Open Road Integrated Media, 2013.

Trevelyan, George Macaulay. *Garibaldi and the Making of Italy.* Longmans, Green & Co., 1911.

United States Treasury Department, Bureau of Narcotics. *Mafia: The Government's Secret File on Organized Crime*. HarperCollins, 2007.

Valentine, Douglas. *The Strength of the Wolf: The Secret History of America's War on Drugs*. Kindle ed. Verso, 2006.

Varese, Federico. *Mafias on the Move: How Organized Crime Conquers New Territories*. Princeton University Press, 2013.

Waldron, Lamar. *Watergate: The Hidden History: Nixon, the Mafia, and the CIA*. Counterpoint Press, 2012.

Ward, Nathan. *Dark Harbor: The War for the New York Waterfront*. Farrar, Straus and Giroux, 2010.

Waugh, Daniel. *Gangs of St. Louis: Men of Respect*. Arcadia Publishing, 2010.

Weintraub, Robert. *The Victory Season: The End of World War II and the Birth of Baseball's Golden Age*. Back Bay Books, 2014.

Whatmough, Joshua. *The Foundations of Modern Italy*. Haskell House Publishers, 1937.

Zarnowitz, Victor. *Business Cycles: Theory, History, Indicators, and Forecasting*. University of Chicago Press, 2007.

Zinn, Howard. *LaGuardia in Congress*. Cornell University Press, 1958.

Index

About the Author

CHRISTINA ANN-MARIE DIEDOARDO is a seasoned criminal defense attorney in California and Nevada, as well as a former investigative reporter and award-winning foreign correspondent. Before graduating cum laude from the William S. Boyd School of Law at the University of Nevada, Las Vegas, in 2005, she worked as a reporter for a host of publications, including the *Las Vegas Review-Journal*, the *San Diego Daily Transcript*, and the *Columbia Missourian*. Christina was born and raised in New York City and now resides in San Francisco.